## ✳ STEP OUTSIDE YOUR COMFORT ZONE

and into Joe Sasto's adventurous world of Italian cooking. From playing with flour and water in his mother's kitchen to running Michelin-starred kitchens, Joe has learned one truth: food has power—the power to evoke memories and create new ones, to bring people together and spark joy. The strict rules he once followed felt limiting, so he made it his mission to help others loosen up, embrace creativity, and feel comfortable carving their own paths in the kitchen.

*Breaking the Rules* is a fresh approach to Italian cuisine, reimagined with Joe's unique flair and playfulness. In this one-of-a-kind cookbook, you'll find everything from classic recipes like meatballs and focaccia to innovative creations such as Pesto Pinwheel Pull-Apart Bread and Corn Cacio e Pepe. And when it comes to pasta, nobody does it better than Joe. With step-by-step guidance, he'll show you how to make various pastas by hand, from delicate tortellini and cappelletti to agnolotti and perfect, pillowy gnocchi. Joe's recipes are designed to inspire both home cooks and experienced chefs. He encourages you to cook with intuition, swap ingredients freely, and let inspiration strike. No escarole? Use kale or spinach. A recipe serves four to six? Make as much as you crave. Extra Sasto Bolo? Turn it into shepherd's pie. Leftover filling? Try a new pasta shape or make a Baked Ricotta Pie.

With stunning photography and Joe's contagious energy, *Breaking the Rules* is a celebration of Italian cooking that invites you to ditch the rule book and make each dish your own. Whether you're an experienced home cook or just getting started, Joe's passion for pasta and inventive cooking will ignite your creativity—and leave you hungry for more.

# BREAKING the RULES

# BREAKING the RULES

## A Fresh Take on Italian Classics

## JOE SASTO

with **THEA BAUMANN**

Photographs by **HUGE GALDONES**

**SIMON ELEMENT**

New York   Amsterdam/Antwerp   London
Toronto   Sydney/Melbourne   New Delhi

## SIMON ELEMENT

An Imprint of Simon & Schuster, LLC
1230 Avenue of the Americas
New York, NY 10020

First Simon Element hardcover edition October 2025

SIMON ELEMENT is a trademark of Simon & Schuster, LLC

For information about special discounts for bulk purchases, please contact Simon & Schuster Special Sales at 1-866-506-1949 or business@simonandschuster.com.

The Simon & Schuster Speakers Bureau can bring authors to your live event. For more information or to book an event, contact the Simon & Schuster Speakers Bureau at 1-866-248-3049 or visit our website at www.simonspeakers.com.

Food Stylist: Mollie Hayward
Culinary Assistants: Wanjoon Chang and Jane Katte
Prop Stylist: Janelle Gonyea
Photo Assistants: Jack Li and Eric Kleinberg
Intern: Tatyana Starks-Harris

Manufactured in China

10 9 8 7 6 5 4 3 2 1

Library of Congress Cataloging-in-Publication Data has been applied for.

ISBN 978-1-6680-5257-0
ISBN 978-1-6680-5258-7 (ebook)

Thank you to the following artists for contributing to this book:
Monsoon Pottery
Kate Parisian Ceramics
BayClay
Civil Stoneware
This Quiet Dust
Ashley Lin Ceramics
Aku Ceramics
Kati von Lehman
Studio M/Marumitsu Poterie
Hana Karim Studio
Minna linens
Yusuke Wakasa
Bennington Potters
Bella Bennett
Trapdoor Studio
Jono Pandolfi
Oyoy
Ed Elsey Woodworking
Red Dog Designs
River Otter Wood Works
Julie Damhus Studio
San Rocco Italia
Janelle Gonyea

*TO MY MOM, CLAUDETTE.* It was her love and support
that started and fueled my entire journey.
Eat Pasta Make Love (but maybe not always in that order).

INTRODUCTION 8     HOW TO USE THIS BOOK 14     PANTRY 16     TOOLS 24

## Chapter One
# CRISPY CRUNCHY

Fried Halibut and Savory Zabaglione .................. 32

Fried Ceci Beans............................................ 35

Rice Paper Cacio e Pepe Chips.......................... 38

Fried Castelvetrano Olives............................... 39

Santorini-Style Tomato Fritters.......................... 40

Fried Maitake Mushrooms with Onion Dip........... 45

Lemon Pepper Chicken Wings.......................... 46

Honey Butter Fried Chicken ............................. 48

Mozzarella en Carrozza................................... 50

Crispy Churros and Fonduta............................. 57

## Chapter Two
# FRESH AND LIGHT

Charred Zucchini Dip, Basil, and
Cherry Tomatoes............................................ 62

Summer Melon Gazpacho ............................... 63

Grilled Apriums, Vinegary Simple Syrup,
Burrata, and Brown Butter Crumble Rumble.......... 66

Cucumber and Plum Salad with Pistachio
and Wasabi ................................................. 71

Grilled Short Rib Lettuce Wraps ........................ 72

Marinated Tomato "Amatriciana" ...................... 75

Roasted Snap Peas and Artichoke Yogurt............. 76

Crunchy Caesar and Garlic Streusel.................... 79

BBQ Shrimp, Calabrian Chile Paste,
Orange, and Fresh Herbs ................................. 80

Kale Salad with Blueberry and Lemon Dressing ..... 83

Endive Salad with Roasted Red Pepper Italian
Vinaigrette, Horseradish, and Hazelnuts.............. 84

## Chapter Three
# BREAKING THE BREAD

Fried Potato, Cheese, and Sausage Pie................. 88

Rosemary and Blackberry Focaccia with
Whipped Mortadella ...................................... 91

Pesto Pinwheel Pull-Apart Bread and Fonduta ....... 98

Sesame Semolina Flatbreads............................ 106

Staff Favorite Cornbread ............................... 107

"Quick and Dirty" Pizza Dough ........................ 108

Garlic Knots............................................... 112

Pepperoni Stromboli..................................... 113

Pantry-Friendly Fancy Toasts........................... 114

## Chapter Four
# SHARING IS CARING

Lamb Chops with Agrodolce Glaze, Walnuts,
and Feta .................................................... 122

Risotto ..................................................... 125

Baked Clams and Rice "Casino"........................ 127

Mom's Meatballs ......................................... 130

Weeknight Short Ribs.................................... 134

Ribeye, Crispy Fingerlings, and All the
Peppercorns Sauce ...................................... 137

Black Garlic Butter Branzino............................ 140

Pork Chops with Mustard Berry Jus.................... 144

Rosemary Chicken Thighs, Raspberry
Bomba, and Anchovy Grilled Romaine................ 146

Mini Salami Meatballs with Whipped Ricotta
and Pesto................................................... 149

Chapter Five

# ON THE SIDE

Carrots with Spicy Yogurt and Carrot Top Pesto .. *154*

Radicchio, Whipped Ricotta, and Macadamia
Nuts .................................................. *161*

Squash, Whipped Ricotta, and Spicy Pumpkin
Seed Crumble Rumble .............................. *162*

Blistered Shishitos and Dashi Mayo ............... *163*

Sweet Potato Wedges and Lemony Ranch .......... *164*

Fresh Corn Polenta with Butter and Chives ......... *167*

Baked Burrata alla Diavola ........................ *168*

Asparagus Cooked in Its Own Juices ............... *171*

Grilled Broccolini, Stracciatella, and
Seeded Crumble Rumble ........................... *173*

Pesto-Rubbed Corn on the Cob .................... *174*


Chapter Six

# DRIED PASTA IS YOUR BEST FRIEND

Sasto Bolo ......................................... *178*

Turkey Bolognese ................................. *182*

Butternut Mac n Cheese ........................... *185*

Pasta alla Norcina ................................. *186*

Beet Bolognese ................................... *188*

Corn Cacio e Pepe ................................ *196*

Pasta alla Nerano ................................. *199*

Whipped Cauliflower and Everything
Bagel Crumble Rumble ............................ *200*

Pasta alla Mezcal ................................. *203*


Chapter Seven

# MADE BY HAND

Grano Treiso Dough ............................... *206*

Brown Butter and Potato .......................... *224*

Braised Pork and Roasted Pepper .................. *226*

Chicken Parm ..................................... *232*

Sweet Potato Maple Miso .......................... *235*

Spicy Pork with Pistachio Crumble Rumble ........ *238*

Kale, Ricotta, and Hot Honey ...................... *239*

Potato Gnocchi ................................... *242*

Ricotta Gnocchi .................................. *244*


Chapter Eight

# SWEET TREATS

Absolute Best Rainbow Sprinkle Cookies ........... *248*

Brown Butter Chocolate Chip Cookies ............. *250*

Almond Flour and Egg White Thumbprints ........ *254*

Pistachio Calzones ................................ *255*

Baked Ricotta Pie ................................. *256*

Sweet Potato Pie .................................. *259*

Matcha Tea-ramisu ................................ *260*

Panettone "Italian Toast" with Strawberries
and Balsamic ..................................... *263*

Mom's Crepes ..................................... *264*

Strawberry Cobbler ............................... *266*

Banana "Ice Cream" with Cinnamon,
Walnuts, and Dates ............................... *268*


Chapter Nine

# ESSENTIAL BASIC RECIPES

White Pepper Marshmallows ....................... *272*

Herby Garlicky Paste .............................. *273*

Praline Paste ..................................... *274*

Basic Pie Dough .................................. *275*

Tomato Raisins ................................... *276*

Garlic Confit ..................................... *277*

Burnt Strawberries ............................... *278*

INTRODUCTION

**MY LOVE OF FOOD CAME FROM MY MOTHER.** I attribute everything—my passion for food, the joy I get from feeding people, my whole career, really—to her. Being the matriarch of an Italian American family, she always had something delicious simmering on the stove. When friends would sleep over on weekends, we'd wake up to a buffet of warm and fluffy crepes (I was a difficult child and wanted mine without brown spots, more on that later . . .) accompanied by all the toppings we could ever imagine. Instead of spending money on movie tickets, my mom would move all the furniture in the living room, clear out a space for a large plastic tablecloth, and cook up a smorgasbord of snacks and dishes for us to all enjoy while watching our favorite shows on the television. We called this tradition "movie picnics" and it's still one of my fondest childhood memories.

I was lucky. From a very young age, my mom and dad showed me that food has power. It has the power to create and evoke memories; the power to bring people together, and to light them up inside. As soon as I was able to walk, I'd find my way into the kitchen, wanting to be at my mom's side. She'd let me mix together flour and water, even though I usually made nothing but a mess. Under her patient guidance, I learned how to hold a peeler, make a filling for lasagna, and fish out the softened onions and garlic from her famous gravy (see Mom's Red Sauce on page 54). But more importantly, she gave me the space to develop my own palate and trust myself in the kitchen.

It wasn't until later in life, when I started running restaurant kitchens, cooking pop-up dinners, and teaching online cooking classes, that I realized if you didn't grow up with my mom or a food family to guide you, learning to cook can feel a little overwhelming. I was surprised to see how nervous and hesitant some people were at first, worried about using the wrong ingredient or making a mistake. And I get it. When I first started working in professional kitchens, I was shocked by all the rules I encountered. I was taught all the "right" ways to make the classic French dishes, and why a demi-glace "had" to be done this way, or a duck butchered that way. I also learned, in no uncertain terms, that there were very strict rules and rituals around making Italian food, especially when it came to pasta. But as I worked my way up the ranks in these Michelin-starred kitchens, I started to feel constrained by all these "rules" and found myself looking for ways to push back on, bend, and sometimes even break them.

Don't get me wrong. I have great respect for the canon of classic French and Italian dishes (heck, I dedicated my entire career to learning those classics), but that's not the way I love to cook. I'm all about experimenting with new techniques and unfamiliar ingredients, using what I have, and being inspired by what I find at the market. I firmly believe that a recipe should only act as a road map. At the end of the day, you are still the one driving the car. My goal with this book is to help make you the most comfortable, confident driver you can be.

In these pages, you'll find simple, delicious recipes that I cook for myself at home interspersed with family recipes and pared-down versions of dishes I've made at my restaurants and pop-ups over the years. They're mostly Italian or Italian-inspired, usually with a little rebellious Sasto spin. Like chicken parm? Wait till you try my Chicken

**"I WAS LUCKY. FROM A VERY YOUNG AGE, MY MOM AND DAD SHOWED ME THAT FOOD HAS POWER."**

"Cooking doesn't need to be intimidating; in fact, it should be fun!"

Parm filling (page 232). Some are easy-peasy, some require a little more thought/patience/practice, but all are delicious, straightforward, and, most importantly, *flexible.*

I provide a list of ingredients, recommended cooking times, and suggested serving sizes (apparently, it's a requirement when writing a cookbook), but when push comes to shove, you're the one behind the wheel. Maybe the recipe calls for escarole, but if you can only find kale, no sweat! (Psst . . . *the recipe will even work with spinach.*) Maybe your broiler has seen better days and the Burnt Strawberries on page 278 aren't even close to burnt after twelve minutes. *Trust yourself and wait until they're as black as you want them.* I can tell you a pasta recipe serves four to six people, but my wife and I have been known to polish off that entire amount, just the two of us, no problem. *Cook as much pasta as you're hungry for.* If you have extra sauce, great! Freeze it for another time or follow some of my tips for leftovers that you'll find throughout the book (see page 15). Extra filling? No problem. Try out a new pasta shape or turn it into Baked Ricotta Pie (page 256).

I want to show you that cooking doesn't need to be intimidating; in fact, it should be fun! Maybe some of these recipes will become part of your regular rotation and others will push you to try something new. You might be here for the classics like meatballs, Caesar salad, focaccia, and chocolate chip cookies (I could live on that menu happily for the rest of my days), or maybe you'll get out of your comfort zone with something like Kale Salad with Blueberry and Lemon Dressing (page 83) or Pesto Pinwheel Pull-Apart Bread (page 98). However you decide to use this book, I hope it inspires you to get in the kitchen, cook, and break the rules. Best-case scenario, you'll experience something life-changing. Worst case? You'll still have something to eat.

# HOW to USE This BOOK

I always say that recipes are like a road map or GPS. They may tell you how to get there, but you still need to drive the car. My goal with this book is to make you feel comfortable in the kitchen, to step into uncomfort, to not feel limited by certain techniques, ingredients, or the words "traditional" or "classic." After all, these words only have meaning instilled by the user. Even seemingly canonical Italian dishes like Bolognese or carbonara will vary slightly depending on who is making them, where they live, who taught them the technique, and what they have in their kitchen that day—all of which, even though different, can still be considered "traditional." All the recipes in this book are designed to make you feel like a chef, but they don't require extensive cooking knowledge and lots of obscure ingredients, and most importantly won't require a ton of time.

As an added bonus, you'll also find suggestions for what to do with leftovers, ideas for how to "Break the Rules" with a different technique or ingredient, and my (sometimes nerdy, but hopefully helpful) pro tips.

## BREAK THE RULES

The Break the Rules boxes are there to remind you that you're in charge. They provide suggestions for how to spin a recipe—usually adding an extra element, employing a cool technique, or swapping in an ingredient—to "chef it up" a little. I included them for anyone who wants to take their cooking a step further, play around a bit, and make dishes the way I would in a restaurant kitchen. But making recipes more complex or "elevated" isn't the only way to break the rules or cook like a chef. I urge you to think of these boxes as a reminder—a hall pass, if you will—to trust your instincts and cook with what you have, or in some cases to still cook even if you might be missing an ingredient or two.

## LEFTOVERS

Nobody likes food waste. As a chef, I'm always looking for creative ways to repurpose leftovers. I have shared some of my favorite ways to do this—like turning leftover Bolognese into shepherd's pie (see page 178) or leftover meatball mixture into smash burgers (see page 151)—in callouts throughout the book.

## PRO TIPS

These are chef-y tricks and techniques I've learned over the years in professional kitchens, my home kitchen, and cooking on the road. Keep in mind, there is always more than one way to do something, but these are an opportunity for me to share the whys of some of my personal favorite techniques and processes and not just the hows.

# PANTRY

A great recipe starts with a well-stocked pantry. Here are some of my pantry staples that you'll see in recipes throughout the book. Some are basics you likely already have, while others are a little more obscure. All can be found at international grocery stores or ordered online.

## CALABRIAN CHILE PASTE

I use this Southern Italian staple to add fruity sweetness and moderate heat to everything from sauces and glazes to marinades, Fancy Mayo (page 43), and more. Tutto Calabria is my favorite brand, but any Calabrian chile paste will work well for the recipes in this book. Just be sure to taste it first and adjust the amount to suit your palate, as the spiciness can vary considerably from brand to brand.

## FLOURS

My home pantry is stocked with too many flours to list here, but the main three I call for in this book are:

### ALL-PURPOSE FLOUR

Any AP flour will work, but I usually use King Arthur.

### 00 FLOUR

Double Zero flour, also called 00, refers to the flour's fineness rather than the type of flour. In Italy and across Europe, grind sizes vary from 00 to 2, with 00 being the finest grind and 2 the coarsest. There are many types of wheat flour available in 00 grind, including semolina (hard durum wheat known as *rimacinata* when finely ground), whole wheat, pastry, pizza, and high-protein flour. But the one most commonly seen in the States, and the type I use to make my pizza dough (page 108), is a grano tenero, or soft wheat. Molino Pasini and Caputo are two of my favorite brands. If you can't find 00 (it's available online and at many grocery stores these days), you can swap in All-Purpose flour.

### BREAD FLOUR

I use bread flour—which has a higher protein content than All-Purpose (from 10 to 13 percent versus 9 to 11 percent)—for all my breads and doughs. Higher protein means higher gluten content, so the resulting doughs will form stronger strands of gluten when kneaded. This creates a better rise with more elasticity, a crustier exterior, and a chewier crumb. Keep in mind that because of its higher protein content, bread flour absorbs liquid better than other flours like AP, so it often requires a slightly higher water-to-flour ratio. Hayden Flour Mills based in Arizona have a wide variety of freshly milled flours and wheats to choose from.

## SICILIAN OREGANO

I use a lot of dried oregano and always stock my pantry with Sicilian oregano, which has a much more intense, earthy, and less vegetal flavor than the stuff you find in the spice section at the grocery store. The name "oregano" is derived from the Greek *oros*, meaning "mountain," and *ganos*, meaning "delight." And what a perfect name for something that grows spontaneously and happily in the sun and coastal air on Sicilian mountainsides! It generally comes on a whole branch; simply turn it upside down to sprinkle into a sauce, on a pizza, or as a final garnish on fish, meat, or vegetables before serving. I buy it at Italian grocery stores or online. If you can't get your hands on any, regular dried oregano will certainly work for all the recipes in this book.

## COLATURA

In simple terms, colatura is an ancient, fermented Roman fish sauce. It is similar in flavor to Southeast Asian fish sauce but is made using only anchovies and salt from the Amalfi coast, resulting in a cleaner, slightly less fishy flavor. I add it to Sicilian Soffritto (page 180) and the marinade for Grilled Short Ribs (page 72), but its uses are endless. You could splash a little over grilled vegetables, meat, or fish, use it to jazz up a batch of bagna cauda or Caesar dressing, or toss it with chile, garlic, parsley, olive oil, and cooked pasta to make one of the easiest weeknight dinners ever, spaghetti con la colatura di alici.

## BALSAMIC VINEGARS

### WHITE BALSAMIC VINEGAR

White balsamic is a lovely everyday vinegar that I use for salad dressings and Pickle Liquor (page 193). It's primarily made in the Italian region of Emilia-Romagna by cooking white Trebbiano grapes at a high pressure and low temperature to retain its mild flavor and pale, golden hue. While this is a great all-purpose vinegar for seasoning and cooking, the closest alternative for me is rice wine vinegar.

### AGED BALSAMIC VINEGAR

Aged balsamic is typically made from pressed Trebbiano and Lambrusco grapes and aged for a minimum of twelve years in a series of successively smaller wooden barrels, each made from a different type of wood. As the vinegar ages, it absorbs flavors from the wood, its acidity mellows, and it becomes thicker and more syrupy in texture. If you can, get one that's old enough to vote. And lastly, don't be fooled by those thick balsamic "glazes" that are usually just a mix of corn syrup, sugar, coloring, and cheap balsamic vinegar.

## AQUERELLO CARNAROLI RICE

Yes, you can use plain old arborio rice from the grocery store and make a perfectly good risotto. However, if you want something special (and virtually foolproof), get yourself some Aquerello. This is a unique Carnaroli Superfino rice grown and prepared by the Rondolino family on their farm in the Vercelli province in Italy. The unparalleled quality of this rice comes from the combination of traditional farming practices and innovative production.

After harvest, the unrefined grains are aged in temperature-controlled silos for between one and seven years, which allows them to absorb more liquid when cooked. They are then whitened with a helix—a gentle polishing method where the rice grains rub against one another, leaving them whole and intact. Finally, the family has a proprietary method of reintroducing the germ back into each grain after being polished, so, unlike most white rice, it retains all of its nutritional value. Maybe most importantly, this rice tastes incredible and cooks up perfectly every time.

## CANNED TOMATOES/TOMATO PASTE

My pantry is always stocked with tomato paste (I like Mutti) as well as crushed and whole canned tomatoes. I use them to make my Chicken Parm filling (see page 232), Sicilian Soffritto (page 180), and many of my dried pasta recipes (see pages 178 to 191). For crushed tomatoes, I only use Bianco DiNapoli, which is a San Marzano variety grown and processed in California by renowned farmer Rob DiNapoli and pizza maestro Chris Bianco. While we're on the subject, it's important to note that buying San Marzano tomatoes doesn't necessarily guarantee a good product. Just as a Cabernet Sauvignon grape needs the correct "terroir" to be turned into a fine wine, the same

is true for tomatoes. The best canned tomatoes come from San Marzano seeds, but they need to be grown in good soil, farmed with care, and processed in good conditions.

## ANCHOVY PASTE

I always keep a tube of anchovy paste in my fridge to add umami goodness to things like the dressing for my Crunchy Caesar and Garlic Streusel (page 79), a quick anchovy dressing (see Rosemary Chicken Thighs, Raspberry Bomba, and Anchovy Grilled Romaine on page 146), or my Sicilian Soffritto (page 180). It's so much easier to use than the whole filets and provides plenty of salty, fishy flavor.

## BLACK GARLIC

This is essentially fermented garlic and can be found peeled, in cloves, or in whole bulbs at many grocery stores and online. I love black garlic and mix it into Black Garlic Butter (page 141), Fancy Mayo (page 43), salad dressing (see Crunchy Caesar and Garlic Streusel on page 79), you name it. It has the essence of garlic without any of the harshness or pungency, plus a slight nuttiness and a burst of natural sweetness. Think of it as the garlic version of a caramelized onion or garlic mixed with molasses.

## FENNEL POLLEN

Fennel pollen is harvested from the tiny blossoms at the end of fennel stalks—the same plant that gives you the bulb for your salad and the seeds for your spice rub. Fennel is native to the Mediterranean, but also grows wild throughout California, so much of the fennel pollen available in the US is foraged in the Golden State. The pollen is a little sweeter (with citrus and honey notes) and less intense than ground fennel seed and is so good sprinkled over grilled pork, fish, or vegetables, Fried Ceci Beans (page 35), pasta dishes, or pizzas.

## YUZU JUICE/YUZU MARMALADE

Yuzu is having a moment, and rightfully so. It has all my favorite attributes of lemon, lime, and orange, with a sweet acidity that brings a unique brightness to any dish. You can buy yuzu juice and yuzu marmalade (I look for Yakama brand and use it to make the glaze for the Lemon Pepper Chicken Wings, page 46, or spread onto toast with some Whipped Ricotta, page 159) at most international grocery stores or online.

## SHIRO DASHI

Think of shiro dashi, which translates to "white soup stock," as a flavor booster and instant soup base. The concentrated liquid is made with dashi, white or light-colored soy sauce, mirin, salt, and sometimes sake or sugar. I stir it into soups, stocks, marinades, dressings, and Fancy Mayo (page 43)—anything that could use a little umami flavor, complexity, and depth. I grab whichever one looks good at the Asian grocery store, but you can also easily find it online.

## OILS

### OLIVE OIL

I've always been a "more butter, more better" person, so I'm not big on fancy finishing oils. Instead, I usually opt for solid, mid-price extra-virgin olive oils—something I can cook, fry, and make dressings with—like Graza, Brightland, or Corto. Look for ones that are bright and deep yellow or green in color and stored in dark boxes or bottles (to help protect them from light damage).

### NEUTRAL OIL

I call for neutral oil for deep frying and searing proteins. My go-to's are grapeseed and avocado, but any oil with neutral flavor and a high smoke point (like canola, vegetable, sunflower, or safflower) will work.

## NONSTICK COOKING SPRAY

I use this as added insurance to make sure certain breads and doughs (like my focaccia—see page 91) don't stick to the bottom of my pan.

## SALT

### KOSHER SALT

When it comes to everyday salt for cooking, Diamond Crystal is my favorite, and the only one that I use. It has a lighter flake than other kosher salts like Morton's, which helps it adhere to food and dissolve more quickly and evenly. You cannot, I repeat, *cannot* swap out one for the other without adjusting the amounts. Doing so will either create a much saltier recipe or a significantly under-seasoned dish. A note on seasoning: I list exact amounts for salt in some of the recipes, but most of the time I'll tell you to "season to taste." I highly recommend you use your fingers (not a saltshaker or grinder), and use the same salt (ideally Diamond Crystal) consistently. When you season this way, you'll learn over time how much saltiness a pinch will add and how to adjust with confidence.

### FLAKY SALT

I also use a flaky salt, like Maldon or Jacobsen, to finish a dish or sprinkle over Brown Butter Chocolate Chip Cookies (page 250). It adds a pop of saltiness and crunch to sliced meats, veggies, cheeses, and desserts.

## DRIED PASTA

There are lots of great dried pasta brands out there these days, but they are certainly not all created equal. Choose dried pasta that is light (almost white) in color and has a rough, sandy texture. If you can, opt for brands with the words "bronze die" or "slow dried" on the package. This means the pasta was extruded through dies made of bronze, which gives the finished product a coarser, more porous texture that sauces cling to better. It tends to be a little more expensive, but the slight increase in cost is well worth it.

## PISTACHIO BUTTER

Pistachio butter has the most distinctive and delicious flavor of all the nut butters. (It's not nutty like peanut butter or dry and chalky like almond butter.) It has a natural sweetness, too, which means you can enjoy it without adding jam, honey, or other sweeteners. A lot of pistachio butters are filled with sugars and oils that make for good gelato but don't work well for most of the recipes in this book, so be sure to pay attention to the ingredient list. I usually stock my pantry with Seed & Shell, but you can use any unsweetened pistachio butter. Worst-case scenario and you can only find the sweetened stuff, you can still use it for recipes like the Spicy Pork with Pistachio Crumble Rumble (page 238), but season with a deft hand and cut it with butter or a meaty stock.

## XANTHAN GUM

Xanthan gum is a fine dining chef's secret weapon. It may sound like molecular gastronomy, but chances are you have some in your home and kitchen already. It's found in most shelf-stable salad dressings, hot sauces, marinades, and even toothpaste! This naturally occurring, hydroscopic (water-loving) powder is made from seaweed and helps create stable emulsions and smoother purees. Ever wonder how the sauce at that fancy restaurant got oh-so silky smooth? A small knife tip of xanthan gum (or XG as we call it in restaurant kitchens) does the trick. Need to keep a cheese sauce warm and stable for the entire length of service and ready to reheat the next day? XG. Looking for a smooth and creamy Italian vinaigrette that doesn't separate after sitting? Want to add some body and thickness to your homemade hot sauce? You guessed it. While not strictly necessary, this easy-to-find, optional add-in will change your whole relationship with sauces and purees.

# CHEESE

While it's not technically a pantry item, I use a lot of grated cheese in my recipes and think it's important to touch on the difference between Parmigiano-Reggiano, Pecorino Romano, and "Parmesan" cheeses.

## PARMIGIANO-REGGIANO

Parmigiano-Reggiano is an aged cow's milk cheese with a rich, nutty flavor and granular texture. It is aged for a minimum of twelve months, often closer to twenty-four or thirty-six months. Like many Italian products, true Parmigiano-Reggiano has PDO (Protected Designation of Origin) status, which means it can only be made in a designated region (Parma, Reggio Emilia, Modena, Bologna, or Mantua, in this case) in compliance with specific requirements (such as cattle diet and aging time).

## PECORINO ROMANO

Pecorino Romano is also a PDO cheese, usually made in Lazio, Sardinia, or Tuscany. It is made with sheep's milk and has a firm texture and a sharp, salty, tangy flavor, making it great for grating over salads and pasta dishes. Pecorino is aged for a minimum of five months for a table cheese, and eight months for a harder, grating cheese.

## "PARMESAN" CHEESE

"Parmesan" is a generic term that refers to any cheese made in the style of Parmigiano-Reggiano. Because Parmesan is not regulated, the quality of the cheese can vary considerably. If you can, look for true Parmigiano-Reggiano and avoid its (usually inferior) imitators.

## A NOTE ON GRATED CHEESE

I call for freshly grated cheese in everything except my Chicken Parm pasta filling (on page 232), where I prefer the texture of the packaged, pre-grated stuff. I normally grate cheddar, provolone, and any other semi-hard cheese on the large holes of a box grater and Pecorino on the small holes. If you are able to find the freshly coarse-grated Parmigiano-Reggiano at a specialty store or deli (it comes in a small plastic container), this works great sprinkled over pasta and won't melt as quickly. If not, buy a whole piece and use the small holes of a box grater.

TOOLS

These recipes are all designed with home cooks in mind, so if your kitchen is decently stocked, you'll be able to make everything in this book with the tools you already have. For anyone who may need to stock up on a few items or is curious about which tools I'm always reaching for in my home kitchen, here's a list of some of my essentials:

## SHEET PANS

I use sheet pans for everything; think of them as the professional cookie baking tray. They fulfill endless purposes and also nest so neatly for storage. At home, I stick with half and quarter sizes (18×13-inch and 13×9-inch, respectively) and always buy ones with rolled steel rims, which prevent the flat bottoms from buckling and twisting in hot ovens. Purchase decent ones and they will last for decades.

## WIRE COOLING RACKS

If you don't already have them, buy a few cooling racks that fit inside your sheet pans. I use them not only for cooling cookies and other baked goods, but also for draining fried foods, dry brining meats, and getting air flow underneath things while roasting in the oven.

## DIGITAL FOOD THERMOMETER

This is an affordable and indispensable tool in my kitchen. I use it to check my fry oil, confirm temps on proteins, and make recipes like Praline Paste (page 274) and White Pepper Marshmallows (page 272).

## DIGITAL FOOD SCALE

I know some home cooks shy away from them, but scales are so much cleaner, faster, and more precise than measuring cups and spoons; especially when it comes to making breads and desserts. I put my bowl or pot on the scale and simply add each ingredient, weighing as I go. They virtually eliminate user error and make cleanup so much easier. I provide imperial measurements for all my desserts and breads, but I highly recommend measuring in grams with a scale.

## TONGS/SPIDER STRAINER

I don't own a traditional colander. When it comes to pasta, a pair of long kitchen tongs (to transfer longer shapes like spaghetti and pappardelle from the pasta cooking pot to the saucepan) and a large spider strainer (to remove shorter ones like campanelle and stuffed pastas) is all you need. Both are easier to store, and you won't risk accidentally tossing your liquid gold (starchy pasta water) down the sink! Get a metal spider so you can use it for lowering things in and out of the fryer, too.

## SPRAY WATER BOTTLE

This is an essential tool for making fresh pasta dough. Sometimes one or two spritzes can be the difference between a perfect dough and one that is tough, crumbly, and just doesn't fully come together. But don't limit its uses to making pasta. You can also use it to keep a paper towel roll-up of herbs damp and fresh or fill it with egg wash and use it to mist the top of Pesto Pinwheel Pull-Apart Bread (page 98) before going into the oven.

## PASTA ROLLING MACHINE (SHEETER) OR ROLLING PIN

*Nonnas* roll out beautiful sheets of dough with a large *mattarello* (rolling pin), but I'll tell you firsthand, it isn't easy and takes lots of practice. I personally spent six hours a day for six months rolling out pasta sheets and making tortellini by hand. For novice pasta makers, I always recommend starting with either an electric or hand-cranked pasta machine. If you have a KitchenAid mixer, their pasta rolling attachment is great. I used it myself for years and it makes rolling out dough quick and easy. (Just be sure to buy directly from KitchenAid to avoid a knockoff look-alike product.) My favorite hand-cranked machine is the Marcato Atlas 150, but there are lots of good-quality ones on the market. If you're feeling confident and want to go the rolling pin route, start with a 12- to 18-inch one and avoid French-style rolling pins with the tapered ends. Once you've got the hang of it, you can upgrade to the 36-inch and longer versions.

## PIZZA/PASTA CUTTERS

I use pizza and pasta cutters to slice pizza and flatbreads, seal stuffed pasta doughs, and make intricate designs in my pasta or pastry. I (unsurprisingly) have quite a collection, but the two I would recommend starting with are a standard, straight-edge pizza wheel and a smaller fluted cutter for pasta. Look for stainless-steel pizza wheels and brass pasta tools, if possible. Ones made with cheaper materials are more likely to bend and dent. If you're looking for a fancy one with a mustache, check out my Sastools by DogHouse Forge from my website.

## LARGE WOODEN CUTTING BOARD

I prefer making pasta on a wooden countertop versus stainless steel or smooth granite/marble. The porous material helps absorb excess moisture and prevents the dough from sticking. If you don't have wooden worktops, a simple solution is to use a large cutting board or to get a cheap 2′ x 4′ x ¾′ piece of food-grade wood from the hardware store and sand it down to remove any rough edges or splinters. One or two quick coatings of food-safe mineral oil will keep it porous and ready for endless pastabilities.

## RICER/FOOD MILL

A potato masher will work in a pinch, but to make proper Potato Gnocchi (page 242), you'll need a ricer or food mill. A handheld ricer that folds into itself works great for mashed potatoes and gnocchi, but it isn't the best multitasker. If you're going to buy a new tool, I'd recommend the more multipurpose food mill, which sits on top of a bowl and turns with a handle. It makes perfect gnocchi and mashed potatoes but is also great for pureeing braised vegetables or blending canned tomatoes for pizza sauce.

## PLASTIC AND METAL DOUGH SCRAPERS

These are intended for moving and scooping dough, but I use them for so much more in the kitchen (like cleaning up debris on the counter, scooping and moving chopped ingredients, and pushing water off a washed cutting board to help it dry faster). I like having a small plastic one for scraping the inside of a dough bowl and a larger metal one for shaping loaves and moving my prepped ingredients, or "mise en place." If you're looking for a fancy one with a mustache, check out my Sastools by DogHouse Forge from my website.

## DISPOSABLE SHOWER CAPS

You can absolutely use plastic wrap or a clean dish towel, but I find disposable shower caps to be the best tool for resting and proofing breads and other yeasted doughs. They fit over any bowl, maintain good humidity, and prevent the dough from drying out or forming a skin. Plus, you can use them multiple times to help prevent waste.

Chapter One

# CRISPY CRUNCHY

Mozzarella
en Carrozza,
PAGE 50

*EVERYONE LOVES FRIED FOOD*—it's probably ingrained in our DNA. And while some of the best is deep fried (like the Lemon Pepper Chicken Wings on page 46), you don't have to heat a large pot of oil every time you want a little crispy crunchy bite. In this chapter, you'll find a whole range of fry techniques (shallow fry, pan fry, oven fry, deep fry), different fry batters (light and crunchy tempura, double-fry Korean chicken, batter and flour dredged), and endless ideas for dunking and dipping; from snacks and apps to main dishes, and everything in between. And because there's nothing worse than badly fried food, I've shared my tips and tricks to help ensure that each bite comes out perfectly crisp and never greasy. Maybe you need an easy party snack like the Rice Paper Cacio e Pepe Chips (page 38), a quick, weeknight dinner like my favorite Mozzarella en Carozza (page 50), or have a hankering for something more decadent like the Honey Butter Fried Chicken (page 48). Whatever mood you're in, you're sure to find something to satisfy that crispy crunchy craving.

✽ When I'm going to eat shellfish or fish, I usually prefer it raw, either quickly marinated or simply sliced thin and served with some well-cooked and seasoned rice. The one exception to this rule? Fried fish. Here I toss halibut in a crunchy tempura batter, fry until golden, and serve with a savory zabaglione. Zabaglione is usually made with whipped eggs, sugar, and sweetened wine and served as an Italian dessert. But because I like to walk the line of savory and sweet, I use the same technique to make a luscious, savory dipping sauce for crispy fried fish (or anything, really). Don't be intimidated by the name; think of it as a cooked, whipped mayonnaise.

# FRIED HALIBUT

## AND

## Savory Zabaglione

### Serves 4 to 6

### Zabaglione

3 large egg yolks

1 tablespoon Sambuca or sherry wine vinegar

1 tablespoon fresh lemon juice

1 teaspoon white sugar

Kosher salt

1 tablespoon finely chopped fresh chives

1 tablespoon finely chopped fresh parsley

### Fish

Neutral oil, for frying

1 cup all-purpose flour

1 cup cornstarch

1 teaspoon baking powder

1 teaspoon fennel pollen or ground fennel seed (optional)

1 teaspoon chile flakes or chile powder, plus extra for dusting

1/2 teaspoon white pepper

1½ cups cold sparkling water, plus more as needed

1 tablespoon vodka (optional)

1½ pounds skinless halibut filet (or rockfish, cod, or tilapia), cut into 1×2-inch pieces

Kosher salt

1 *Make the Zabaglione:* Combine the egg yolks, Sambuca, lemon juice, and sugar in a large, heat-proof bowl. Fill a medium pot with 1 inch of water (choose one that will hold the bowl comfortably without letting the bottom touch the water) and set over medium heat. When the water is simmering, set the bowl on top, reduce the heat as needed to maintain a gentle simmer, and cook, whisking vigorously, until the eggs are cooked, aerated, and frothy, 2 to 3 minutes. Remove the bowl from the heat, season to taste with salt, and stir in the chives and parsley.

2 *Cook the Fish:* Fill a large, wide, heavy-bottomed pot about a third of the way with oil and set over medium heat. Place a sheet pan fitted with a wire cooling rack near the stove.

3 In a large bowl, whisk together the flour, cornstarch, baking powder, fennel pollen or seed (if using), chile flakes, and white pepper. Whisk in the sparkling water and vodka (if using) in a steady stream, adding more water as needed to make a thin, smooth batter. Be careful not to overmix.

*RECIPE CONTINUES*

**4** When the oil reaches 350°F on a food thermometer, season the fish pieces with salt, then dip them, one by one, into the batter and lift to allow any excess to drip off completely. Gently place them into the hot oil, dragging them back and forth through the oil for a few seconds before releasing, allowing the batter to set. (This will prevent the fish from sinking and sticking to the bottom of the pan.) Fry until golden and crispy, 1 to 2 minutes. Using tongs or a spider, immediately transfer the fried fish to the wire rack and season with additional salt and chile flakes. Continue coating and frying, being sure not to overcrowd the pan, until all the fish is cooked.

**5** Serve the hot fish with zabaglione for dipping.

**PRO TIP** The addition of vodka is a restaurant secret for fry batters, as alcohol has a different boiling/evaporation point than water. Because vodka is more volatile than water, it evaporates more quickly, drying out the batter faster and creating a much crispier exterior.

**BREAK THE RULES**

If you have a little extra time, give your halibut a salt cure or dry brine instead of seasoning right before battering. Put the halibut pieces on a parchment-lined sheet pan and season generously all over with salt. Cover with plastic wrap and place in the fridge to cure for 1 hour and follow the recipe as written (just don't season with salt before dipping them into the batter).

❋ I have a thing for snacking. And anything with an alluring combination of crispy, spicy, sweet, and sour is hard for me to resist. One of my favorite ways to satisfy this craving is with the classic Italian drinking snack, fried ceci beans. They're quick to make, the amount of spice can be varied to your personal taste, and, once you try them, you'll have a hard time eating only one. The only thing that could make these better is a crisp, cold, authentically Italian Peroni or negroni to drink them with.

# FRIED CECI BEANS

Serves 4 to 6

2 (15-ounce) cans garbanzo beans, drained and rinsed

3 tablespoons extra-virgin olive oil

2 teaspoons ground smoked paprika

1 teaspoon kosher salt

½ teaspoon chile flakes

½ teaspoon ground coriander

½ teaspoon white sugar

1 medium lime, zest grated

1. Preheat the oven to 375°F and place the drained chickpeas on a clean dish towel to dry.

2. Transfer the chickpeas to a large sheet pan, toss with the olive oil, and roast until golden and crispy, 15 to 20 minutes. In a large bowl, whisk together the paprika, salt, chile, coriander, and sugar.

3. Spoon the chickpeas into the bowl with spices and toss to season. Garnish with lime zest and serve immediately.

## BREAK THE RULES

Add ½ teaspoon fennel pollen and ⅛ teaspoon citric acid to the spice mix—it lends a really nice herbal, citrus-y flavor.

Fried Maitake
Mushrooms
with
Onion Dip,
PAGE 45

Fried Ceci
Beans,
PAGE 35

Fried
Castelvetrano
Olives,
PAGE 39

Rice Paper Cacio e Pepe Chips, PAGE 38

Santorini-Style Tomato Fritters, PAGE 40

❀ Have you ever tried fried rice paper chips? Rice paper wrappers (which are available in the Asian section of most grocery stores these days) are typically used to make spring and summer rolls, but this crispy Italian-inspired chip is my new favorite way to eat them. I think this recipe may have been an early version of my puffed pasta chips, Tantos, which are also fried, puffed, and dusted with delicious seasonings. While Tantos are made from actual wheat and water (just like pasta), this technique is much simpler. Once fried, I shower the crispy rice paper in black pepper, salt, Parmigiano, and Pecorino to mimic the flavors of the classic pasta dish cacio e pepe. This cacio e pepe version is probably my favorite, but I also love them sprinkled with cumin, coriander, and paprika for a Southwest flair or five spice powder and ground Sichuan peppercorns for a tingly twist. I usually serve them with Whipped Ricotta (page 159) for dipping, but they're a great snack or app on their own, too.

# Rice Paper CACIO E PEPE CHIPS

Serves 4 to 6

- Extra-virgin olive oil, for frying
- 6 rice paper wrappers
- Kosher salt and freshly ground black pepper
- 1/2 cup freshly grated Parmigiano-Reggiano
- 1/2 cup freshly grated Pecorino Romano

1. Heat ½ inch of oil in a medium Dutch oven or saucepan (it can be a little smaller than the diameter of the rolls, as they'll immediately shrink when they touch the hot oil) over medium-high heat and place a sheet pan fitted with a wire rack near the stove.

2. When the oil is very hot but not smoking (400°F), carefully drop in a rice paper wrapper with your fingers—it will puff up instantaneously!—then use tongs to remove it to the prepared cooling rack. Immediately season with a good pinch of salt, lots of black pepper, and about 1 tablespoon each Parmigiano and Pecorino. Continue frying and seasoning until all the wrappers are cooked.

3. Serve immediately or store in an airtight container for 1 day.

❀ These little fried morsels make an unstoppable poppable party snack or appetizer. The trick is using a mix of panko and Italian breadcrumbs, which makes the perfect crunchy coating. The coarseness of the panko provides texture and crunch and the fineness of the breadcrumbs fills in any gaps, ensuring the entire olive is coated.

# FRIED Castelvetrano OLIVES

### Serves 4 to 6

Neutral oil, for frying

2 (10-ounce) jars extra-large pitted Castelvetrano olives (I love Pearls)

1 cup all-purpose flour

2 large eggs, beaten

1 cup panko breadcrumbs

1 cup seasoned Italian breadcrumbs

Kosher salt

**1** Fill a large, wide, heavy-bottomed pot about one-third of the way with oil and place a sheet pan fitted with a wire cooling rack near the stove. Turn on the heat to medium.

**2** Drain the olives from their brine, but do not dry them (the moisture will help the breading stick better). Place the flour in a large shallow bowl or sheet pan, the eggs plus 2 tablespoons of water in another, and the panko and Italian breadcrumbs in a third. Season each with a small amount of salt to taste. Use tongs or your fingers and work in batches to roll the olives in the flour mixture, then the egg mixture, then the breadcrumb mixture. (If you want a thicker, crunchier coating, move the olives back into the eggs and then the breadcrumbs again.)

**3** When the oil reaches 350°F on a food thermometer, add about one-third of the olives to the pot and fry, moving them around with a spider or slotted spoon every so often, until golden and crispy, 3 to 5 minutes.

**4** Remove to the prepared wire rack and season with salt. Continue breading and frying until all the olives are cooked. Serve immediately.

## BREAK THE RULES

Serve these with Pepperoni Mayo (page 43) for dipping.

✽ *Domatokeftedes* are Santorini-style tomato fritters—a combination of ripe tomatoes, fresh herbs, and feta cheese fried until light and crispy. These types of fritters are commonplace in Greece, but people sometimes forget how close Southern Italy is to Greece and how similar their cuisines often are. They tend to highlight many of the same ingredients, like ripe tomatoes, which grow so beautifully there. This is my "Italian" version of the Greek fritter—tons of herbs, no feta, and lots of fresh tomato flavor.

Since tomatoes are the star of the show here, I recommend using the freshest ones you can get. Hothouse tomatoes will work, but the fritters really taste best in the summer with a ripe San Marzano or sweet sungolds. Be mindful that the amount of liquid they'll release depends on the variety—small tomatoes such as grape or cherry won't release much, while a larger heirloom, for example, will release a lot. I like to let the batter sit for at least 30 minutes, as the tomatoes will continue to release their juices and loosen it up (don't be afraid to leave the batter on the looser side). As the flour absorbs the extra tomato juice, it will increase in tomatoey goodness!

# Santorini-Style TOMATO FRITTERS

### Serves 4 to 6

## Fritters

- 1½ pounds tomatoes, diced (and seeds removed if using large tomatoes)
- 5 scallions (green and white parts), thinly sliced
- ¼ cup roughly chopped fresh parsley
- ¼ cup roughly chopped fresh dill
- 2 tablespoons finely chopped fresh mint
- 2 tablespoons finely chopped fresh basil
- 2 teaspoons dried oregano
- 1 teaspoon kosher salt, plus more as needed
- Freshly ground black pepper
- 1½ cups all-purpose flour, plus more as needed
- 1½ teaspoons baking powder

## To Fry and Finish

- Extra-virgin olive oil, for frying
- 1 cup Spicy Lemon Mayo (page 43), for serving (optional)

**1** *Make the Fritters:* In a large mixing bowl, combine the tomatoes, scallions, parsley, dill, mint, basil, and oregano and season lightly with salt and pepper. In a small bowl, whisk together the 1 teaspoon salt, the flour, and the baking powder. Add the flour mixture to the tomato mixture and mix well with a spatula until everything is combined. Taste for seasoning, adding more salt and pepper if desired. Cover and refrigerate for at least 1 hour and up to 3 days to let the flavors marry (preferred), or use immediately.

**2** *Cook the Fritters:* Heat 1 inch of oil in a large skillet over medium-high heat and place a paper towel–lined plate next to the stove. If the batter seems dry, add a little water (it should be the consistency of pancake batter).

**3** When the oil is hot but not smoking (375°F), carefully drop a heaping tablespoon of batter into the pan and let fry until the bottom is golden and the fritter won't fall apart when flipped, 3 to 4 minutes. Use a spatula to carefully flip each fritter and cook on the second side until evenly golden and crispy, 2 to 3 more minutes. Remove to the prepared plate to absorb any excess oil and season with salt. Continue with the remaining batter, adding more oil as needed, until all the fritters are cooked.

**4** Serve hot with the Spicy Lemon Mayo (if using) for dipping.

# AIOLI and FANCY MAYO

The terms "aioli" and "mayo" get thrown around interchangeably. I hate to be a stickler (a garlicky, creamy sauce is delicious no matter what you call it), but I'd be remiss if I didn't take this opportunity to break down the difference:

Aioli (which originated in Catalonia and means "garlic oil" in Catalan) is made by pounding raw garlic into a thick paste, then gradually adding olive oil, creating a pungent, creamy, semi-emulsified sauce.

To make mayo, you slowly and steadily whisk or blend oil into egg yolks until thick and creamy, then often season with garlic, lemon, and mustard or other spices. I love them both but, here, we're focusing on homemade mayo or, as I like to call it, *fancy* mayo. It's quick and simple to make and is infinitely better than anything you can buy in a jar. The basic recipe will transform your sandwiches, dressings, and even a simple tuna salad, but I've also included lots of variations that will pack even more punch and flavor. I usually make this in the small bowl of a food processor (if your bowl is too big, the blades may not be able to catch and whip together the yolks and oil properly), but you can also use a tall jar and an immersion blender. Just remember to be patient. If you rush the oil at the beginning, you'll end up with a separated mess instead of a lovely, creamy condiment. Also, did I mention you can make any of the flavored mayos by seasoning up store-bought mayonnaise instead of making your own? (I promise I won't tell anyone your secret.)

# FANCY MAYO

*Makes about 1 cup*

1 large egg, at room temperature

1 tablespoon Dijon mustard

1 tablespoon red or white wine vinegar

1/4 teaspoon kosher salt, or more to taste

1 cup neutral oil (preferably grapeseed, safflower, or canola)

1 teaspoon fresh lemon juice (optional)

1  Place the egg in the small bowl of a food processor or, if using an immersion blender, in the bottom of a tall jar. Blend for 20 seconds, or until smooth. Add the mustard, vinegar, and the 1/4 teaspoon salt and blend again for 20 seconds. Use a spatula to scrape down the sides and bottom of the bowl or jar. With the food processor or immersion blender running continuously, begin adding the oil, one tiny drop at a time, until you've added about 1/4 cup (this is critical for proper emulsification).

2  When you notice that the mixture is beginning to thicken, you can be a little less strict: With the machine still running, start adding the oil in a slow steady stream, making sure it has time to incorporate into the mixture as you pour.

3  When all the oil has been added, scrape the bottom and sides of the bowl or jar and process for an extra 10 seconds. If the mayo seems too thin, slowly stream in more oil (with the processor or immersion blender running) until the mayo is luscious and thick. Taste for seasoning and add salt, lemon juice (if using), or extra vinegar to taste. Use immediately or store in an airtight container in the fridge for up to 1 week.

## VARIATIONS

### Pepperoni Mayo

Cut 1/4 cup sliced pepperoni into thin strips and fry in a skillet with a splash of olive oil until crispy, 3 to 5 minutes. Add 1 tablespoon tomato paste and 3 cloves of Garlic Confit (page 277) when doing the final blend in step 3, then stir in the crispy pepperoni strips.

### Green Goddess Mayo

Add 1/4 large avocado, 1 tablespoon finely chopped fresh tarragon, 2 tablespoons finely chopped fresh dill, and 2 tablespoons finely chopped fresh parsley when doing the final blend in step 3.

### Saffron Mayo

Bloom a pinch of saffron in 1 teaspoon of room temperature water for 5 minutes. Add the saffron water, the zest of 1/2 medium lemon, and lots of black pepper when doing the final blend in step 3.

### Chipotle Mayo

Add 1 chipotle chile in adobo sauce, 1/2 teaspoon ground cumin, and 2 tablespoons finely chopped fresh cilantro when doing the final blend in step 3.

### Spicy Salty Mayo

Add about 6 thin slices of fresh jalapeño (or to taste), 1 teaspoon colatura or fish sauce, and the zest of 1 medium lime when doing the final blend in step 3.

### Roasted Garlic Mayo

Add 4 cloves Garlic Confit (page 277) and the zest of 1/2 medium lemon when doing the final blend in step 3.

### Black Garlic Mayo

Add 4 cloves black garlic, a dash of soy sauce, and the zest of 1/2 medium lime when doing the final blend in step 3.

### Spicy Lemon Mayo

Add 3 cloves of Garlic Confit (page 277), 2 teaspoons Calabrian chile paste, and 2 tablespoons finely chopped preserved lemon when doing the final blend in step 3.

### Dashi Mayo

Add 2 teaspoons dashi, 1 teaspoon fish sauce, juice of 1/2 medium lime, 1/2 teaspoon white sugar, and 1 teaspoon toasted sesame oil when doing the final blend in step 3.

AIOLI
& FANCY
MAYO

PAGE 43

Aioli

Spicy
Salty
Mayo

Dashi
Mayo

Chipotle
Mayo

Green
Goddess
Mayo

Back
Garlic
Mayo

Pepperoni
Mayo

Spicy
Lemon
Mayo

Roasted
Garlic
Mayo

✿ This recipe is a tribute to my time in the kitchen at Lazy Bear, the two-Michelin-starred restaurant in San Francisco. Originally, we made this dish with tempura-fried string beans that I would hand select from the Ferry Building Farmer's Market two to three times a week. The hot, crunchy string beans dipped into the cold, savory onion dip were always a big hit on the tasting menu. After the short spring season, we played around with different seasonal vegetables to replace the string beans. Maitakes—a meaty, cultivated mushroom with consistent size, shape, and year-round availability—were always my favorite. But then again, just about anything served alongside this creamy, herby dip (a play on that little nostalgic blue box "French Onion Dip" that we all grew up with) would be good.

# FRIED MAITAKE MUSHROOMS

## WITH ONION DIP

Serves 4 to 6

### Dip

½ cup crème fraîche

½ cup mayonnaise

2 teaspoons granulated garlic

1 teaspoon dried parsley

½ teaspoon onion granules

½ teaspoon dried dill

⅛ teaspoon ground celery seed

1 medium lemon, zest grated and juiced

1 small bunch scallions, whites minced and greens sliced on a long bias

1 tablespoon thinly sliced fresh chives

Kosher salt and freshly ground black pepper

### Mushrooms

Neutral oil, for frying

1 cup all-purpose flour

1 cup cornstarch

1 teaspoon baking powder

1½ cups cold sparkling water, plus more as needed

1 tablespoon vodka (optional)

1 pound fresh maitake or oyster mushrooms, cut or torn into bite-size pieces

Kosher salt

**1** *Make the Dip:* In a medium bowl, use a whisk to whip the crème fraîche until it holds soft peaks, about 1 minute. Fold in the mayonnaise, granulated garlic, parsley, onion granules, dill, celery seed, lemon zest and juice, minced scallion whites, and chives. Mix well and season to taste with salt and pepper. Cover and place in the fridge to chill and stiffen, and place the sliced scallion greens in a bowl of ice water to curl.

**2** *Make the Mushrooms:* Heat about 2 inches of oil in a medium, heavy-bottomed pot or Dutch oven over medium-high heat and place a sheet pan fitted with a wire cooling rack near the stove. In a large bowl, whisk together the flour, cornstarch, and baking powder. Whisk in the sparkling water and vodka (if using) in a steady stream, adding more water as needed to make a thin, smooth batter. Be careful not to overmix.

**3** When the oil reaches 350°F on a food thermometer, work in batches to dip the mushroom pieces in the batter, then place directly into the oil, making sure not to overcrowd the pot. Cook until golden brown, 3 to 4 minutes. Use a slotted spoon to remove the pieces and place on the prepared cooling rack. Season immediately with salt. Continue dipping and frying until all the pieces are cooked.

**4** Remove the scallion tops from the ice water and drain on a clean dish towel. Garnish the mushrooms with scallion tops and serve hot with the onion dip for dunking.

Chicken wings are one of my favorite food groups—if I see them on a menu I am ordering them regardless. This is my version of everyone's favorite lemon pepper chicken. It's the perfect combination of crispy, juicy, and flavorful. When I am feeling extra fancy, I take the time to trim the ends off the chicken drums, pushing all the meat to the bottom of the bone, creating a plump little chicken lollipop for eating and a cute bone handle for holding.

# Lemon Pepper CHICKEN WINGS

Serves 4 to 6

Neutral oil, for frying

*Dredge Mixture*

- 1 cup all-purpose flour
- 1 cup cornstarch
- 2 teaspoons lemon pepper seasoning
- 2 teaspoons granulated garlic
- 2 teaspoons onion granules
- 2 teaspoons freshly ground black pepper

*Fry Batter*

- 1 cup all-purpose flour
- 1 teaspoon lemon pepper seasoning
- 1 teaspoon granulated garlic
- 1 teaspoon granulated onion
- 1 teaspoon freshly ground black pepper
- 1 teaspoon baking powder
- 1 teaspoon kosher salt
- 1½ cups cold sparkling water, plus more as needed
- 2 pounds chicken wings

1 Heat about 6 inches of neutral oil in a large, heavy-bottomed pot or Dutch oven over medium heat and place a sheet pan fitted with a wire cooling rack near the stove.

2 *Make and divide the Dredge Mixture:* In a large bowl, whisk together the flour, cornstarch, lemon pepper seasoning, garlic powder, onion powder, and black pepper. Divide the mixture between 2 large mixing bowls.

3 *Make the Fry Batter:* In a third large bowl, whisk together the flour, lemon pepper seasoning, garlic powder, onion powder, black pepper, baking powder, and salt. Whisk in the sparkling water in a steady stream, adding more as needed to make a thin, smooth batter. Be careful not to overmix.

4 When the oil reaches 315°F on a kitchen thermometer, toss the wings in one of the bowls with the seasoned cornstarch mixture. Remove with clean fingers or tongs, shaking off any excess flour, then dip the wings into the batter in batches, letting any excess drip off as you remove them with tongs. Transfer to the unused bowl of cornstarch and flour mixture. Turn to coat them evenly, then place directly into the preheated frying oil in batches, making sure not to overcrowd the pot.

5 Fry the wings until the batter is set and only lightly golden but not cooked through, 2 to 4 minutes. Use a slotted spoon to carefully remove the wings and place on the prepared cooling rack. Continue battering, dredging, and frying until all the wings have been par-cooked.

6 Turn the heat under the pot up to medium-high. When the oil reaches 375°F, add the wings to the pot in batches and fry until dark golden and cooked through, another 2 to 4 minutes. Remove to the wire rack to drain off excess oil, season with salt, and serve immediately.

**PRO TIP**   Be sure to keep an eye on your oil temp and not overcrowd your pot when deep frying! Fried food is crunchy because when the water in the batter hits the hot oil, it rapidly turns to steam and pushes outward, causing the fry bubbles. If the pan is overcrowded or the oil isn't hot enough, the water won't convert to steam fast enough and the oil can seep into the food instead of creating a crispy crunchy exterior, leaving you with a greasy bite.

**BREAK THE RULES**

Brush the finished wings with a sweet and tangy yuzu glaze before serving: Combine 1/2 cup yuzu marmalade, 1/4 cup yuzu juice, 2 tablespoons honey, and 2 tablespoons unsalted butter in a saucepan. Bring to a simmer, then cook over medium heat, stirring constantly, until reduced and bubbling, 5 to 7 minutes. Let cool slightly, season with salt and lots of freshly ground black pepper, and generously brush over each wing before serving.

❉ I think we can all agree with my sentiment "more butter, more better." Yes, even when it comes to something inherently rich, over the top, and decadent like fried chicken. My friends Josh and Christine have a very successful fried chicken shop in Chicago called Honey Butter Fried Chicken. The name comes from dipping the crispy, hot pieces of chicken into the whipped honey butter they serve alongside their cornbread. Inspired by this perfect pairing, I made my own version, where a sweet, spicy, and sticky honey butter sauce glazes all the crispy nuggets of chicken.

After countless trials and errors, my preferred technique for fried chicken is a Korean-style double fry. The first fry at a low temperature sets the batter and partially cooks the chicken and the second, high-temp fry creates a super crispy, almost glass-like crunch and finishes cooking the chicken while still keeping it juicy.

# Honey Butter
# FRIED
# CHICKEN

### Serves 4 to 6

Neutral oil, for frying

**Honey Butter Sauce**

8 tablespoons (4 ounces) unsalted butter

2 medium garlic cloves, minced

1 to 2 tablespoons Calabrian chile paste (depending how spicy you want it)

2 tablespoons soy sauce

1/4 cup honey

**Fry Batter and Chicken**

1/2 cup all-purpose flour

1/2 cup cornstarch

1 teaspoon baking powder

Kosher salt and white pepper

1 large egg

1/2 cup cold sparkling water, plus more as needed

2 pounds boneless, skinless chicken thighs, cut into 1- to 2-inch pieces

**To Finish**

1 bunch fresh chives or 3 scallions, thinly sliced

**1** Heat about 6 inches of oil in a large, heavy-bottomed pot or Dutch oven over medium heat. Place a sheet pan fitted with a wire cooling rack near the stove.

**2** *Meanwhile, make the Honey Butter:* Heat the butter in a large saucepan or Dutch oven (large enough to toss all the chicken pieces in later) over medium-high heat until melted and bubbling. Stir in the garlic and cook, stirring, until fragrant and softened, about 1 minute. Add the chile paste and cook, stirring constantly to make sure nothing sticks, just until fragrant. Add the soy sauce, stir to combine, then stir in the honey and bring to a simmer. Cook, stirring constantly, until the mixture has reduced a bit and is thick and bubbly, 1 to 2 minutes. Turn off the heat and cover to keep warm.

**3** *Make the Fry Batter:* In a large bowl, whisk together the flour, cornstarch, and baking powder, and season with salt and white pepper. Whisk in the egg, then stir in the sparkling water in a steady stream, adding more as needed to make a thin, smooth batter. Be careful not to overmix. Season the chicken pieces generously with salt and add to the batter.

**4** When the oil reaches 315°F on a kitchen thermometer, use tongs to remove the chicken pieces from the batter, letting any excess drip off, and place directly into the oil, making sure not to overcrowd the pot. Fry the chicken pieces in batches, moving them around a bit with tongs as they cook to make sure they're not sticking, until lightly golden and crispy but not cooked through, 2 to 3 minutes. Use a slotted spoon or tongs to carefully remove the pieces and place on the prepared cooling rack. Continue battering and frying until all the pieces have been par-cooked.

**5** Turn the heat under the pot to medium-high. When the oil reaches 375°F, add the chicken back to the pot in batches and fry until very crispy, golden brown, and cooked through, another 2 to 3 minutes. Remove to the cooling rack and immediately season with salt.

**6** Turn the heat under the honey butter sauce to high. When bubbling, add the chicken and toss to coat. Serve hot with chives or scallions to garnish.

**PRO TIP** This double fry method is great when you're having guests over or prepping and planning ahead for dinner. You can brine, batter, and do the initial lower-temp fry a few hours ahead. When you're ready to serve and eat, all that's left to do is flash fry the chicken at 375° for a few minutes and toss with the honey butter sauce.

## BREAK THE RULES

For extra juicy chicken, start with a wet brine: Combine 1 cup warm water, ¼ cup kosher salt, 2 tablespoons brown sugar, 2 tablespoons sliced ginger, 2 sprigs fresh rosemary, and 8 peeled and smashed garlic cloves in a large bowl. Whisk until the salt and sugar have dissolved. Add 1 cup ice water to cool down the mixture, then add the chicken pieces. Cover and refrigerate for 30 to 45 minutes and follow the recipe as written (just don't season with salt before dipping them into the batter).

❀ Mozzarella en carrozza is a classic Italian appetizer that translates to "mozzarella in a carriage"—a nod to the golden, crispy bread that encases the gooey, melted cheese. Some consider this dish to be the godfather of the mozzarella stick, with its cheesy center, crunchy exterior, and marinara dipping sauce. They say the name comes from its resemblance to a horse carriage's reins when you tear open a sandwich and hold two long strands of gooey mozzarella.

Don't be scared by the anchovy filet. This secret addition, which you'll find in all the aperitivo shops in Italy, melts into the gooey cheese, adding a wonderfully salty bite.

# Mozzarella en Carrozza

*Serves 4 to 6*

- 8 slices soft, white sandwich bread
- 8 ounces fresh mozzarella cheese, cut into 8 slices
- 4 anchovies in olive oil
- 1 large egg
- 1/2 cup whole milk
- 1/2 teaspoon granulated garlic
- 1/2 cup all-purpose flour
- 1/2 cup Italian breadcrumbs
- Kosher salt and freshly ground black pepper
- Extra-virgin olive oil, for frying
- 1 cup Mom's Red Sauce (page 54) or your favorite store-bought marinara, to serve

1 Take a slice of bread and place one piece of mozzarella on top, tearing it as needed to fill in the center of the bread. Place an anchovy in the middle, then top with another slice of mozzarella and another slice of bread. Press down firmly on the sandwich to make sure everything holds together, then use a serrated or sharp knife to carefully cut off the crusts and make one cut diagonally, resulting in two small triangles. Repeat with the remaining bread, cheese, and anchovies.

2 *Prepare the breading station:* In a shallow dish, whisk together the egg, milk, and granulated garlic. Place the flour and breadcrumbs in separate shallow dishes. Season each to taste with salt and pepper.

3 Coat a large skillet or sauté pan generously with olive oil (you want the oil to come about halfway up the sandwiches when you fry them) and set over medium heat. Working one at a time, dip the sandwiches into the flour, shaking off any excess, then the egg mixture, then the breadcrumbs. Place as many sandwiches as will fit into the hot pan and cook until the bread is golden and the cheese is melted and gooey, 2 to 3 minutes per side. Continue cooking, spooning out any loose breadcrumbs in the pan and adding more oil as needed, until all the sandwiches are fried.

4 Serve hot with Mom's Red Sauce for dipping.

# MOM'S RED SAUCE

There is nothing more nostalgic than Mom's Red Sauce or, as we called it in our house, Sunday gravy. She made a big batch of it every week, using some for dinner that night and carefully packing up the leftovers into empty Polly-O ricotta containers to stash in the fridge and freezer for meals throughout the week. Sometimes she'd slowly stew meatballs, short ribs, or pig's feet in the flavorful sauce, and other times she'd cook it quickly and simply like this.

For the longest time, I thought everyone called this type of tomato-based sauce "gravy." Because my own family's Italian American lexicon was so ingrained, it never occurred to me that, for many, gravy is something you serve with roast chicken or pour over mashed potatoes at Thanksgiving. I guess that's why I've never loved the word "traditional"—after all, tradition is something personal, made by individuals and repetition. What's traditional in your house won't necessarily be traditional in mine, even if we live on the same street. But I digress . . . whether you call it gravy, red sauce, or marinara, this sauce has been a staple in my life and my kitchen since I can remember.

After my mom passed away, my sisters and I attempted to make her gravy several times. We went by memory and smell but could never get it just right. Had she used special tomatoes? A certain olive oil? And then we remembered the little plate of garlic and onions next to the stove.

My mom's family was French, so when she married into a big Italian family, she wanted to learn their recipes. Red Gravy, or Sunday Sauce, is typically loaded with onions and garlic but, despite loving their flavor and aroma, they didn't sit well in my mom's stomach. So rather than blending them into the sauce like most recipes tell you to, she developed her own method of frying the onions and garlic in olive oil until golden and translucent, then spooning them out and using that now-flavorful oil as the base for the gravy. Removing these golden aromatics totally changes the sauce, letting the pure tomato flavor shine through. The onions and garlic would sit on a small plate next to the big pot of sauce all day on Sunday. Whenever we would come into the kitchen hungry and curious about the much-anticipated Sunday dinner, my mom would put out a loaf of Italian bread and the little golden morsels to tide us over—the perfect pre-dinner snack for a house full of hungry (and sometimes impatient) people.

It's my go-to red sauce and I always keep a stash in my freezer, just like Mom. I spread it on pizzas and Stromboli (page 113), dunk Garlic Knots (page 112) or Mozzarella en Carrozza (page 50) in it, spoon it over pasta stuffed with Kale and Ricotta filling (page 239), or toss it with dried pasta for a quick, cozy dinner.

# MOM'S RED SAUCE

*Makes about 3 cups*

½ to 1 cup extra-virgin olive oil
1 medium white onion
6 large garlic cloves, peeled
1½ teaspoons dried oregano
1 teaspoon dried thyme
1 (28-ounce) can crushed tomatoes
Kosher salt and white sugar
1 large bunch fresh basil leaves, torn

**1** In a large, wide Dutch oven or sauté pan, heat enough oil to generously coat the bottom of the pan over medium-high heat.

**2** While the oil heats up, remove both ends of the onion, slice it in half (tip to root end), and peel. Working parallel to the root, cut each half into roughly 1-inch slices. Add the onion slices and garlic to the hot oil (they should start to sizzle immediately) and cook, stirring often, until the edges begin to brown and the onions are soft and translucent in the center, 5 to 8 minutes. Use a spider or slotted spoon to remove the onions and garlic to a plate and set aside. Reduce the heat to low.

**3** Add the oregano and thyme and cook, swirling the pan to help the flavors infuse, for about 30 seconds. Carefully add the crushed tomatoes and season to taste with salt and a pinch of sugar. Bring the sauce to a gentle simmer and cook, stirring occasionally, for 20 to 30 minutes. (The oil will separate—that's okay!)

**4** Turn off the heat and stir in the basil. Taste for seasoning and use immediately, or cool and store in the fridge for up to 5 days or in the freezer for up to 6 months.

**PRO TIP** This sauce can be used as a base and built upon by adding ground sausage, chopped beef, short ribs, pork ribs, pig's feet, or any meat of your choice—just sear in the oil after the onions and garlic are removed, add aromatics and the tomato, and braise accordingly.

**LEFTOVERS?**

If you don't want to eat the onions and garlic while you're cooking (you're a fool), refrigerate them or transfer to zip-top bags or ice cube trays and freeze for later. Add them to a pot of rice, scrambled eggs, or your next braise; turn them into a Fancy Toast (see Blueberries & Caramelized Onions on page 119); or blend them with mustard, lemon juice, and thyme to make a quick vinaigrette.

✿ One of my favorite things about traveling to Tijuana, Mexico, is eating the freshly fried, sugar-dusted churros you can buy from the hand-pushed churro fry-carts rolling up and down the rows of cars waiting to cross the border back into California. There are few things better than a hot, fresh, crispy churro. I love the sweet version as much as the next guy (and often serve these with a quick chocolate ganache—melt down some chocolate hazelnut spread with a pinch of chile powder and cinnamon, and you're in business, my friends), but I think they're even better seasoned with salt and dipped into cheesy Fonduta (page 143). Now, have you ever had a savory churro?

# Crispy CHURROS AND FONDUTA

Serves 4 to 6

## Churro Batter

½ cup whole milk

8 tablespoons (4 ounces) unsalted butter, cut into ½-inch pieces

1 teaspoon kosher salt

1 cup all-purpose flour, sifted

3 large eggs

## To Fry and Finish

Neutral oil, for frying

Flaky salt

Fonduta (page 143)

**1** *Make the Churro Batter:* Combine ½ cup water and the milk, butter, and salt in a small saucepan over medium-low heat. Cook, stirring often, until the butter has melted, then increase the heat to medium-high. Bring the mixture to a boil, then turn off the heat and stir in the all-purpose flour, using a wooden spoon or spatula to incorporate the flour into the liquid.

**2** When the mixture is smooth, turn the heat back on to low and cook, stirring constantly, until a film forms on the inside of the pot and the dough forms a nice ball (or until a food thermometer reads between 165 and 175°F), about 2 minutes.

**3** Transfer the dough to a stand mixer fitted with the paddle attachment. Mix on low for 1 minute, or until the dough is no warmer than 145°F. Turn the mixer up to medium-low and start adding the eggs, one at a time, waiting about 20 seconds between each addition to ensure they are fully incorporated. Scrape down the sides and bottom of the bowl as needed. Transfer the dough to a piping bag (or zip-top bag).

RECIPE CONTINUES

# BREAK THE RULES

Add a little rye flour for a more complex, nuttier flavor: Use ⅓ cup rye flour and ⅔ cup all-purpose for the churro batter.

**4** Line a large sheet pan with parchment paper. Cut a 1-inch hole at the end of the piping bag and squeeze the batter into 3-inch-wide circles on the parchment paper. Transfer to the freezer for 20 to 30 minutes, or until firm but not frozen.

**5** *Fry the Churros:* Heat about 2 inches of oil in a medium, heavy-bottomed pot or Dutch oven over medium-high heat and place a sheet pan fitted with a wire cooling rack near the stove. Use scissors or a sharp knife to cut the parchment paper lined with now partially frozen churros into squares (one churro per square). When the oil reaches 350°F on a food thermometer, add as many churros (while they are still on their parchment squares) as will comfortably fit, being careful not to overcrowd the pan. After a minute, use metal tongs to fish out the parchment squares (they will naturally detach from the churros soon after they hit the hot oil) and continue to cook the churros, flipping halfway through, until golden brown on both sides, 2 to 3 minutes. Use a slotted spoon to remove the churros to the prepared cooling rack and immediately season with flaky salt. Continue frying until all the batter is cooked and serve hot with warm Fonduta for dipping.

**PRO TIP** Freeze any unused piped churro dough completely, then transfer to a zip-top bag and store, ready to fry, for up to 2 months.

## LEFTOVERS?

Have extra churro dough? Make Parisienne gnocchi! Bring a saucepan of salted water up to a boil. Hold the piping bag directly over the pot and dip a sharp paring knife into the hot water. Gently squeeze out the dough, and use the hot wet knife tip to cut the filling into little 1-inch dumplings, letting them fall directly into the boiling water. (Work quickly and periodically dip your knife back into the hot water as needed.) Allow all the gnocchi to float to the top, then simmer until cooked through, another 2 to 3 minutes.

Chapter Two

# FRESH and LIGHT

Roasted
Snap Peas
and Artichoke
Yogurt,
PAGE 76

*I CALLED THIS CHAPTER* "Fresh and Light" because it's full of recipes that are, well, just that. But by now hopefully you know me, so don't expect sad salads and boring sides. All the dishes—like Cucumber and Plum Salad with Pistachio and Wasabi (page 71), Roasted Snap Peas and Artichoke Yogurt (page 76), and BBQ Shrimp, Calabrian Chile Paste, Orange, and Fresh Herbs (page 80)—are full of big, impressive flavors and satisfying crunch. It's the type of simple cooking I gravitate toward in the warmer months, when seasonal produce like stone fruit, snap peas, tomatoes, and melons need very little manipulation to let them shine. This food fills me up without ever weighing me down; just what I want to eat on a long summer night, or at a backyard picnic with friends.

❈ This is my riff on "zucchini ghanoush," a dish that my friend Dave Viana made for me years ago. It's inspired by baba ghanoush—the Mediterranean dip made from roasted, grilled, or smoked eggplant blended with tahini, olive oil, lemon juice, garlic, and salt—but this version celebrates another summer vegetable, zucchini. Unlike eggplant, whose charred skin needs to be peeled off before blending, the whole zucchini can go straight into the blender after broiling, so you preserve even more of that roast-y, toasty charred element, which gives this dip lots of depth and flavor. I always serve this with Sesame Semolina Flatbreads (page 106) or Rice Paper Cacio e Pepe Chips (page 38), but store-bought pita or lavash would also be great.

# Charred Zucchini Dip, Basil, and Cherry Tomatoes

*Serves 4 to 6*

- 3 whole sprigs fresh thyme plus picked leaves from 1 sprig
- 4 small or 2 large zucchini, stems removed and halved
- 1 tablespoon extra-virgin olive oil, plus more for garnish
- Kosher salt and freshly ground black pepper
- 3 cloves Garlic Confit (page 277)
- 3 tablespoons lemon juice (from 1 large or 2 small lemons)
- 1 tablespoon honey
- 1 teaspoon dried oregano
- 1 teaspoon za'atar
- 1 medium ripe heirloom or 1 cup cherry tomatoes, cut into wedges or halved, for garnish
- Torn fresh basil leaves, for garnish
- Flaky salt

1. Preheat the oven to 400°F.

2. Lay a large sheet of aluminum foil on a sheet pan and place 3 thyme sprigs in the center. Place the zucchini halves on top, drizzle over the olive oil, and season generously with salt and pepper. Toss to combine, arrange the zucchini pieces skin side up in a single layer, and fold up the edges of the foil to make a little pouch. Roast in the oven until tender, about 25 minutes. Carefully peel open the foil packet, exposing all the zucchini pieces, and broil for 2 to 3 minutes to give the skin a bit of char. Remove from the oven and let cool to room temperature.

3. Transfer the zucchini (discard the thyme sprigs) to a high-powered blender and add the garlic, picked thyme leaves, lemon juice, honey, oregano, and za'atar. Blend on high until very smooth, about 2 minutes.

4. Add salt and pepper to taste and spoon the dip into a shallow bowl or onto a small serving platter. Top with tomatoes and basil, and finish with a drizzle of olive oil and a pinch of flaky salt.

## Break the Rules

Add a pinch of xanthan gum (see page 21) to the dip for an extra smooth and silky texture.

✿ There are countless variations of gazpacho—a soup (or drink) made of raw and blended vegetables—but most rely on a base of ripe tomatoes. Because I can't help but toe the line between sweet and savory, I decided to try a version where ripe melons are the star. I blend them with a little tomato and cucumber, thicken it up with toasted bread and nuts, balance the sweetness with acid from the vinegar, and bring freshness with basil, mint, and cilantro. The result is a perfect, refreshing twist on your classic tomato gazpacho.

Now that you know that a good gazpacho isn't limited to tomatoes, play around and have a little fun with it. Let's get crazy. Experiment with watermelon, cantaloupe, or a blend of melons! Heck, I've even made this with peeled peaches . . . and it was quite divine.

# SUMMER MELON

## GAZPACHO

Serves 4 to 6

2 tablespoons plus 2 tablespoons plus ½ cup extra-virgin olive oil, plus extra for garnish

2 slices day-old bread, crusts removed and torn into pieces

¾ cup raw almonds, roughly chopped

1 medium shallot, thinly sliced

2 medium garlic cloves, thinly sliced

1 ripe cantaloupe, seeded, skin removed, and diced (about 4½ cups)

2 large, vine-ripe tomatoes, roughly chopped

2 medium Persian cucumbers, peeled, seeded, and diced

Leaves from 2 fresh basil sprigs (about ¼ cup), plus extra for garnish

Leaves from 2 fresh mint sprigs (about ¼ cup), plus extra for garnish

Leaves from 2 fresh cilantro sprigs (about ¼ cup), plus extra for garnish

Ice cubes, for chilling (optional)

2 tablespoons sherry or red wine vinegar, or more to taste

Salt and freshly ground black pepper

1 Heat 2 tablespoons of the oil in a medium skillet over medium heat. Add the bread and cook, tossing and turning as needed to cook evenly, until golden and crisp, 2 to 3 minutes. Remove to a plate to cool slightly.

2 Add the almonds to the pan and cook, tossing often, until fragrant and toasted, about 2 minutes. Remove to the plate with the bread (but reserve ¼ cup for garnish). Reduce the heat to low, add 2 more tablespoons of olive oil to the pan, and stir in the shallot and garlic. Cook for 30 seconds, just until fragrant and starting to soften. Remove to the plate with the bread and almonds.

3 In a blender or food processor, combine the melon, tomatoes, cucumbers, basil, mint, cilantro, the remaining ½ cup of olive oil, and the reserved bread, almonds, shallot, and garlic. Blend until smooth, 2 to 3 minutes. If the gazpacho seems too thick, add a little water or a few ice cubes to thin it out.

4 Transfer the soup to a large bowl (pass it through a fine-mesh sieve first for a smoother, more refined consistency), add the vinegar, and season to taste with salt and pepper. Cover with plastic wrap and refrigerate for at least 1 hour and up to 2 days.

5 Divide among serving bowls, drizzle over a little olive oil, and garnish with reserved toasted almonds and fresh herbs.

Summer
Melon
Gazpacho,
PAGE 63

✿ Most recipes in this book celebrate the best, peak-season produce. And while this will be most delicious made with the best stone fruit you can find, the nice thing about this recipe is that the vinegary simple syrup will transform even a less desirable, underripe, out-of-season piece of fruit into something, well . . . worth calling Mom about. Just be sure to go straight from the grill to the syrup so the open pores of the fruit absorb as much of the flavor as possible. I'm partial to apriums (a hybrid fruit of apricots and plums) because they're perfectly bite size, but any stone fruit would work. And feel free to swap out the burrata with Whipped Ricotta (page 159) or any creamy cheese.

# GRILLED APRIUMS,

## VINEGARY SIMPLE SYRUP, BURRATA, AND BROWN BUTTER CRUMBLE RUMBLE

Serves 4 to 6

### Simple Syrup

1/2 cup rice wine or white balsamic vinegar

1/4 cup white sugar

### Apriums

1 pound fresh apriums, halved and pitted

2 tablespoons extra-virgin olive oil

Kosher salt and freshly ground black pepper

### Crumble Rumble

3 tablespoons unsalted butter

1/4 cup Garlic Streusel (page 68)

### To Finish

1 (8-ounce) ball burrata

Flaky salt and freshly ground black pepper

Fresh mint or Thai basil leaves, to garnish

1 *Make the Simple Syrup:* In a medium saucepan, combine the vinegar, sugar, and 1 cup of water. Bring to a simmer over medium heat, whisking every so often to help dissolve the sugar. Turn off the heat and cover to keep warm.

2 *Grill the Apriums:* Preheat a grill or grill pan to high heat. In a medium bowl, toss the apriums with the olive oil and season with a little salt and pepper. Place on the hot grill and cook, until charred on the outside but not mushy, 1 to 2 minutes. Immediately transfer to the hot syrup and let soak in for 5 to 10 minutes.

3 *Make the Crumble Rumble:* Melt the butter in a small saucepan over medium heat and cook, swirling the pan occasionally, until it is golden brown and smells nutty, 3 to 5 minutes. Remove from the heat and stir in the Garlic Streusel.

4 *To Finish:* Tear the burrata into large pieces and arrange on a serving plate or platter. Use a slotted spoon to drain the apriums from the syrup and place on top of the cheese. Sprinkle the brown butter crumble over the top, season with flaky salt and black pepper, and garnish with fresh herbs.

## BREAK THE RULES

For an extra crumbly, nutty, and buttery crumble rumble, add 2 tablespoons of dehydrated milk powder to the melted butter and allow it to toast until brown.

LEFTOVERS?

Don't toss your simple syrup! Use it again for this recipe (the flavors will get better every time you do it) or mix 1 ounce simple syrup with 2 ounces of your favorite spirit and top with soda water to make a super refreshing summer cocktail.

# CRUMBLE RUMBLE

Crumble Rumble is the affectionate term I use to describe the crispy, crunchy, textural topping I put on just about everything. I start with my Garlic Streusel base, which provides great texture and a baseline crunch, then dress it up with extra flavor components to complement whatever dish I'm sprinkling it over. You'll find Crumble Rumble variations throughout the book, but I encourage you to experiment and come up with your own perfect versions, too. Here's the base recipe and some ideas to get you started . . .

## GARLIC STREUSEL

### Makes about 2 cups

2 cups panko
4 cloves Garlic Confit (page 277)
1½ teaspoons white sugar
1 teaspoon kosher salt
2 tablespoons unsalted butter, softened
2 tablespoons extra-virgin olive oil

1 Preheat the oven to 325°F and line a sheet pan with parchment paper.

2 Combine the panko, Garlic Confit cloves, sugar, salt, butter, and olive oil in the bowl of a food processor. Blend until the mixture is crumbly and looks like streusel, about 30 seconds.

3 Transfer to the prepared sheet pan and bake, rotating the pan and stirring halfway through, until evenly golden brown, 12 to 15 minutes. Use immediately or store in an airtight container at room temperature for up to 2 weeks.

## DO YOU WANT . . .

### Salty?
Add flaky salt, smoked salt, or citrus salt.

### Sweet?
Add extra sugar, brown sugar (for that BBQ vibe), or candied nuts.

### Spicy?
Add chile flakes that bring flavor, too, like Urfa, chipotle powder, Aleppo, or Espelette.

### Tingly?
Add Sichuan chile pepper, Sichuan pepper oil, pink peppercorns, or wasabi powder.

### Sour?
Add citric acid or grated black lime.

### Chewy?
Add dried fruits like apricots, cherries, or raisins (try grilling or smoking them for added flavor).

### Seedy?
Add sesame seeds, hemp seeds, flax seeds, and/or poppy seeds.

### Nutty?
Add candied or toasted nuts like pistachios, hazelnuts, or peanuts. Or keep it nut free with toasted sesame seeds or brown butter.

### Extra crunchy?
Add crispy rice cereal or corn flake cereal (toasted in brown butter if you're feeling fancy) or crispy fried onions.

# GARLIC STREUSEL

## DO YOU WANT . . .

**SPICY**

Gochugaru

Chile Flakes

Chipotle Chile Powder

Urfa Chile

**NUTTY**

Pistachios

Peanuts

Hazelnuts

**SOUR**

Citric Acid

**TINGLY**

Pink Peppercorns

Wasabi Powder

Sichuan Chile Pepper

**SEEDY**

Sesame Seeds

Poppy Seeds

Flax Seeds

Hemp Seeds

**CRUNCHY**

Crispy Rice Cereal

Fried Onions

Corn Flake Cereal

**SALTY**

Smoked Salt

Flaky Salt

**CHEWY**

Dried Cherries

Dried Apricots

❋ If ever there was a "just trust me" category for recipes, this one would definitely be in there. I know the combination of flavors may sound . . . odd, obscure, unique? But believe me when I say that you will love this salad. The pistachio wasabi combo—a perfect intersection of Italian and Japanese flavors—just works so well, especially in conjunction with the crunchy cucumber and sweet plum. I sometimes double the dressing so I have some in the fridge to toss with arugula for a quick salad or spread on a sandwich. It's that good.

# CUCUMBER
## AND
# PLUM SALAD
## WITH
## Pistachio and Wasabi

### Serves 4 to 6

## Salad

4 Persian cucumbers

3 tablespoons kosher salt

2 medium, ripe plums, pitted and thinly sliced

3 tablespoons shelled and toasted pistachios, roughly chopped

3 tablespoons wasabi peas, roughly chopped

## Dressing

¼ cup unsweetened pistachio butter

1 tablespoon soy sauce (preferably white)

1 teaspoon wasabi paste

1 teaspoon honey, or more to taste

Kosher salt and freshly ground black pepper

**1** Cut the cucumbers into roughly 1-inch oblique pieces, slicing on a 45° angle and turning the cucumber as you cut. Place in a medium bowl and toss with the salt. Transfer to a basket strainer set over the bowl and allow to drip and drain for 20 to 30 minutes.

**2** *Make the Dressing:* In a medium bowl, vigorously whisk together the pistachio butter, soy sauce, wasabi paste, and honey. (The mixture may look broken and clumpy, but the butter will thin out with water and re-emulsify from whisking.) Taste for seasoning, adding more honey, salt, or pepper to taste.

**3** *Assemble the Salad:* Rinse the cucumbers under cold water to remove any excess salt, then toss in a large bowl with the dressing. Transfer to a serving platter or bowl, top with plum slices, and sprinkle over the pistachios and wasabi peas.

## BREAK THE RULES

Mix the pistachios and wasabi peas with 1 tablespoon dried plum powder before sprinkling over the finished salad.

�֍ I try to avoid turning on my stove or oven in the summertime, so I'm always looking for hearty, protein-rich dinners that I can cook on the grill. This is one of my favorites. I marinate the meat in the morning or the night before (or buy pre-marinated short ribs from a Korean grocery store!); then all I have to do is prep my lettuce, veg, and herbs and quickly grill up my meat. These are fun to make for friends because everyone can pick and choose from the garnishes on the table, making their own perfect wrap.

# Grilled SHORT RIB LETTUCE WRAPS

*Serves 4 to 6*

## Ribs

¼ cup soy sauce

2 tablespoons brown sugar

2 tablespoons toasted sesame oil

2 tablespoons Calabrian chile paste

1 teaspoon colatura or fish sauce

2 large garlic cloves, minced

2 scallions (white and light green part), thinly sliced

1 stalk lemongrass, smashed (optional)

2 tablespoons finely chopped fresh rosemary

1 teaspoon grated fresh ginger

1½ pounds flanken beef short ribs

## To Finish

1 large head Bibb or butter lettuce, leaves separated, washed, and dried

Thinly sliced vegetables, such as cucumber, carrot, and radishes

Fresh herbs, such as mint and cilantro leaves

**1** *Make the Ribs:* In a shallow baking dish or large resealable bag (something large enough to hold the short ribs), combine the soy sauce, sugar, sesame oil, chile paste, colatura, garlic, scallions, lemongrass (if using), rosemary, and fresh ginger. Add the short ribs, tossing in the mixture to make sure they are evenly coated. Cover and refrigerate for at least 1 hour and up to 12.

**2** Preheat a grill or grill pan to medium-high heat. Remove the short ribs from the fridge and let sit at room temperature for 15 minutes. When the grates are hot, cook the short ribs until they have nice grill marks and reach your desired level of doneness (2 to 3 minutes per side for medium-rare). Remove to a cutting board to rest, then cut into large pieces.

**3** *To Finish:* Arrange the Bibb lettuce leaves, sliced vegetables, fresh herbs, and meat on a large serving platter and let everyone make their own wraps.

## BREAK THE RULES

Add some texture with a little Crumble Rumble: Melt 4 tablespoons unsalted butter in a small saucepan over medium heat. Cook, swirling the pan occasionally, until the butter is golden brown and smells nutty, 3 to 5 minutes. Remove from the heat and stir in 2 tablespoons soy sauce, 2 tablespoons brown sugar, 2 teaspoons chile flakes, and 1 teaspoon toasted sesame seeds. Toss with ¼ cup Garlic Streusel (page 68) and sprinkle over the finished lettuce wraps.

Give your cucumber, carrot, and radish a quick pickle (see Pickle Liquor on page 193).

❄ You hear "amatriciana," you think pasta with cured pork jowls, right? Well, think of this as a light, summery, salad version of that famous dish. I took all the elements of the Roman pasta sauce—pork, tomato, chile, and Pecorino—and made an "amatriciana" that I'm more than happy to eat on even the hottest summer night. Use the juiciest heirloom tomatoes you can find (or any mix of ripe, summertime tomatoes) and serve with bread to sop up the mixture of rich guanciale fat, sweet tomato juice, and lemony dressing.

# Marinated TOMATO "AMATRICIANA"

### Serves 4 to 6

3 large heirloom tomatoes (about 2 pounds)

1 bunch fresh chives, finely chopped

4 fresh parsley sprigs, leaves removed and finely chopped, plus extra for garnish

2 fresh dill sprigs, leaves removed and finely chopped, plus extra for garnish

1 medium shallot, diced

1 medium lemon, zest grated

2 tablespoons extra-virgin olive oil

1 tablespoon sherry vinegar

Kosher salt and freshly ground black pepper

4 ounces guanciale or pancetta, cut into ¼ x 1-inch pieces

2 tablespoons freshly grated Pecorino Romano

**1** Cut the tomatoes into large, nonuniform pieces, removing any stem bits. In a large bowl, toss the tomatoes with half the chives, half the parsley, half the dill, the shallot, lemon zest, olive oil, and vinegar. Season generously with salt and pepper and let marinate at room temperature for 30 minutes.

**2** Heat a medium skillet over medium-low heat. Add the guanciale and cook gently, stirring every so often, until the pieces are golden and most of the fat has cooked out, 12 to 15 minutes. Stir in the remaining chives (set a tablespoon or so aside for garnish), parsley, and dill and turn off the heat.

**3** Arrange the tomatoes on a serving platter and pour over the warm, herby fat and crispy guanciale. Grate over the Pecorino and garnish with the reserved chives and extra chopped parsley and dill.

## BREAK THE RULES

For a little kick, add 1 teaspoon Calabrian chile oil to the tomato marinade.

❇ I get excited every year when I start to see snap peas popping up at the farmers' market, a sure sign of spring and the end of winter. I love any vegetable I can eat whole, and I find their sweetness and crunch so uniquely satisfying. I could munch on raw snap peas all day, but because they're so good raw, I think people often forget that they're also supremely delicious cooked. Here, I roast them in a hot oven until deeply caramelized on one side, then serve over a bright and refreshing artichoke and yogurt sauce. This makes a great appetizer for a crowd, but I've also been known to eat a whole plate myself, with some focaccia (page 91) to scoop up the delicious sauce.

# Roasted SNAP PEAS

## AND

### ARTICHOKE YOGURT

Serves 4 to 6

1 pound snap peas, ends and strings removed

2 tablespoons extra-virgin olive oil

1 small lemon, zest grated and juiced

Kosher salt and freshly ground black pepper

½ cup whole milk Greek yogurt

¼ cup artichoke paste or finely chopped jarred artichoke hearts

Flaky salt

**1** Preheat the oven to 450°F and line a large sheet pan with parchment paper.

**2** In a large bowl, toss the snap peas with olive oil and about half of the lemon zest. Season to taste with salt and pepper. Transfer to the prepared sheet pan (set aside the mixing bowl to use later) and roast, undisturbed, until nicely caramelized, 9 to 11 minutes.

**3** Mix together the yogurt and artichokes in a medium bowl. Season to taste with salt and pepper and spoon onto a serving plate or platter.

**4** Transfer the cooked snap peas back to the mixing bowl and toss with lemon juice and flaky salt to taste. Spoon over the yogurt, garnish with remaining lemon zest, and serve immediately.

**BREAK THE RULES**

Toss the snap peas with 2 tablespoons Herby Garlicky Paste (page 273) before roasting and top with a drizzle of chile crunch.

✿ Everyone loves a Caesar salad. Even the mediocre ones are sort of good in a bad, nostalgic way, right? I've made a lot of Caesars over the years and, after lots of tweaking, I've finally perfected all the elements I am looking for in my dressing. The additions of various garlics, creamy tahini, and a little Calabrian chile paste are what sets mine apart. Then all that's left to do is toss it with whole, crunchy little gem leaves, grate over some fresh Parmigiano-Reggiano, and finish with a little Garlic Streusel (page 68) for crunch. This recipe makes extra dressing, but I've never had trouble getting through it.

# Crunchy CAESAR AND GARLIC STREUSEL

Serves 4 to 6

## Dressing

3 large garlic cloves, peeled

2 tablespoons Dijon mustard

2 tablespoons tahini

2 teaspoons rice wine or white balsamic vinegar

2 teaspoons Worcestershire sauce

1 teaspoon Calabrian chile paste

1 teaspoon anchovy paste

1 medium lemon, zest grated and juiced

2/3 cup extra-virgin olive oil

1/2 cup avocado (or other neutral) oil

1 cup freshly grated Parmigiano-Reggiano

Kosher salt and freshly ground black pepper

## Salad

3 large little gems or small hearts of romaine, leaves separated, washed, and dried

1/4 cup Garlic Streusel (page 68)

Freshly grated Parmigiano-Reggiano

**1** *Make the Dressing:* Place the garlic, mustard, tahini, vinegar, Worcestershire sauce, chile paste, anchovy paste, and lemon zest and juice in a high-powered blender. Blend to combine, then slowly stream in the olive and avocado oils and blend until creamy, 1 to 2 minutes. Add the Parmigiano and blend for a second or two so the dressing retains some texture. Season to taste with salt and lots of black pepper.

**2** *Assemble the Salad:* In a large bowl, toss the lettuce leaves with enough dressing to coat them evenly. Transfer to plates or a serving platter, top with Garlic Streusel, and finish with freshly grated Parmigiano.

**BREAK THE RULES**

Make a black Caesar dressing: Swap out 1 clove of fresh garlic for 4 cloves black garlic and 2 cloves Garlic Confit (page 277).

**LEFTOVERS?**

Use any leftover dressing as a dip for crudités, a sauce for pizza, or a spread for a sandwich.

❀ What's fun about this BBQ shrimp recipe is that it's inspired by New Orleans–style BBQ shrimp, which isn't cooked on the grill at all. In my version, head-on shrimp are seared on one side in a hot pan, removed, then finished in a quick and addictive pan sauce made of butter, garlic, chile, coriander, sherry vinegar, orange juice, and tons of fresh herbs. The final dish is a saucy, wonderful mess that begs to be eaten with your hands. Don't forget some Sesame Semolina Flatbreads (page 106) or a baguette to sop up any extra sauce.

# BBQ SHRIMP,

## Calabrian Chile Paste,

### ORANGE, AND

### FRESH HERBS

Serves 4 to 6

- 1 pound large, shell-on and head-on shrimp
- Kosher salt and freshly ground black pepper
- 1 tablespoon plus 3 tablespoons unsalted butter
- 4 medium garlic cloves, minced
- 1 tablespoon Calabrian chile paste
- 1 tablespoon coriander seeds, crushed
- 1 small orange, zest grated and juiced
- 2 tablespoons sherry vinegar
- 1 tablespoon finely chopped fresh dill
- 2 tablespoons finely chopped fresh parsley
- Crusty bread, for serving

1 Use scissors to cut a split down the back of each shrimp shell. Starting just below the head, use the tip of a knife to remove the vein, but leave the shells intact (this helps protect the shrimp from overcooking). Place in a large bowl and season with salt and pepper.

2 Heat 1 tablespoon of butter in a large skillet over medium-high heat. When the butter has melted and the pan is hot, add the shrimp in a single layer. Cook, without turning, until they develop a golden crust on one side, about 2 minutes. Remove to a large plate and reduce the heat to medium.

3 Add the remaining 3 tablespoons of butter to the skillet and let it cook until foamy and lightly brown, 1 to 2 minutes. Add the garlic and cook, stirring, until fragrant, about 30 seconds. Stir in the chile paste, coriander, and orange zest and add the shrimp back to the pan. Cook, tossing to combine, for another minute or so. Stir in the orange juice and sherry vinegar and use a wooden spoon to scrape up the bottom of the pan to deglaze and incorporate any browned bits.

4 Cook, tossing to evenly coat the shrimp, until the sauce has thickened slightly and the shrimp are just cooked through, about 2 more minutes. Turn off the heat, sprinkle in the dill and parsley, and gently toss once more to combine. Transfer to a platter and serve immediately with crusty bread on the side for dipping.

✻ This is another recipe that fuses Italian and Japanese flavors, here with nori and Tuscan (also called dino or black) kale. Most people associate nori with their sushi, but I use it to add crunch, saltiness, and umami flavor to all kinds of dishes. The salty nori and sweet, tangy lemon and blueberry dressing all work together to balance out the intense earthiness that raw kale tends to have. A little shallot, crispy fried onions (yes, the ones you use at Thanksgiving for green bean casserole), a handful of salty feta, and crunchy sliced almonds brings it all together. And before you ask, you don't need to use the blueberry dressing on this salad, but once you try it, you'll be wanting to put it on all your greens.

My tip for working with kale is to season it with salt and then really, truly massage it. Seriously, it is hard to overdo it. Let your hands do the heavy lifting, tenderizing the leaves and helping break down the cell structure, so it's not a workout for your jaw when you go to eat it.

# KALE SALAD

## WITH BLUEBERRY AND LEMON DRESSING

Serves 4 to 6

### Salad

1 medium shallot, thinly sliced

1 large bunch dino kale, stalks removed

Kosher salt

½ cup fresh blueberries

¼ cup crumbled feta cheese

¼ cup sliced almonds, toasted

¼ cup crispy fried onions

4 small (snack-size) sheets seasoned nori, thinly sliced or crumbled

Flaky salt and freshly ground black pepper

### Dressing

½ cup fresh blueberries

1 medium lemon, zest grated and juiced

2 tablespoons extra-virgin olive oil

1 tablespoon honey

1 teaspoon Dijon mustard

1 medium garlic clove, minced

1 small (snack-size) sheet seasoned nori, roughly torn

Kosher salt and freshly ground black pepper

**1** Place the shallot in a bowl of ice water and set aside. Thinly slice the kale and toss in a large bowl with a couple of good pinches of salt. Use your hands to mix the salt in with the kale, massaging until the leaves begin to wilt and the liquid begins to draw out, about 30 seconds. Transfer to a colander or basket strainer to drain while you prepare the dressing.

**2** *Make the Dressing:* Combine the blueberries, lemon zest and juice, olive oil, honey, mustard, garlic, and nori in a high-powered blender. Blend on high until smooth, about 1 minute, then season to taste with salt and pepper.

**3** *Assemble the Salad:* Drain the shallot from the ice water and quickly dry on a clean dish towel or paper towel. Gently squeeze out any excess liquid from the kale, then toss in a large bowl with the shallot and enough dressing to coat evenly. Add the blueberries, feta, almonds, fried onions, and nori. Season to taste with flaky salt and black pepper and serve immediately.

❉ I love endives, but I know a lot of people are turned off by this bitter and obscure-looking vegetable. One of the best ways to bring out its natural flavor and combat its bitterness is by pairing it with high levels of acid. In this salad, we get that from the intense, punchy vinaigrette made with lots of red wine vinegar. A little grated fresh horseradish adds a hint of spice, hazelnuts bring welcome texture, and fresh dill rounds everything out. If you can't find endive, radicchio or arugula work really well in its place.

# ENDIVE SALAD

## WITH ROASTED RED PEPPER ITALIAN VINAIGRETTE, HORSERADISH, AND HAZELNUTS

Serves 4 to 6

### Dressing

1 large roasted red bell pepper (jarred or homemade)

1/4 cup extra-virgin olive oil

2 tablespoons red wine vinegar

1 medium garlic clove, minced

1 teaspoon Dijon mustard

1/2 teaspoon dried oregano

1/2 teaspoon dried basil

1/2 teaspoon dried thyme

Kosher salt and freshly ground black pepper

### Salad

4 medium endives

About 2 tablespoons freshly grated raw horseradish root

1/4 cup hazelnuts, toasted and roughly chopped

1/4 cup shaved (with a peeler) Pecorino Romano

2 tablespoons fresh dill fronds

**1** *Make the Dressing:* Combine the bell pepper, olive oil, vinegar, garlic, mustard, oregano, basil, and thyme in a high-powered blender. Blend on high until smooth, about 1 minute, then season to taste with salt and pepper.

**2** *Assemble the Salad:* Trim the root end from the endives and separate each one into individual leaves. In a large bowl, toss the endives with enough dressing to coat them evenly. Transfer to a serving platter, grate over the fresh horseradish, and garnish with hazelnuts, Pecorino, and dill. Serve immediately.

## BREAK THE RULES

Sub 1 clove of black garlic for the raw garlic in the dressing.

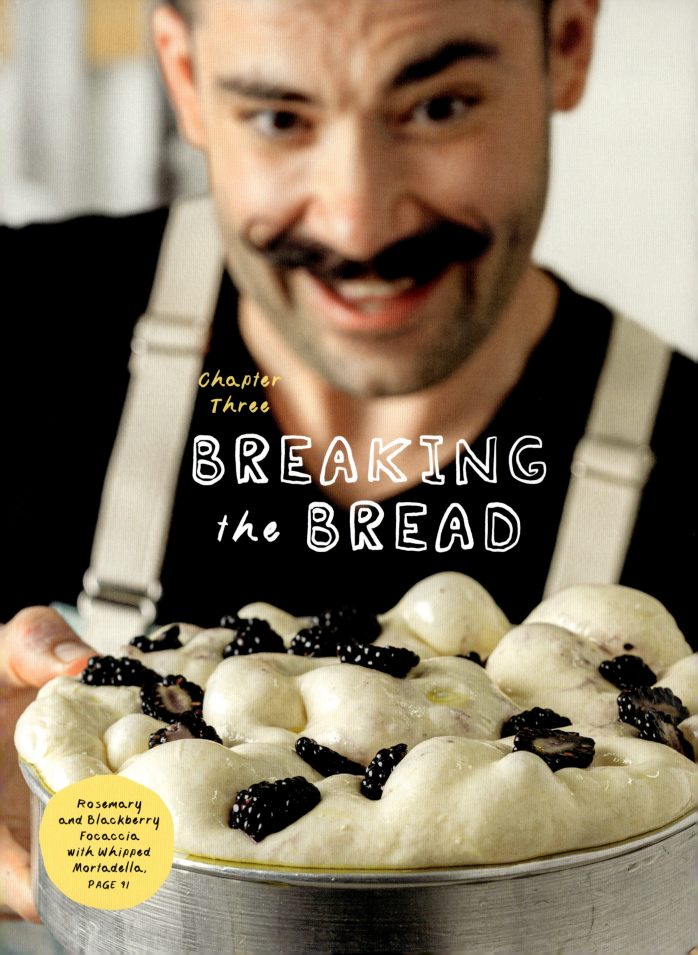

Chapter
Three

# BREAKING
## the BREAD

Rosemary
and Blackberry
Focaccia
with Whipped
Mortadella,
PAGE 91

*I KNOW, I KNOW,* baking bread sounds scary. But trust me, it's not. While my Focaccia (page 91) may take a bit of practice to truly master, this chapter is full of bread recipes for bakers of any skill level. I have breads that can be eaten as a side dish and breads that can be eaten as a meal. I even devoted an entire section to the infamous Fancy Toast (page 114), perfect for any leftover bread (or your favorite store-bought loaf). There's certainly the option to get a little advanced with tangzhongs, bigas, and multi-day rises, but there are also plenty of recipes— like my addictive Staff Favorite Cornbread (page 107) or easy Sesame Semolina Flatbreads (page 106)—that you could easily whip up any night of the week. And quite possibly my favorite part about this section: None of the recipes require a sourdough starter, so now everyone can make bread (no excuses)!

This is my version of Placinta con Patate, a traditional Italian fry bread that features layers of thinly sliced potatoes and a savory mixture of meat, cheese, and tomato sauce. I make mine with boiled and riced potatoes, but the great thing about this recipe is how versatile it is. You could make a simple version with just cheese and tomato sauce or add any cooked meats or vegetables you like. You can even make my sweet and salty version—I stuff the dough with provolone, then glaze it with honey and butter in the pan after frying. Eat these hot out of the pan, at room temperature, or reheated in the oven or toaster oven.

# FRIED POTATO, CHEESE, AND SAUSAGE PIE

Serves 4 to 6

## Dough

2 cups all-purpose flour

1/2 cup warm water

1 1/2 teaspoons olive oil

1/2 teaspoon kosher salt

## Filling

2 medium Yukon Gold potatoes, peeled

1 whole sprig fresh rosemary

2 whole garlic cloves, peeled

Kosher salt

1/4 pound spicy Italian sausage, casings removed

1 teaspoon sweet paprika

Freshly ground black pepper

1 (8-ounce) can tomato sauce

6 ounces freshly grated provolone

## To Cook and Finish

2 tablespoons unsalted butter, melted and slightly cooled

1 medium garlic clove, minced

1 tablespoon finely chopped fresh parsley

Vegetable oil or extra-virgin olive oil, for frying

**1** Preheat the oven to 375°F.

**2** *Make the Dough:* In a large bowl, combine the flour, water, olive oil, and salt. Use your hands to mix everything together, then knead until a smooth ball forms, 5 to 8 minutes. Cover with plastic wrap and set aside at room temperature to rest.

**3** *Make the Filling:* Place the potatoes in a large pot, cover with water, and set over medium-high heat. Add the sprig of rosemary and the 2 whole garlic cloves, and season generously with salt. Bring up to a simmer and cook until the potatoes are fork tender, about 30 minutes.

**4** Heat a large, wide skillet or sauté pan over medium heat. Crumble in the sausage and cook, breaking it up with a spoon, until golden brown and cooked through, 3 to 5 minutes. Transfer to a plate and set aside.

**5** Drain the potatoes, discard the garlic and rosemary, and immediately press the potatoes through a hand ricer. Stir in the paprika, season with salt and pepper to taste, stir in the cooked sausage, and set aside to cool slightly.

*RECIPE CONTINUES*

**6** Uncover the dough, turn it out onto a well-floured work surface, and divide into 4 small balls. Use a rolling pin to roll each ball into an 8-inch circle, adding more flour as needed to prevent the dough from sticking.

**7** Spread a thin layer of tomato sauce on the base of each "pie." Spoon in about ¼ cup of the potato sausage mixture and top with grated provolone. Fold the edges of the dough up and over the center, meeting in the middle to encase the filings. Press together to seal. Combine the melted butter, minced garlic, and parsley in a small bowl and set near the stove.

**8** *Cook the Pies:* Line a large sheet pan with parchment paper and place it near the stove. Heat a couple of tablespoons of vegetable or olive oil in a nonstick skillet over medium heat. Add as many pies as will comfortably fit (you'll have to do this in batches) and cook until lightly golden brown on both sides, about 3 minutes per side. Transfer to the prepared sheet pan and brush both sides with the garlic and parsley butter. When all the pies have been pan-cooked, place the sheet pan in the oven and cook for 15 to 20 minutes, or until golden brown and slightly puffed.

**9** Serve hot or at room temperature.

✳️ If you follow me on social media, you've likely seen me make focaccia. It's a bit of an obsession. I love dimpling the dough with my fingers and getting creative with sweet and savory iterations. Focaccia is not the easiest dough to work with, but it also isn't the hardest. It requires a lot of patience and a little faith—you have to trust the no-knead process. Unlike other doughs, which require a good deal of active kneading, focaccia relies on lots of rest time and several series of small folds. At first, it won't look like it's coming together, but as you do the stretches and folds, letting the gluten develop slowly over time, it will start to get shiny and puffy, and you'll know you're on the right track. This is a wetter dough, so be sure to rinse your hands with water as you stretch and fold to help avoid it sticking to your fingers.

Blackberry focaccia with whipped mortadella is a signature of mine, but feel free to change up the toppings. I love a simple olive oil and flaky salt combo, but you could top this with anything from olives and Tomato Raisins (page 276) to peanut butter and jelly. I usually cook mine in a 10-inch round pan, but it also works in a 9x13-inch cake pan (it will just get a little less height).

I highly encourage you to use a kitchen scale when making bread; however, I did include imperial measurements for all the "holdouts."

---

1½ cups (360g) plus 3 tablespoons (40g) warm water

3¾ cups (450g) bread flour

¼ cup plus 3 tablespoons (50g) specialty flour, such as red fife, einkorn, or durum semolina

2 teaspoons (6g) instant yeast

1½ teaspoons (6g) white sugar

1 tablespoon plus 2 teaspoons (13g) kosher salt

¼ cup plus 2 tablespoons (75g) extra-virgin olive oil, plus extra for greasing the pan and drizzling

Nonstick cooking spray

½ cup fresh blackberries

Leaves from 1 sprig fresh rosemary

Whipped Mortadella (recipe follows)

---

1 Pour the 1½ cups of warm water into the bowl of a stand mixer. Add the bread flour and specialty flour and mix with the paddle attachment on low speed until the dough is shaggy and combined, about 1 minute. Remove the paddle attachment, cover the bowl with a disposable shower cap (or clean dish towel), and leave on the counter to rest for 30 minutes.

2 When only 20 minutes have passed, combine the yeast, sugar, and remaining 3 tablespoons of warm water in a small bowl. Stir to dissolve and leave to activate and bubble for 10 minutes.

3 Add the yeast mixture to the mixing bowl fitted with the dough hook. Mix on medium-low speed for 5 minutes, using a spatula or plastic bench scraper to scrape down the sides and bottom of the bowl halfway through, until the

---

Rosemary and Blackberry

FOCACCIA

WITH

WHIPPED MORTADELLA

Serves 4 to 6

RECIPE CONTINUES

dough is loose, no longer shaggy, and the water and flour have combined into a sticky mass around the hook. Cover with the shower cap (or clean dish towel) and rest for 20 minutes.

**4** Turn the mixer back on to medium-low and slowly sprinkle in the salt and drizzle in the olive oil. Mix for 8 minutes, using a spatula or plastic bench scraper to scrape down the sides and bottom of the bowl halfway through, until the dough is homogenous, soft, and supple. The oil should be fully absorbed and the dough shouldn't look greasy. Remove the dough hook, cover the bowl with the shower cap (or clean dish towel), and rest for 30 minutes.

**5** Wet your hands with water. Grab the dough from the top edge of the bowl and stretch it up and over into the center toward the bottom of the bowl. Turn the bowl 25° and repeat the motion. Do this 6 more times, turning the bowl and folding down from the top, wetting your hands each time so the dough doesn't stick.

**6** Carefully turn the dough out, folded sides down, into a large bowl or wide, 6-quart plastic container. Cover tightly with a shower cap (or with the lid) and rest for 30 minutes.

**7** After the dough has rested, you'll begin a series of coil folds, every 30 minutes, for the next 2 to 4 hours (depending how warm your kitchen or proofing area is). With wet hands, grab the dough from the center, stretching and pulling it up into the air. Allow the end farthest away from you to tuck underneath, then gently place the dough down on top of the fold, taking care not to deflate the dough. Turn the bowl 180° and repeat the motion, grabbing the thicker portion of dough, pulling it up and allowing the remaining third to tuck underneath. Rotate the container 90° and repeat this entire process again, turning the bowl and stretching up from the center, wetting your hands as needed to keep them from sticking. Cover and let rest for 30 minutes.

**8** Repeat this process for about 2 hours (after the first series of coil folds), resting for 30 minutes, then doing 4 coil folds, until the dough has doubled in size. You want an ambient temperature of around 80°F, so be sure to keep your dough in a warm spot (ideally between 80 and 90°F) in the kitchen. I like to use a turned-off oven with the light on and a pan of hot water on one of the racks, or inside the turned-off oven or microwave. If your kitchen is closer to 70 to 80°F, this bulk fermentation stage may take closer to 4 to 6 hours.

**9** After the last coil fold, cover the dough and transfer to the fridge to rest overnight (approximately 12 to 16 hours).

**10** The next day, preheat the oven to 425°F and grease a 10-inch round cake pan generously with olive oil and pan spray. Transfer the refrigerated dough to the pan, cover with plastic wrap or a clean dish towel, and let rest for 1 hour. Use your hands to gently stretch the dough toward the edges of the pan, cover, and let rest for 1 more hour, or until the dough has relaxed and doubled in size. Again, if your kitchen is cold, it may take closer to 3 or 4 hours total.

**11** Top the focaccia with the blackberries and rosemary leaves, drizzle generously with olive oil, then use your fingers to press into the dough, making large dimples throughout. Bake until golden brown and bubbling, about 30 minutes. Use a metal spatula to immediately transfer the focaccia to a wire rack to cool and keep the bottom crispy. Let cool for at least 20 minutes before cutting, then serve with Whipped Mortadella to spread onto each piece.

**PRO TIP** Because salt retards the yeast and inhibits the initial gluten development, I always wait and add it after the first mix.

# BREAK THE RULES

The night before you want to start your dough, mix together 100g of water and 100g whole wheat or specialty flour and a pinch of instant yeast. Cover and let sit at room temperature for at least 12 hours. Add to the dough during your first mixing stage in step 1.

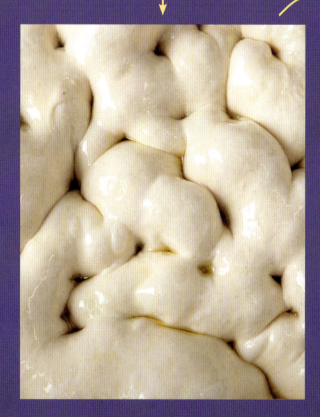

# WHIPPED MORTADELLA

*Makes about 1 cup*

The hardest part about making this addictive spread is likely going to be tracking down the mortadella. You can find it at most Italian delis, some butcher shops, and online. Pink curing salt, while not strictly necessary, is easy to find online. It keeps proteins pink after cooking and will stop your whipped mortadella from oxidizing and turning gray after a day or two; just be sure to not eat the salt straight.

⅓ pound mortadella, diced
⅓ cup whole milk, plus more as needed
Pinch freshly grated nutmeg
Pinch ground white pepper
Pinch pink curing salt (optional)
¼ cup heavy whipping cream
Kosher salt

1 Place the mortadella in a high-powered blender.

2 In a small saucepan, heat the milk over medium until warm but not quite simmering (remove it when you start to see a few bubbles around the edges of the pot). Pour into the blender and season with nutmeg, white pepper, and curing salt (if using). Blend on high for 2 minutes, or until very creamy and smooth (depending on the power of your blender, you may need to add another tablespoon or 2 of hot milk to keep it moving).

3 Set a sieve over a medium bowl and place the bowl in an ice bath. Pass the mortadella mixture through the sieve, using a spatula to press everything through.

4 While the mortadella mixture chills, place the heavy cream in a medium bowl and whisk to medium peaks, 2 to 3 minutes.

5 Fold the cream into the mortadella mixture and taste for seasoning, adding salt and more pepper or nutmeg if needed. Transfer to an airtight container and leave to set and chill in the fridge for at least 1 hour.

✤ I developed this recipe when I was looking for a signature bread to serve at a restaurant I was opening in LA. We wanted to do something fun and unique and a little bit nostalgic, so we came up with the idea of a savory "cinnamon roll" style bun. It's the same brioche recipe I would use for classic cinnamon rolls, but instead of sprinkling over brown sugar and cinnamon, I spread on herby pesto, and in place of the cream cheese icing, I drizzle over Fonduta (page 143). I usually cook these all together in a 9x9-inch pan, but you can also do them in small, individual baking pans.

# Pesto Pinwheel PULL-APART BREAD

## AND FONDUTA

*Makes 9 buns*

### Tangzhong

2 tablespoons (15g) bread flour

2 tablespoons (30g) water

4 tablespoons (60g) whole milk

### Bread Dough

2½ cups (300g) bread flour, plus extra for rolling out the dough

¼ cup (50g) white sugar

1 tablespoon (9g) instant yeast

¾ teaspoon (3g) kosher salt

½ cup (120g) whole milk, at room temperature (or microwaved on high for about 45 seconds)

1 large egg plus 1 large egg yolk, at room temperature (see Pro Tip on page 251)

3 tablespoons (50g) unsalted butter, softened, plus extra for greasing the bowl and pan

### To Assemble and Finish

½ cup Classic Pesto (page 104) or your favorite store-bought pesto

1 large egg

1 tablespoon whole milk

½ cup Fonduta (page 143)

**1** *Make the Tangzhong:* Combine the bread flour, water, and milk in a small saucepan over medium heat. Cook, stirring constantly with a small spatula, until it has thickened into a paste, about 2 minutes.

**2** *Make the Bread Dough:* Combine the bread flour, sugar, instant yeast, and salt in the bowl of a stand mixer fitted with the hook attachment and mix to combine. With the mixer running on low, slowly pour in the milk and eggs, then add the tangzhong, mixing to combine. Increase the speed to medium-low and mix until the eggs are incorporated, 1 to 2 minutes. Add the butter, ½ tablespoon at a time, and mix until the dough is smooth and doesn't stick to the sides, 4 to 5 minutes total.

**3** Lightly grease a large mixing bowl with butter and transfer the dough to the bowl. Cover with a shower cap (or a damp, clean kitchen towel) and leave in a warm place to rest until the dough has doubled in size, 1 to 1½ hours.

*RECIPE CONTINUES*

**4** Lightly grease a 9-inch square pan with butter. Use your fist to punch down the dough, then transfer to a lightly floured work surface. Use a rolling pin to roll the dough out into a 14x10-inch rectangle, adding a small amount of flour as needed to prevent sticking. Spread the pesto evenly over the dough, making sure to leave a 1-inch border at the top. Carefully roll the rectangle up into a log, starting at the bottom and working your way up.

**5** Use a long piece of dental floss, string, or twine to slice the log into 9 even "buns." Arrange in the prepared pan, making sure to leave a couple of inches between the buns (they will expand as they rest and cook). Cover with an inverted pan of the same size or a clean dish towel and leave in a warm place to rest and rise until doubled in size, 1 to 2 hours depending on how warm your kitchen is.

**6** Preheat the oven to 350°F. Whisk together the egg and milk and brush over the tops of the buns. Bake until golden brown, 25 to 30 minutes. Drizzle with Fonduta and serve immediately.

**PRO TIP** Tangzhong pre-gelatinizes the starches in the flour so they can absorb more water, which gives you a moister, softer end result.

# PESTO

When most people think of pesto, they think of the classic, Genovese version, made with basil, pine nuts, Parmigiano-Reggiano, olive oil, a little garlic, and salt. But unless I'm eating it on the Ligurian coastline (preferably made by an Italian *nonna* and served with trofie pasta), I usually put my own spin on it.

Like most "classic" or "traditional" recipes, I prefer to look at pesto as a technique, rather than a recipe. I break it down into its individual elements, so I can mix and match to make it suit what I'm cooking and what ingredients I have in my fridge and pantry. I also trade the mortar and pestle for a food processor or blender (don't tell Nonna!), which I think results in a much more consistently smooth and vibrantly green sauce. Here's my guide to making pesto and a basic recipe to use as a jumping off point:

## THE ELEMENTS

GREENS: The green component is the base of every successful pesto, but it doesn't have to be limited to basil. Any combination of herbs or greens will work—kale, pea tendrils, beet greens, carrot tops, spinach, cilantro, and mint are all great.

NUTS/SEEDS: The nut or seed of your pesto is going to provide body and texture. The more you add, the thicker, creamier, and more emulsified your pesto will be. This helps keep things rich and nutty, and provides a nice mouthfeel. Next time you're feeling adventurous, try using more nuts or seeds than the herb component for a fun twist on the classic.

ACID: I generally try to avoid any type of citrus juice, vinegar, or acid when making a pesto, and prefer to use the zest. While the acid in guacamole, for example, prevents the oxidation of the fruit, adding acid to a green puree or pesto will cause the degradation of the chlorophyll and you'll lose that bright green color. If you do want to add some acid, save it until just before you use the sauce.

**CHEESE:** The French make a pesto without any dairy or cheese, often referred to as a pistou. While I am half French, I have a firm belief that more cheese is generally more better. I usually lean toward hard cheeses such as Pecorino or Parmigiano when making pesto, but a crumbled feta or goat would provide a lovely rich and creamy result.

**UMAMI:** For lack of a better description, I like to think of this component as the added zing, whether it comes from raw grated garlic, roasted garlic cloves, half a jalapeño, or a spoonful of miso paste. This element gives you the option to add some heat, spice, or complexity to your pesto.

**OIL/WATER:** This is where my pesto took the hardest right turn away from traditional, as I tend to lean more on water, rather than oil, to emulsify it. The reason is that I am often looking to get as many uses out of it as possible—saving some for a marinade, some for pasta, and some to use as a base for my grilled veggies. From that base, I can always add more oil, breaking the emulsion, or I can serve it as a dip or spread for an appetizer. I don't particularly love the mouthfeel of a broken oily pesto, and so I will opt for more ice water to help the pesto blend, rather than extra oil.

**BALANCE:** Just like in life, your pesto is going to require balance. Taste and decide the prominent direction your pesto is going in—bitter, spicy, or herbaceous. I often lean on honey here. A few drops can bring the missing sweetness from your summer basil or counteract the earthiness that spicy beet tops bring.

# CLASSIC PESTO

*Makes about 2 cups*

3 cups fresh basil leaves
1/4 cup pine nuts
Grated zest of 1/2 medium lemon
1/3 cup grated Parmigiano-Reggiano
1 medium garlic clove
3/4 cup extra-virgin olive oil
Ice water, as needed
Kosher salt and freshly ground black pepper
Honey, to taste

**1** Bring a large pot of water to a boil and season lightly with salt, and fill a large bowl with ice water.

**2** Starting with the heartiest of the greens (like kale, English peas, pea tendrils, etc.), add them to the pot and cook, stirring occasionally with a wooden spoon, until tender, about 2 minutes. (If you're only using soft herbs, skip this step.) Add the soft herbs and greens (basil, dill, fennel fronds, etc.) to the pot and cook until wilted and bright green, 1 more minute.

**3** Use a spider to remove all the greens and transfer to the prepared ice bath (this will stop the cooking process and help the greens retain their bright color). Stir with a spoon to evenly disperse the cold water and eliminate any hot pockets.

**4** Drain the greens from the water bath and use your hands to squeeze out any excess water. Roughly chop the greens and place in a blender or food processor.

**5** Add the nuts, acid, cheese, umami element, and olive oil. Blend on high (or pulse in a food processor), adding ice water as needed to keep everything moving, until homogenous and broken down, about 2 minutes. Taste for seasoning and balance, adding salt, pepper, and honey to taste.

**6** Use immediately or transfer to an airtight container in the fridge for up to 5 days.

❋ I like to think of these as a pita-style flatbread crossed with a sesame bastone that you might find in a bakery on Arthur Ave. in New York City. They're a great introduction to the world of bread making. Because this dough has a low hydration (unlike focaccia, for example) and is not enriched with anything (like butter, egg, or milk), it's extremely forgiving and easy to work with. Once cooked, the flatbreads can be topped with just about anything. I've done these with uni and clams on *Top Chef All Stars*, I've used them to make little pizzas, I've finished them with sweetened cream cheese or chocolate hazelnut spread and fresh fruits, and I often keep a batch of cooked-off ones in my freezer to turn into sandwiches or wraps as needed for the week.

# Sesame
# SEMOLINA FLAT-BREADS

## Makes 8 flatbreads

¼ cup plus 3 tablespoons (75g) semolina (or any flour), plus extra for rolling out the dough

1⅓ cups plus ½ cup (265g) bread flour (or all-purpose)

2 tablespoons sesame seeds, untoasted (optional)

2 teaspoons (7g) instant yeast

1½ teaspoons (5g) kosher salt

2 teaspoons (16g) honey (or white sugar)

1 teaspoon (5g) extra-virgin olive oil, plus extra for greasing the bowl

½ teaspoon toasted sesame oil

Neutral oil, for frying (optional)

**1** Combine the semolina, bread flour, sesame seeds (if using), yeast, and salt in the bowl of a stand mixer fitted with the dough hook attachment. Mix to combine. In a small bowl or liquid measuring cup, combine 1 cup of water with the honey, olive oil, and sesame oil. Whisk together to dissolve the honey, then add to the dry ingredients and mix on low speed until a sticky, slightly shaggy ball has formed, about 4 minutes. Increase the speed to medium and mix until a soft, smooth dough has formed, about 6 minutes.

**2** Lightly grease a large mixing bowl with olive oil and transfer the dough to the bowl. Cover with a shower cap (or clean kitchen towel) and leave in a warm place to proof until doubled in size, about 1 hour. Use your fist to punch down the dough, then divide into 8 equal balls (about 75 grams each). Use your hands or a rolling pin to stretch or roll each dough ball into a 6x8x¼-inch flatbread, dusting with additional flour as needed to keep it from sticking.

**3** Heat a large cast-iron or nonstick pan over medium-high heat. If frying, add a thin layer of neutral oil to the pan. Cook the flatbreads (either in a dry skillet or with the oil) for 1 to 2 minutes per side, or until blistered and slightly puffed. Transfer to a plate and cover with a clean dish towel to keep warm. Continue with remaining flatbreads and serve warm.

✿ I still get calls and texts from former cooks and chefs I've worked with asking for this cornbread recipe. I used to make it for family meal in my restaurant days because it's quick, easy, and is guaranteed to be the most delicious, moistest cornbread you've ever had. I think the secret is the copious amounts of crème fraîche in the batter. I prefer a sweet cornbread, but you can always scale down (or up!) the sugar. Or throw in some cheddar and jalapeños if you're going that savory, Americana route. I know, crème fraîche is one of those "luxury ingredients," and I would sometimes get in trouble for using up our supply in the restaurant. Sour cream works in a pinch, but I urge you to try it with the real French stuff at least once.

## Staff Favorite CORN-BREAD

### Serves 6 to 8

Nonstick cooking spray

1 cup (175g) fine-grind cornmeal

1¼ cups (150g) all-purpose flour

4 teaspoons (13g) kosher salt

½ teaspoon (3g) baking soda

12 tablespoons (6 ounces) unsalted butter, melted and cooled

¾ cup (170g) white sugar

2 large eggs, at room temperature

1¼ cups (300g) crème fraîche (or sub sour cream)

1 teaspoon finely chopped fresh rosemary

1 Preheat the oven to 325°F. Spray a 9x9-inch baking pan or 10-inch cast-iron skillet with cooking spray and line with parchment paper.

2 In a medium bowl, whisk together the cornmeal, all-purpose flour, salt, and baking soda.

3 In a large bowl, whisk together the melted butter and sugar until smooth. Crack in the eggs one at a time, whisking well after each addition, and continue to whisk until the mixture is pale, 3 to 5 minutes. Whisk in the crème fraîche until just combined (the mixture may start to look broken—don't worry), then stir in the dry ingredients and the rosemary. Stir with a spatula or wooden spoon until just combined, then transfer to the prepared pan. Use a spatula to evenly spread the batter out to the edges.

4 Bake for 35 to 38 minutes, or until the edges are lightly browned and a toothpick inserted into the center of the cake comes out clean (or with just a few crumbs still clinging). Let cool on a wire rack for at least 30 minutes, then carefully invert the cake and either serve warm or cool to room temperature on the wire rack.

❊ There are certainly times for store-bought pizza dough, but if you have a couple of hours and a stand mixer, you can make something infinitely better with very little effort. My mom would call anything she made quickly and easily that would normally take a few hours or even a few days "quick and dirty." This dough is simple to make, easy to work with, and can be turned into pizza, Garlic Knots (page 112), Pepperoni Stromboli (page 113), Pistachio Calzones (page 255), and more. Like all yeasted doughs, mix time, rest time, and exact ingredient amounts will vary depending on the temperature in your kitchen, your tools, and your ingredients, so watch your dough and adjust as needed. That said, I find this recipe to be pretty foolproof. This makes great last-minute, day-of pizza, but it's even better if you can plan a day or two in advance (see the Breaking the Rules box)!

If you're not planning to use all 4 dough balls, skip the last rest in step 3 and transfer to airtight containers (32-ounce black rectangular takeout containers work well) after shaping. Store in the freezer and thaw overnight before using.

# "QUICK AND DIRTY" PIZZA DOUGH

*Makes 4 pizza dough balls*

1½ cups plus 3 tablespoons (390g) warm water (90°F)

2 tablespoons (24g) extra-virgin olive oil

1 tablespoon (15g) white sugar

2 teaspoons (6g) instant yeast

3¼ cups plus 2 tablespoons (500g) bread flour

¾ cup plus 1 tablespoon (100g) 00 flour

4 teaspoons (13g) kosher salt

Nonstick cooking spray

**1** Combine the water, oil, sugar, and yeast in the bottom of the stand mixer bowl with the hook attachment. Add the bread flour and 00 flour and mix on low speed until fully combined, 2 to 3 minutes. Cover the bowl with a shower cap (or plastic wrap or a clean dish towel) and let rest on the counter for 20 minutes.

**2** Turn the mixer back on to low speed, gradually add the salt, and mix for 1 minute. Increase the speed to medium-low and mix for another 3 minutes. Turn off the machine and scrape down the sides of the bowl and the dough hook. Continue mixing on medium speed for 4 minutes, then increase the speed to medium-high for 4 minutes. The dough should look very smooth and soft. Remove the dough hook, cover the bowl, and let rest for another 20 minutes.

**3** Divide the dough into 4 balls (about 260g each) and shape on a clean work surface, using your hands to gently drag each ball into a taut, tight, and smooth round. Spray 4 small containers (I use 6-inch disposable aluminum tins with lids) with cooking spray, place the dough balls inside, and cover with the lid or plastic wrap. Let sit in a warm spot in your kitchen for at least 2 hours and up to 4 before using.

**PRO TIP**  I keep a container of equal parts all-purpose and white rice flour in my pantry to use as bench flour when I'm rolling this dough into pizzas, calzones, Stromboli (page 113), or Garlic Knots (page 112).

**BREAK THE RULES**

After shaping the dough in step 3, cover and refrigerate overnight—this slower cold proof allows the dough to develop additional flavor. When you're ready to cook, remove the dough from the fridge and let it proof at room temperature for at least 2 and up to 4 hours.

Pepperoni Stromboli, PAGE 113

"Quick and Dirty" Pizza Dough, PAGE 108

Garlic Knots, PAGE 112

�֍ I have a soft spot for old-fashioned pizza parlor garlic knots, and considering these are one of my most requested appetizers, I'm clearly not alone. I'll even admit that I've caught my girlfriend eating the leftovers, directly from a bag, cold out of the fridge. Because I always have some Black Garlic Butter (page 141) in my fridge, I usually go the "Break the Rules" route, but the Pecorino and fresh herbs take these up a notch even without it.

# GARLIC KNOTS

Serves 4 to 6

### Knots

1 ball "Quick and Dirty" Pizza Dough (page 108) or 1 store-bought ball pizza dough

All-purpose flour, for dusting

White rice flour, for dusting

3 tablespoons unsalted butter, softened

### Garlic Butter

3 tablespoons unsalted butter

1 large garlic clove, minced

### To Finish

2 tablespoons finely chopped fresh dill

2 tablespoons finely chopped fresh parsley

¼ cup grated Pecorino Romano

Kosher salt and freshly ground black pepper

**1** If using refrigerated pizza dough or store-bought, place the dough on a work surface dusted with a little flour, cover with a large, inverted bowl or clean dish towel, and leave near a warm spot on the counter for at least 1 hour to rest and rise. If using freshly made and proofed pizza dough, place on a work surface dusted with a little flour and proceed to step 2.

**2** Preheat the oven to 425°F and line a sheet pan with parchment paper.

**3** *Make the Knots:* Roll the dough into an 18x6-inch rectangle. Brush with some of the butter, and use a pizza cutter or large knife to cut down the center lengthwise, making two even 18x3-inch rectangles. Now cut vertically, making 1-inch-wide strips, then roll and tie into a knot and transfer to the prepared sheet pan. Brush the tops with the remaining butter and bake until golden brown, 18 to 20 minutes.

**4** *Make the Garlic Butter:* Heat the butter in a small saucepan over medium heat. When the butter has melted, stir in the minced garlic and cook, stirring, until fragrant but not at all browned, about 1 minute. Turn off the heat and set aside.

**5** *To Finish:* Remove the knots from the oven and immediately toss them in a large bowl with the garlic butter; stir with a spoon or spatula to thoroughly coat. Add the chopped dill, parsley, and Pecorino, and season to taste with salt and pepper. Stir again to evenly coat and serve immediately.

## BREAK THE RULES

Substitute Black Garlic Butter (page 141) for the garlic butter.

❧ Another Italian American classic. Often confused with a calzone, a stromboli is unique because of the rolled layers that the dough and filling create. I fill mine with pepperoni and mozzarella before rolling up and baking until golden and melty, but there are zero rules when it comes to stromboli fillings. I highly recommend Mom's Red Sauce (page 54) for dunking, but if you don't have time to make some, a good store-bought marinara works in a pinch.

2 balls "Quick and Dirty" Pizza Dough (page 108) or 2 store-bought balls pizza dough

All-purpose flour, for dusting

White rice flour, for dusting

Extra-virgin olive oil, for brushing

½ pound freshly grated mozzarella

4 ounces sliced pepperoni

1 large egg, at room temperature

1 tablespoon whole milk

1 tablespoon sesame seeds

2 teaspoons dried Italian herbs

Mom's Red Sauce (page 54) or your favorite marinara, for dipping

## Pepperoni STROMBOLI

### Serves 2 to 4

**1** If using refrigerated pizza dough or store-bought, place the dough on a work surface dusted with a little flour, cover with a large, inverted bowl or clean dish towel, and leave near a warm spot on the counter for at least 1 hour to rest and rise. If using freshly made and proofed pizza dough, place on a work surface dusted with a little flour and proceed to step 2.

**2** Preheat the oven to 425°F and place a baking sheet inside.

**3** Use a rolling pin to roll each piece of dough into a 10x14-inch rectangle, making the sides as even as possible. Brush the rectangles with a little olive oil, then place a quarter of the mozzarella in an even layer down the center of each, leaving a 1-inch border on the bottom and sides and a 2-inch border on the top. Arrange a quarter of the pepperoni on top of the cheese, then make another layer each of cheese and pepperoni. Starting at the bottom, carefully and tightly roll up both of the stromboli, folding in the sides as you roll to keep the filling enclosed.

**4** Whisk together the egg and milk in a small bowl. Carefully remove the baking sheet from the oven and line with parchment paper. Transfer the stromboli to the baking sheet, cut 3 slits into the top of each one with a sharp knife to let steam escape, and brush the tops evenly with the egg wash. Sprinkle over the sesame seeds and Italian herbs and bake for 20 to 25 minutes, or until the tops are golden brown and the filling is bubbling.

**5** Let rest for 5 minutes, then slice and serve with Mom's Red Sauce for dipping.

# PANTRY-FRIENDLY FANCY TOASTS

This section is an homage to my dear friend Carrie Baird, the undisputed queen of Fancy Toasts, who I met while competing on *Top Chef* in Denver. The great thing about these toasts is that any meal can be made into a toast and any toast can be transformed into a meal. Having a quality loaf of bread is key here, whether that be a freshly baked batard of sourdough, a pan loaf of Japanese milk bread, or a slab of focaccia. This isn't the time to use a bag of pre-sliced white bread.

## BLACK GARLIC EGG SALAD

Serves 2 to 4

¼ cup Black Garlic Mayo (page 43)
2 tablespoons finely chopped celery
4 hard-boiled eggs, peeled
Kosher salt and freshly ground black pepper
4 slices good sourdough, lightly toasted
4 tablespoons unsalted butter, softened
Fresh herbs (I like chives, dill, and/or parsley)

1 In a medium bowl, stir together the Black Garlic Mayo and celery with a fork. Add the eggs and use the fork to roughly mash them (you want them to still be a little chunky). Season to taste with salt and pepper.

2 Slather the warm bread with butter, and spoon over the egg salad. Finish with fresh herbs and enjoy.

# FONDUTA & HERB OIL

Serves 2 to 4

4 thick slices good sourdough, lightly toasted
1/3 cup Fonduta (page 143)
1/4 cup Green Herb Oil (page 231)

Drizzle the warm bread with Fonduta and herb oil and eat immediately.

# GOOD BREAD, GOOD BUTTER, GOOD ANCHOVIES

Serves 2 to 4

4 slices good sourdough or Danish-style grainy bread, lightly toasted
4 tablespoons salted butter (preferably cultured), softened
12 salt-packed anchovies
1 medium Meyer lemon, thinly sliced, or grated zest and juice of 1 medium lemon
Flaky salt and freshly ground black pepper

Slather the warm bread with butter, and top each piece with 3 anchovies. Garnish with whole Meyer lemon slices or regular lemon zest and juice, then finish with a little flaky salt and black pepper.

# GREEN EGGS & HAM

Serves 2 to 4

Extra-virgin olive oil
1/2 cup leftover sliced salami trimmings (or ham, mortadella, or bacon), cut into strips
2 tablespoons Classic Pesto (page 104) or your favorite store-bought pesto
6 large eggs
Kosher salt and freshly ground black pepper
4 slices good sourdough, lightly toasted

1 Heat a medium nonstick skillet over medium-high heat. Add 1 tablespoon of olive oil and the salami and cook, stirring often, until crispy, 2 to 3 minutes. Use a slotted spoon or spatula to remove the salami to a plate, leaving the rendered fat in the pan.

2 Add the pesto and another tablespoon of olive oil to the pan and give them a good stir. When the pesto is sizzling, crack in the eggs, season with salt and pepper, and scramble, stirring quickly with a spatula, until just set, 1 to 2 minutes. Spoon the eggs onto the warm bread and top with crispy salami.

PRO TIP   If your scrambled eggs are "done and cooked" in the pan to your liking, they will be overcooked by the time you get them to the plate. So err on the side of undercooked in the pan—they will continue cooking from the residual heat and end up perfect.

CONTINUES

Pistachio
Butter &
Bacon,
PAGE 118

Tomato
Paste &
'Nduja,
PAGE 118

Black
Garlic Egg
Salad,
PAGE 114

Green Eggs & Ham, PAGE 115

Pepperoncini Tuna Salad, PAGE 119

Blueberries & Caramelized Onions, PAGE 119

Good Bread, Good Butter, Good Anchovies, PAGE 115

Fonduta & Herb Oil, PAGE 115

# PISTACHIO BUTTER & BACON

## Serves 2 to 4

4 slices good sourdough, very lightly toasted (you want the bacon to be the crunchy element here)
½ cup pistachio butter
6 slices cooked bacon (see Pro Tip)
Honey, to garnish

Slather the warm bread with pistachio butter, crumble over the crispy bacon, and drizzle with honey.

PRO TIP    I like to lay my bacon out on a sheet pan and cook in a 400°F oven until crispy. It's less messy than cooking in a skillet and I always end up with evenly cooked bacon.

# TOMATO PASTE & 'NDUJA

## Serves 2 to 4

¼ cup plus 1 tablespoon 'nduja
3 tablespoons tomato paste
4 slices good sourdough, lightly toasted
½ cup assorted color cherry tomatoes, halved
Small fresh basil leaves or buds (optional)

In a small bowl, mix together the 'nduja and tomato paste with a spoon until homogenous. Spread the 'nduja paste onto the warm toast and garnish with cherry tomatoes and basil (if using).

# BLUEBERRIES & CARAMELIZED ONIONS

Serves 2 to 4

1 cup caramelized onions (left over from Mom's Red Sauce, page 54)
2 tablespoons Worcestershire sauce
4 slices good sourdough, lightly toasted
1/3 cup fresh blueberries
Flaky salt and freshly ground black pepper

In a small bowl, toss together the caramelized onions and Worcestershire sauce. Spoon over the warm bread slices, top with fresh blueberries, and finish with flaky salt and black pepper.

# PEPPERONCINI TUNA SALAD

Serves 2 to 4

1 (5-ounce) can tuna, drained
1/4 cup Fancy Mayo (page 43) or mayonnaise (preferably Kewpie)
1 tablespoon Dijon mustard
2 tablespoons finely chopped jarred pepperoncini, plus 1 tablespoon juice
2 tablespoons finely chopped cucumber or celery
2 tablespoons finely chopped fresh herbs (such as parsley, dill, or basil) (optional)
4 slices good sourdough, lightly toasted

In a medium bowl, stir together the tuna, Fancy Mayo, mustard, pepperoncini, cucumber, and herbs (if using). Season to taste with salt and pepper and spoon onto the warm bread.

Baked Clams and Rice "Casino," PAGE 127

Chapter Four

# SHARING IS CARING

MY MOM'S COOKING always brought the whole family together, especially at dinnertime. Unlike at a lot of my friends' households, both my parents were adamant that we eat dinner together as a family every night. This sense of food as community became instilled in me at a young age and is what inspired me to become a chef. My mom showed me that sharing *is* caring, and that feeding people is one of the purest, most genuine expressions of love. While all the dishes in this book are designed to be shared with people you care about, these larger-format ones are especially well-suited to it. That said, I've definitely eaten all of these on my own—after all, you deserve a little sharing and caring, too.

❀ Lamb chops are one of those ingredients that intimidate a lot of people, but they're actually a great protein to cook at home. They're usually easy to find and cook up quickly and beautifully on the grill. And because these ones are coated with a sweet and sour (*agrodolce* in Italian) glaze, you don't have to worry about cooking them perfectly—a little extra time on the grill will only make them more sticky, caramelized, and delicious. Serve these as a decadent appetizer or alongside Crunchy Caesar and Garlic Streusel (page 79) or the Kale Salad with Blueberry and Lemon Dressing (page 83) for a light dinner.

# LAMB CHOPS

## WITH AGRODOLCE GLAZE, WALNUTS, AND FETA

*Serves 4 to 6*

### Lamb Chops

- 8 lamb chops (about 1 inch thick)
- 1/4 cup extra-virgin olive oil, plus more for the grill grates
- Kosher salt and black pepper

### Glaze

- 2 tablespoons unsalted butter
- 1/2 cup honey
- 4 garlic cloves, minced
- 2 tablespoons minced shallot
- 1 teaspoon minced fresh ginger
- 1/2 cup red wine vinegar
- 1/2 cup white sugar
- 1/4 cup Calabrian chile paste

### To Finish

- 1/2 cup walnuts, crushed or roughly chopped
- 4 ounces feta, crumbled

1 Preheat a grill or grill pan to medium-high heat.

2 Toss the lamb chops with the olive oil and season with salt and pepper. Cover and set aside at room temperature.

3 *Make the Glaze:* In a medium saucepan, melt the butter and honey over medium-low heat until bubbling. Add the garlic, shallot, and ginger and cook, stirring, until fragrant, about 1 minute. Add the vinegar, sugar, and chile paste, whisking constantly to combine. Reduce the heat to low and cook, whisking often, until the glaze has thickened and looks sticky, 5 to 7 minutes.

4 *Cook the Lamb:* Pour a couple tablespoons of oil on a clean kitchen towel and rub that over the grates of the grill or grill pan to coat. Brush both sides of the lamb chops with the chile glaze and grill for 3 to 4 minutes per side for medium-rare. Remove to a plate or serving platter and let rest for 5 minutes.

5 *To Finish:* Serve hot, drizzled with any remaining chile glaze and garnished with walnuts and feta.

**PRO TIP** Don't worry if you don't have a grill—these can be made by searing the chops in a pan or roasting on a rack in the oven and lacquering on the glaze.

### BREAK THE RULES

Add 1 tablespoon of sweet white miso paste to the glaze when you add the chile paste and serve over a bed of Whipped Feta (page 159) instead of garnishing with crumbled feta.

❁ I learned to make risotto from a maestro. Michael Tusk, the chef/owner of Quince restaurant in San Francisco, has an unparalleled knowledge of the traditions of Italian cuisine, especially when it comes to risotto. When I worked in his kitchen, only a handful of us were ordained to touch the risotto pan, and when we did, it had to be made according to a very strict set of rules and rituals. When Marc Vetri came to cook a guest chef dinner at the restaurant one night, he threw all those rules out the door. He started the risotto, then stopped it midway. He stirred it a bit, then walked away, while we enjoyed an espresso, leaving it to simmer unattended. And yet, the resulting risotto was perfection. I was so used to obsessively standing over the pot, giving the precious grains my constant care and attention, and here was Vetri essentially letting the risotto cook itself.

The key, I later learned, is the Acquerello rice he was using—a special type of Carnaroli rice that is grown, harvested, and packed at the Tenuta Colombara estate in Piemonte, Italy (see more info on page 18). It's now the only rice I use to make risotto. If you can get your hands on some Acquerello (it's available online and at some specialty food shops), use this recipe as a guide but don't stress too much about the constant stirring. If you're using grocery store Carnaroli or Arborio, follow the directions as written and you'll end up with perfect, three-Michelin-star-worthy risotto every time.

# RISOTTO

### Serves 4 to 6

### Risotto Base

4 cups chicken or vegetable broth or water

2 tablespoons extra-virgin olive oil

1 tablespoon unsalted butter

1 small white onion, minced

1 small shallot, minced

2 garlic cloves, minced

1½ cups Carnaroli rice

½ cup dry white wine

Kosher salt

### To Finish

1 cup grated Parmigiano-Reggiano

4 tablespoons cold unsalted butter, cut into ¼-inch dice

**1** *Make the Risotto Base:* In a medium saucepan, heat your cooking liquid of choice over medium heat until it comes to a simmer. Reduce the heat to low to keep it warm.

**2** In a large, heavy-bottomed skillet or saucepan, heat the olive oil and butter over medium heat. Add the onion and cook, stirring often, until translucent, 3 to 4 minutes. Add the shallot and minced garlic and cook, stirring, until fragrant, 1 to 2 minutes. Add the rice and stir to coat it evenly with the oil and butter. Toast the rice, stirring often to make sure it cooks evenly, until the edges become slightly translucent, 2 to 3 minutes.

*RECIPE CONTINUES*

**3** Pour in the wine and cook, stirring continuously, until the raw alcohol flavor has cooked off and the rice has absorbed all the wine, about 2 minutes. Begin adding warm broth to the rice, 1 ladleful at a time. Allow each ladleful of broth to be mostly absorbed by the rice before adding the next (if you scrape your wooden spoon through the rice, you should be able to see the bottom of the pot for just a moment before the risotto fills it back in) and stir continuously. Continue adding broth, 1 ladleful at a time, until all the liquid is gone and the rice is tender and creamy, 18 to 20 minutes; "al dente" with a slight bite is traditional for risotto. (If you're running low on broth, add a little warm water to the saucepan to stretch it.)

**4** *To Finish:* Remove the pan from the heat, aggressively stir in the Parmigiano and the cold, diced butter, beating the risotto with a spoon until creamy. Season to taste with salt (keep in mind that risotto will set up and thicken quickly), divide among plates or bowls, and serve immediately.

**PRO TIP** A proper risotto should pool loosely out on a wide plate and not stand up like porridge or oatmeal in a bowl or, God forbid, a ring mold. It is best to make it a little thinner in the final stages before going to the plate.

## VARIATIONS

### Pea (or any green vegetable)

Blanch 1¼ cups frozen peas in boiling water for 30 seconds. Drain and set aside ¼ cup for garnish. Add the 1 cup of peas to a high-powered blender along with about 3 tablespoons of roughly chopped fresh dill and the grated zest of ½ medium lemon. Blend until smooth, about 1 minute, then season to taste with salt and pepper. Stir the puree and reserved blanched peas into the risotto along with the Parmigiano and butter in step 4.

### Saffron

Before starting the risotto, crush a pinch of saffron into a small bowl and add 2 ice cubes. As the ice melts, it will bloom the saffron. Stir the saffron water and grated zest of ½ medium lemon into the risotto along with the Parmigiano and butter in step 4. Finish the dish with a drizzle of olive oil.

### Balsamic & Parm

Stir in about 2 tablespoons of aged balsamic vinegar and add extra butter and Parmigiano in step 4. Finish the dish with shaved Parmigiano cheese and an extra drizzle of balsamic.

**LEFTOVERS?**

Have leftover risotto? Turn it into Baked Clams and Rice "Casino" (page 127)! Instead of cooking the rice, mix 2 cups of leftover risotto with the smoked paprika and tomato paste, then follow the recipe as written starting at step 3 (just don't forget to preheat the oven).

❋ I don't know if it's the Italian American in me, but whenever I think of clams, I automatically think of clams casino. Maybe it's because I ate so many of them growing up. The one thing I never loved about the dish is all the breadcrumbs—they were always too dry and bland. To remedy this, I started using creamy leftover risotto (or well-seasoned short-grain rice) as the base and mixing in the flavorful clam cooking liquid. It's a game changer. In true casino style, I spoon the filling into the empty clam shells before topping with breadcrumbs and baking. If that feels too fussy, just transfer the filling to a baking dish, sprinkle over the breadcrumb mixture, and throw it in the oven.

# BAKED CLAMS
## AND RICE
## "CASINO"

### Serves 4 to 6

1 cup Carnaroli rice

2 cups chicken broth

2 tablespoons plus 2 tablespoons extra-virgin olive oil

1 dried bay leaf

1 tablespoon tomato paste

1 tablespoon smoked paprika

24 cherrystone or littleneck clams (about 2½ pounds)

4 medium garlic cloves, minced

Kosher salt and freshly ground black pepper

Rock salt (or crumpled aluminum foil), for balancing the clams while baking

¼ cup breadcrumbs

2 tablespoons unsalted butter, softened

½ large or 1 small bunch fresh Italian parsley, finely chopped (about ½ cup)

¼ cup grated Parmigiano-Reggiano

2 tablespoons dried oregano

**1** Preheat the oven to 400°F.

**2** Rinse the rice in a fine-mesh strainer and place it in a medium pot with the chicken broth, 2 tablespoons of the olive oil, the bay leaf, tomato paste, and smoked paprika. Bring to a boil, stir to combine everything, then reduce the heat to low and cover the pot with a tight-fitting lid. Cook for 18 to 20 minutes, or until the water has been absorbed and the rice is tender. Let stand for 5 minutes, then remove the bay leaf and transfer to a large bowl to cool.

**3** Rinse the clams under cold running water and use a small kitchen brush to remove any sand or grit. Discard any that are open or don't close when tapped. Place the clams in a large pot and add enough water to barely come up the sides of the clams. Cover, bring to a boil, and cook for 3 to 4 minutes, or until the clams have just opened. Use a slotted spoon or spider to transfer them to a large bowl or sheet pan and discard any that remain closed.

**4** Strain the clam cooking liquid through a fine mesh sieve or coffee filter and set aside.

*RECIPE CONTINUES*

**5** Remove the cooked clams from their shells, roughly chop them, and add to the bowl with the rice. Add the garlic and the reserved clam juice. Stir everything together to combine and season to taste with salt and pepper. Use a spoon or spatula to spoon the rice mixture into each clam shell, packing it down slightly.

**6** Line a rimmed baking sheet or large baking dish with an even layer of rock salt and arrange the stuffed clam shells on top.

**7** In a small bowl, mix together the breadcrumbs, remaining 2 tablespoons olive oil, softened butter, chopped parsley, Parmigiano, and oregano and season to taste with salt and pepper. Sprinkle the breadcrumb mixture over the clams.

**8** Bake until the stuffing is golden brown and crispy, 10 to 15 minutes. Serve immediately.

**BREAK THE RULES**

Stir ¼ cup 'nduja into the rice mixture when you add the garlic and chopped clams in step 5.

"Plate like a chef" by pulsing the parsley stems and leftover rock salt in a food processor to make a striking green salt that will hold the clams in place on your serving platter.

✿ What Italian American kid doesn't love meatballs? I'm certainly no exception, and my mom made some of the best. Unlike Mom's Red Sauce (page 54), which I follow to the letter every time, I've taken a few liberties with this one. The main difference is that I use the panade method, which sounds fancy, but it just means that I mix the ricotta, eggs, breadcrumbs, and cooked onion and garlic into a paste before folding it into the meat. Pre-mixing these ingredients helps ensure that they'll incorporate evenly into your meatballs. And because I think meatballs can get dry if they're braised for too long, I prefer to cook them just until tender, 35 to 45 minutes. You can absolutely serve these over spaghetti, but my preferred way to eat them is sprinkled with Parmigiano-Reggiano with fresh Focaccia (page 91) on the side for scooping and dipping.

# MOM'S MEATBALLS

### Serves 4 to 6

## Meatballs

3 tablespoons extra-virgin olive oil, plus more for frying

1/2 medium white onion, minced

3 garlic cloves, finely chopped

1/4 cup ricotta

2 large eggs

1/2 cup panko

1 pound ground beef (80/20)

1 pound ground pork

1/2 large or 1 small bunch fresh Italian parsley, finely chopped (about 1/2 cup)

1 tablespoon dried oregano

1 tablespoon dried thyme

1 teaspoon Calabrian chile paste or chile flakes

2 teaspoons kosher salt

Freshly ground black pepper

1 cup freshly grated Parmigiano-Reggiano

1/2 cup freshly grated Pecorino Romano

## Sauce

1/2 medium white onion, cut into 1-inch slices

2 medium garlic cloves, finely chopped

1/2 teaspoon chile flakes

1 tablespoon tomato paste

1 (28-ounce) can crushed tomatoes

Kosher salt and freshly ground black pepper

## To Finish

Freshly grated Parmigiano-Reggiano

Focaccia (page 91), for serving (optional)

**1** *Make the Meatballs:* Heat the 3 tablespoons of oil in a large sauté pan or Dutch oven over medium heat. Add the onion and garlic to the pot and cook, stirring often, until translucent and starting to soften, 3 to 5 minutes. Set aside to cool slightly.

**2** In a medium bowl, use a spatula or wooden spoon to mix together the ricotta and eggs. Add the breadcrumbs, mix to combine, then stir in the onion and garlic mixture (this is your panade!).

**3** Place the beef and pork in a large mixing bowl. Add the panade, parsley, oregano, thyme, chile paste, and salt, and season generously with black pepper. Use a spatula or your hands to mix everything together very well, then stir in the Parmigiano and Pecorino.

**4** Use your hands to roll the meatballs into 20 equal balls, each a little larger than a golf ball. Be sure not to pack them together too tightly or your balls will be dense.

**5** Heat a generous layer of olive oil in the same Dutch oven you cooked the onions in over medium-high heat. Add the meatballs to the pot in batches and cook, turning with tongs or a large spoon, until nicely browned on all sides, 6 to 8 minutes. Remove to a large plate or sheet pan and continue until all the meatballs have been seared.

**6** *Make the Sauce:* Add the onion, garlic, and chile flakes to the meatball pot and cook, stirring often, until the onion is translucent and starting to soften, about 5 minutes. Remove the onion and garlic. Stir in the tomato paste and cook, stirring constantly to ensure it doesn't burn, until fragrant, 1 to 2 minutes. Add the crushed tomatoes and bring the sauce to a simmer. Cook, stirring occasionally, until the sauce has reduced slightly and the raw tomato flavor has cooked off, about 15 minutes.

**7** Return the meatballs to the pot and bring to a simmer. Cook, stirring often to make sure nothing is sticking to the bottom of the pot, until the sauce has reduced slightly and the meatballs are tender, 35 to 45 minutes. Season the sauce to taste with salt and pepper and serve the meatballs with grated Parmigiano and homemade focaccia (if using) on the side.

**BREAK THE RULES**

Grind your own meat (using a blend of brisket, chuck, and short rib) and add ¼ pound prosciutto to the mix.

Mom's
Meatballs,
PAGE 130

❋ I developed this recipe during my pop-up days, when I was regularly cooking dinners for eighteen-plus people. Short ribs are famously good to make for a crowd because they lend themselves to large batch cooking and are universally adored. The key to a good short rib is twofold: getting a hard sear on the meat and blending the braising vegetables into the sauce. The caramelized meat gives the dish an added layer of flavor and the vegetables help thicken the sauce, creating a luscious gravy that coats and glazes the ribs. I like to add a little squid ink to the sauce at the end (see Break the Rules on page 145) and serve over mashed potatoes or whipped cauliflower (see the recipe for Whipped Cauliflower and Everything Bagel Crumble Rumble on page 200)—the stark contrast of black and white looks great on the plate.

# Weeknight SHORT RIBS

### Serves 4 to 6

2½ pounds bone-in beef short ribs

Kosher salt and freshly ground black pepper

2 tablespoons neutral oil

1 medium white onion, roughly chopped

2 medium carrots, peeled and roughly chopped

2 stalks celery, roughly chopped

6 garlic cloves, smashed

½ pound whole cremini mushrooms

1 (6-ounce) can tomato paste

2 sprigs fresh rosemary

3 sprigs fresh sage

4 sprigs fresh thyme

½ cup dry red wine

1 tablespoon Worcestershire sauce

1 bunch dino kale, stems removed and roughly chopped

**1** Set the Instant Pot to sauté and season the short ribs generously with salt and pepper. When the pot is hot, add the oil and short ribs and cook until deeply golden brown on all 6 sides, about 18 minutes total. Depending how large your Instant Pot is, you may need to do this in batches.

**2** Remove the short ribs to a plate and add the onion, carrot, celery, garlic, and mushrooms to the pot. Cook, stirring often, until the veggies are just starting to soften, 3 to 5 minutes. Add the tomato paste and cook, stirring constantly, for 1 minute to cook off the raw tomato flavor. Tie the rosemary, sage, and thyme together with twine and add to the pot. Pour in the wine and cook until the liquid is bubbling and the raw alcohol has cooked off, 2 to 3 minutes. Add back in the short ribs and season with a little more salt and pepper. Stir in the Worcestershire sauce and kale, seal up the pot, and pressure cook on high for 45 minutes.

*RECIPE CONTINUES*

**3** Allow the pressure to release from the pot, then open and remove the short ribs to a plate. Remove and discard the herb bundle. Set a strainer or colander over a large pot and carefully strain the vegetable mixture, catching all the cooking liquid in the pot. Reserve the cooked vegetables.

**4** Place the pot over medium-high heat and bring the cooking liquid up to a simmer. Cook, stirring occasionally, until the liquid has reduced by about half, 10 to 15 minutes. Transfer the reserved vegetables and reduced cooking liquid to a high-powered blender and blend until smooth, 1 to 2 minutes.

**5** Return the sauce to the pot and add the short ribs. Bring to a simmer, taste for seasoning, and serve.

**PRO TIP** I prefer to use an electric pressure cooker (like an Instant Pot), which cuts the cooking time by two-thirds and results in the same luscious and tender final product. But if you don't have a pressure cooker, you can sear the ribs and cook the veg in a large Dutch oven, then cover and braise in a 300°F oven for 3 to 4 hours until fork tender.

**BREAK THE RULES**

Add 1 tablespoon of squid ink to the blended sauce for a unique flavor and dramatic look.

Add ½ cup Sicilian Soffritto (page 180) instead of the tomato paste for a richer and deeper flavor.

**LEFTOVERS?**

Give any leftover short ribs a quick blend in a food processor with a little bit of the sauce and use as a filling for pasta.

�֎ Ribeye is, hands-down, my favorite cut of beef. It's got great flavor, good marbling, and a nice fat cap, not to mention it slices up beautifully. The leaner filet tends to be more expensive, and the New York Strip always seems chewy. Little known fact, but when the USDA is grading cows and separating them into Prime, Choice, and Select categories, the only cut or "steak" they look at to determine the grade of the entire cow is the ribeye. If they're using that as their gold standard, I don't see a reason to be eating any other cut of beef. Some say a good ribeye doesn't need anything in the way of accouterments; I say some crispy potatoes and a creamy peppercorn sauce can only make things better.

# RIBEYE, CRISPY FINGERLINGS,

## AND ALL

## THE PEPPERCORNS

## SAUCE

### Serves 4

### Ribeyes

2 (1- to 1½-inch-thick) bone-in ribeye steaks

1 tablespoon neutral oil

Kosher salt

2 tablespoons unsalted butter

### Potatoes

1½ pounds fingerling potatoes

3 large garlic cloves, peeled and smashed

½ small bunch fresh thyme

1 sprig fresh rosemary

½ teaspoon baking soda

1 tablespoon apple cider vinegar

Kosher salt

2 tablespoons extra-virgin olive oil

### All the Peppercorns Sauce

2 tablespoons whole peppercorns (I like a mix of pink, white, green, and black)

2 tablespoons unsalted butter

1 medium shallot, minced

3 medium garlic cloves, minced

¼ cup Madeira or cognac

1 cup chicken or beef broth

½ cup crème fraîche

2 tablespoons Dijon mustard

Kosher salt

Fresh lemon juice, to taste

2 tablespoons finely chopped fresh parsley

2 tablespoons finely chopped fresh chives

**1** Preheat the oven to 450°F and remove the ribeyes from the fridge.

**2** *Cook the Potatoes:* Place the potatoes in a medium pot and cover with water. Add the garlic, thyme, rosemary, baking soda, and apple cider vinegar and season very generously with salt. Bring to a boil over medium-high heat, then reduce to a simmer and cook until the potatoes are tender and easily pierced with a knife, about 15 minutes. Drain and transfer to a sheet pan to cool.

**3** *Toast peppercorns for the Sauce:* Heat a medium skillet over medium heat. Add the peppercorns and cook, swirling the pan often to make sure they toast evenly, until fragrant, 2 to 3 minutes. Transfer to a mortar and pestle and grind into a coarse powder. Set aside.

**4** *Back to the Potatoes:* When cool enough to handle, place the potatoes on a cutting board and use your palm (or the bottom of a coffee mug) to gently but firmly smash each one. Return to the sheet pan, toss with the olive oil, and season generously with salt. Roast until crispy and golden, 12 to 15 minutes.

*RECIPE CONTINUES*

**5** *Cook the Ribeyes:* Heat the oil in a large stainless steel or cast-iron skillet over medium-high heat and place a clean wire rack set in a rimmed baking sheet near the stove. Season the steaks generously with salt. When the oil is just smoking, add the ribeyes, pressing down firmly to ensure full contact with the hot pan, and cook until they develop a nice crust, about 3 minutes per side. Add the butter to the skillet and continue cooking, tilting the pan and spooning the melted butter over the steaks, until a thermometer inserted into the center registers 125°F, about 2 minutes longer. Transfer the steaks to the wire rack to rest.

**6** *Make the Sauce:* Reduce the heat to medium-low and add the butter to the pan. Stir in the shallot and garlic and cook, stirring constantly, until fragrant and starting to soften, about 1 minute. Turn off the heat, add the Madeira, and use a long match or lighter to carefully ignite the alcohol. Turn the heat back to medium-low, add the broth, and cook until slightly reduced, 1 to 2 minutes. Stir in the crème fraîche and mustard and whisk to combine. Let the sauce simmer for a minute or so, then stir in the peppercorns, season to taste with salt and lemon juice, and stir in the parsley and chives.

**7** Cut the steak into thick slices. Arrange the crispy fingerlings on a serving platter, place the steak on top, and pour over the peppercorn sauce. Serve immediately.

**PRO TIP** Adding baking soda to the potato water helps the exteriors of the potatoes break down more, creating a starchy slurry that leads to an extra-crisp exterior when roasted.

**BREAK THE RULES**

Toss the potatoes with 3 tablespoons Herby Garlicky Paste (page 273) before roasting and drizzle them with fontina Fonduta (page 143) before serving.

❈ Branzino is one of my favorite fish to cook, particularly if I'm looking for a nice, crispy skin. Also known as European sea bass, this mild white fish has firm flesh, is very low in fat, and is easy and quick to cook. Here, the fish is pan-seared, basted in a delicious Black Garlic Butter, and served over sautéed spinach. It feels like restaurant cooking but requires only one pan and is ready in under 10 minutes. But don't let the fancy-sounding branzino scare you off; black garlic butter is delicious on everything from salmon to halibut, too.

# Black Garlic Butter BRANZINO

### Serves 4

2 tablespoons extra-virgin olive oil, plus extra for brushing the fish

1 large garlic clove, peeled

1 pound fresh Bloomsdale or baby spinach

Kosher salt and freshly ground black pepper

4 skin-on branzino filets

4 tablespoons Black Garlic Butter (recipe follows)

Lemon wedges, to serve

**1** Heat the olive oil in a large skillet over medium-high heat and stab the garlic clove with the tines of a fork. Stir the spinach into the pan, season to taste with salt and pepper, and cook, stirring often with the garlic clove fork, until the spinach has wilted and cooked down, no more than 2 to 3 minutes. Divide among serving plates and cover with a clean dish towel to keep warm. Wipe out the pan with a paper towel.

**2** Dry the skin of the branzino filets with a paper towel then brush with a little olive oil and season with salt. Heat the same skillet over medium-high heat and place the fish, skin-side down, in the pan (depending on the size of your pan, you may need to do this in batches or use 2 skillets). Cook, pressing down with a spatula to help the skin make contact with the pan, until the skin is starting to crisp, about 1½ minutes. Add the butter and cook until foamy, about 30 seconds, then flip the filets and cook, tilting the pan a bit and spooning the butter over the fish, until just cooked through, about 1 minute.

**3** Divide the fish among the serving plates. Pour over any black garlic butter left in the pan and finish with a squeeze of fresh lemon juice. Serve with lemon wedges.

# BLACK GARLIC BUTTER

Makes about ½ cup

This butter is one of my favorite condiments, period. It's the best of your classic garlic butter without the pungent raw garlic flavor. Plus, you get added complexity from the fermented black garlic. I toss Garlic Knots (page 112) in it, spread it on Fancy Toasts (page 114), and spoon it over Fresh Corn Polenta (page 167). I always have a jar of this in my fridge and firmly believe that you should, too.

6 black garlic cloves

8 tablespoons (4 ounces) unsalted butter (preferably cultured), softened

1 tablespoon white miso paste

1 medium Meyer (or regular) lemon, zest grated

1 tablespoon freshly ground black pepper

Press the black garlic through a fine-mesh sieve to remove any skins and make a smooth paste. In a small bowl, mash together the garlic paste, butter, miso paste, lemon zest, and black pepper until homogenous and irresistible.

**BREAK THE RULES**

Add 3 cloves Garlic Confit (page 277) for even more complexity and garlicky goodness.

# FONDUTA

The easiest way to understand fonduta is to think of it as Italian nacho cheese. Or, if you're French, Italian fondue. You'll normally find fonduta in the northwestern region of Piedmont, at the base of the Alps. It is typically made with fontina cheese, thickened with egg yolks, and served with local truffles, though my simplified technique makes it more of an everyday sauce. I blend grated cheese with warm milk, cream, or half and half (depending how rich I want my fonduta to be), add a little Garlic Confit (page 277) or granulated garlic, then add a pinch of xanthan gum to keep it stable. That's it! This base recipe comes together in minutes and adds the perfect creamy, cheesy layer to just about anything—drizzle it over grilled vegetables, meats, fish, pastas, and, of course, bread.

What I love most about this fonduta is its versatility. You can use any cheese you like in place of the Parmigiano-Reggiano and Pecorino Romano and change up the seasonings to suit your palate and the rest of your menu. I've added a pinch of smoked paprika or curry powder, black garlic, or even roasted squash for my Butternut Mac n Cheese (page 185). Use all whole milk for a lighter fonduta, all cream for a richer one, or half and half for a nice middle ground. You can also easily adjust the consistency, adding more hot milk or cream to make it thinner, or more cheese to thicken it. Xanthan gum gives the sauce an extra thick and creamy texture and makes it easier to hold stable and smooth for longer periods but is not strictly necessary.

# FONDUTA

*Makes about 1 cup*

1 cup freshly grated Parmigiano-Reggiano (or any cheese)

½ cup freshly grated Pecorino Romano (or any cheese)

2 cloves Garlic Confit (page 277) or 1 teaspoon granulated garlic

¾ cup half and half, milk, or heavy cream

Pinch xanthan gum (optional)

Kosher salt

**1** Place the Parmigiano, Pecorino, and Garlic Confit in a blender.

**2** In a small saucepan, heat the half and half over medium and turn off the heat just before it reaches a simmer. Turn the blender to high and slowly stream in half of the warm half and half (or milk or heavy cream). Add the xanthan gum (if using) and continue adding half and half, a little at a time (depending how thick you want the fonduta, you may only need ½ cup total), until the mixture is silky and smooth. Season to taste with salt and use immediately, keep warm in a pot with a lid over very low heat, or cool and refrigerate until ready to use.

❊ This is a serious bang-for-your-buck recipe. It looks and tastes like something you would get at a high-end restaurant but is surprisingly easy (and affordable!) to cook at home. Pork chops, like any protein, really benefit from a good sear, so make sure you give them ample time in the pan to get that good caramelization before flipping. And don't be afraid to eat pink pork, as long as you trust your butcher; a medium pork chop is a thing of beauty.

# PORK CHOPS

## WITH

## MUSTARD BERRY JUS

### Serves 4

### Pork Chops

4 (1-inch-thick) bone-in pork chops

2 teaspoons kosher salt

1 teaspoon white sugar

2 tablespoons neutral oil

2 tablespoons unsalted butter

1 medium shallot, thinly sliced

1 small bunch fresh thyme

### Mustard Berry Jus

2 tablespoons honey

1 cup fresh blackberries, sliced in half

¼ cup chicken stock, bourbon, or water

2 tablespoons Dijon mustard

3 tablespoons cold unsalted butter, cut into ½-inch dice

½ medium lemon, juiced

Kosher salt and freshly ground black pepper

3 tablespoons finely chopped fresh parsley

**1** *Cook the Pork:* Pat the pork chops dry with a paper towel. Combine the salt and sugar in a small bowl and sprinkle evenly over the pork chops.

**2** Heat the oil in a very large stainless steel or cast-iron skillet over medium-high heat and place a clean wire rack set in a rimmed baking sheet near the stove. When the oil is just smoking, turn the chops on their sides, and use tongs to transfer to the hot pan, fat edge side down. Cook, holding with tongs to keep them from falling over, for about 1 minute, or until some of the fat has cooked out into the pan and the edges are crisp. Carefully lay the chops flat in the pan and cook, turning occasionally, until starting to brown, about 2 minutes per side. Add the butter, shallot, and thyme to the skillet and continue cooking, tilting the pan and spooning the foaming butter mixture over the chops, until deeply golden brown on both sides and the thickest part of the chop registers 135°F on a food thermometer, 2 to 3 minutes longer. Transfer the chops to the wire rack to rest.

**3** *Make the Sauce:* Reduce the heat to medium and add the honey and sliced blackberries to the pan with the rendered pork fat and roasted butter. Once the honey starts to bubble and darken in color, add the chicken stock (or bourbon or water) and cook, scraping the bottom of the pan to release any stuck bits, until it has reduced slightly, 1 to 2 minutes. Add the mustard and cold butter and cook, swirling the pan vigorously to help mix in the butter, for about 1 minute. Add the lemon juice, season to taste with salt and pepper, and then stir in the chopped parsley.

**4** Divide the chops among plates or transfer to a serving platter and pour over the pan sauce.

## BREAK THE RULES

For more flavorful chops, do a dry brine: After seasoning the pork chops with salt and sugar in step 1, transfer them to a wire rack set in a rimmed baking sheet and refrigerate, uncovered, for at least 8 hours and up to 24. Then follow the recipe as written.

Add a splash of liquid shio koji or Yondu to the blackberry sauce at the end and garnish the dish with pickled peppers (see Pickle Liquor on page 193).

✿ I learned about bomba—a spicy sauce typically made with Calabrian chiles, oil, and vegetables like peppers, artichoke, or eggplant to help soften the heat—on a recent trip to Italy. It's sort of like the Italian version of sambal or gochujang chile paste. Because I love incorporating fruits into savory applications, I tried swapping in a basket of ripe, juicy raspberries I had in the fridge for the vegetable component and came up with this bright, just slightly sweet and sour twist. It offers a great counterpart to the herby chicken, warm, slightly softened romaine, and salty anchovy dressing. Think of this like an elevated spicy chicken Caesar salad.

# Rosemary CHICKEN THIGHS,

## RASPBERRY BOMBA, AND ANCHOVY GRILLED ROMAINE

### Serves 4 to 6

### Chicken
6 bone-in, skin-on chicken thighs

2 fresh rosemary sprigs, leaves removed and roughly chopped

2 teaspoons kosher salt

1 teaspoon freshly ground black pepper

2 teaspoons neutral oil

2 tablespoons unsalted butter

### Bomba
1 pint raspberries

1 tablespoon Calabrian chile paste

1 small lemon, zest grated and juiced

3 tablespoons extra-virgin olive oil

1 tablespoon honey

Kosher salt

### Grilled Romaine and Anchovy Dressing
1 teaspoon anchovy paste

1 teaspoon Dijon mustard

1 tablespoon lemon juice

4 tablespoons extra-virgin olive oil

Kosher salt and black pepper

2 large little gems or small hearts of romaine, core left and quartered

**1** Preheat the oven to 375°F.

**2** Place the chicken thighs on a large plate. Combine the rosemary, salt, and pepper in a mortar and pestle and grind until the rosemary has broken down and released its oils. If you don't have a mortar and pestle, finely chop the rosemary and mix together in a small bowl with the salt and pepper. Rub the rosemary mixture all over the chicken thighs and let sit for 20 to 30 minutes.

**3** *Make the Bomba:* Combine the raspberries, chile paste, lemon zest and juice, olive oil, and honey in a medium bowl. Use a fork to mash the raspberries and mix everything together; the mixture should be a little chunky still but well combined. Season to taste with salt and set aside.

**4** *Make the Dressing:* Whisk together the anchovy paste, mustard, and lemon juice in a small bowl. Slowly drizzle in the olive oil, whisking constantly until it thickens, then season to taste with salt and pepper.

*RECIPE CONTINUES*

**5** *Cook the Chicken:* Heat the neutral oil in a large stainless-steel or cast-iron skillet over medium-high heat. Add the chicken thighs, skin-side down, and cook without moving until most of the fat has rendered out of the skin and they release easily from the pan when lifted, about 10 minutes. Use tongs to flip the thighs, add the butter, and transfer the pan to the oven. Cook until the chicken is crispy and the thickest part of the largest thigh registers 155°F on a food thermometer, about 15 minutes. Remove to a plate to rest and let the internal temperature come up to 165°F.

**6** Place the same skillet over medium-high heat and season the romaine quarters with salt and pepper. Add the romaine to the pan and cook, pressing down with a spatula to help it sear, until nicely charred on both cut sides but still crunchy, 2 to 3 minutes.

**7** Spoon the bomba onto a serving platter, spreading it out evenly with a large spoon. Arrange the chicken thighs on top, then top with the grilled romaine spears. Drizzle over the anchovy dressing and serve immediately.

✣ I like to think of these little mini meatballs (or *polpette* as the Italians would say) as shortcut meatballs. Most recipes start with unseasoned meat, so you need extra time to build flavor with a soffritto of onion, garlic, and herbs. But because this recipe uses pre-seasoned salami as the base (something like a fennel-y finocchiona or a spicy soppressata is ideal, but you could even use pepperoni if that's all you have), the flavor is already built in. I serve these family-style on a bed of Whipped Ricotta (page 159) drizzled with Classic Pesto (page 104), but they also make a fun party appetizer—just add fancy toothpicks unless you want everyone to eat with their hands, which would be completely acceptable as well.

# Mini SALAMI MEATBALLS

## WITH WHIPPED RICOTTA AND PESTO

### Serves 4 to 6

## Meatballs

1/2 pound thinly sliced finocchiona (or any salami)

2 standard ice cubes (about 2 tablespoons each)

1/2 pound ground pork

1 large egg

1/4 cup freshly grated Parmigiano-Reggiano

1/4 cup freshly grated Pecorino Romano

1/4 cup finely chopped fresh parsley

2 slices white sandwich bread, crusts removed and torn into small pieces

1 tablespoon Italian seasoning

1 teaspoon whole milk or water

1/8 teaspoon freshly grated nutmeg, plus more to taste

Kosher salt and ground white pepper

3 tablespoons extra-virgin olive oil

## To Finish

1 cup Whipped Ricotta (page 159)

1/4 cup Classic Pesto (page 104) or your favorite store-bought pesto

1 *Make the Meatballs:* Place the salami and two ice cubes in the small bowl of a food processor and blend, stopping to scrape down the sides as needed, until a fairly smooth paste forms, about 2 minutes. (You can alternatively finely chop the salami, using the edge of your knife to press and smear the meat until it forms a fine paste.)

2 In a large bowl, combine the salami paste, ground pork, egg, Parmigiano, Pecorino, parsley, bread, Italian seasoning, and milk. Use your hands to mix everything together until homogenous, 1 to 2 minutes, then stir in the nutmeg and season with salt and pepper. Roll the mixture into tiny meatballs, just a little larger than a marble (you should get about 50), and place on a large plate.

3 *Cook the Meatballs:* Heat the olive oil in a large skillet or sauté pan over medium-high heat. Add the meatballs (you may need to do this in batches, depending on the size of your pan) and cook, shaking the pan and/or flipping with tongs often so they brown on all sides, until golden brown and cooked through, 5 to 7 minutes.

*RECIPE CONTINUES*

**4** Spread the whipped ricotta out in an even layer on a serving dish, arrange the meatballs on top, and drizzle over the pesto.

**PRO TIP** Taste the meat mixture for seasoning by poaching a small meatball in simmering water for 2 minutes.

## BREAK THE RULES

If you can find it, sub in ¼ pound sliced mortadella for half of the salami. It gives these meatballs a delicious flavor and smooth texture.

Use pea tendrils and fresh English peas as the main green component in your pesto.

## LEFTOVERS?

Any leftover raw meatball mixture makes a great filling for pasta or mini smash burger sliders. Throw leftover cooked meatballs into a breakfast hash or sub sandwich.

Chapter Five

# ON THE SIDE

Sweet Potato
Wedges
and Lemony
Ranch,
PAGE 164

*I'M NOT MUCH FOR* the old-school format of eating a starter, main, and dessert. I much prefer to order a bunch of small plates or appetizers. That way, I get a little variety and a chance to try more things.

So, although this chapter is called "On the Side," please don't think of these as just "side dishes." All the recipes could easily be stand-alone meals or be paired together to make a full spread for a crowd. For example, the Blistered Shishitos and Dashi Mayo (page 163), Baked Burrata alla Diavola (page 168), and Grilled Broccolini, Stracciatella, and Seeded Crumble Rumble (page 173) make perfect, hearty party snacks. And I've eaten a large bowl of the Fresh Corn Polenta with Butter and Chives (page 167) for dinner many nights, but also love to serve it alongside any of the mains from the "Sharing Is Caring" chapter (page 120). These hearty, homey, vegetable-forward dishes are a celebration of good ingredients treated well, with a little bit of that Sasto flair thrown in for good measure.

�֍ This is my favorite way to cook the cute, whole baby carrots you'll find at the farmers' market in late spring and early fall. (No, I'm not talking about the smooth processed things that come in bags at the grocery store and your school lunch box.) Because this dish utilizes the whole vegetable from root to stem, it's also a great way to pay respect to the farmers who grow them. By scrubbing but not peeling the carrots, then roasting them with fat, honey, herbs, and garlic, you end up with wonderfully crispy skin and super tender centers. If you can't find baby carrots, any root vegetable would work here—big carrots, parsnips, sunchokes, or potatoes are all great—just cut them into smaller, more manageable pieces so they roast evenly.

# CARROTS

## WITH

## SPICY YOGURT

## AND CARROT TOP

## PESTO

*Serves 4 to 6*

4 bunches baby or 2 bunches large rainbow carrots

1/4 cup extra-virgin olive oil

2 tablespoons honey

1 small bunch fresh thyme

2 garlic cloves, peeled and crushed

Kosher salt and freshly ground black pepper

1/2 cup whole milk Greek yogurt

1/2 teaspoon Calabrian chile paste

1/4 teaspoon brown sugar

1/4 cup Classic Pesto (page 104) or your favorite store-bought pesto

**1** Preheat the oven to 425°F and line a large sheet pan with parchment paper.

**2** Remove the tops from the carrots (and reserve for carrot top pesto if you're breaking the rules—see below), leaving just a small green tip. Place the carrots in a large bowl of warm water and thoroughly scrub with a green sponge or kitchen brush. Dry them well on a clean dish towel and, if using large carrots, cut them in half, then into 2-inch pieces on a diagonal.

**3** Toss the carrots in a large bowl with the olive oil, honey, thyme, and garlic cloves. Season to taste with salt and pepper and transfer to the prepared sheet pan. Roast until golden and just tender, 15 to 18 minutes, shaking the pan every few minutes to ensure even cooking.

**4** Whisk together the yogurt, chile paste, and brown sugar in a medium bowl. Season with salt and pepper to taste.

**5** Spread the pesto out in an even layer on a serving dish, arrange the carrots on top (discard the thyme and garlic cloves), and drizzle over some of the yogurt sauce.

## BREAK THE RULES

Use 1/4 cup melted duck fat instead of the olive oil for roasting the carrots. It adds an unexpected meatiness to a sometimes sweet and routine vegetable.

Use the carrot tops as the green element in your pesto!

# WHIPPED CHEESE

I grew up eating ricotta ravioli and Mom's Red Sauce (page 54). It was actually my mom's favorite pasta, so it will always be one of my go-to comfort foods. You can, of course, buy premade "quattro formaggi" tortellini or ravioli (my mom often did), but a proper, homemade ricotta filling is a real treat to eat. Unlike some of the packaged options, where the cheese mixture can get a little grainy or separated, this one is oozy, cheesy, and smooth every time.

I learned this technique from my friend Missy Robbins, an incredible pasta chef based in New York City (if you haven't been to her restaurants Lilia and Misi, I insist you make a trip to the Big Apple as soon as possible to try them).

To make it, you take a nice ricotta (my preference is Bellwether Farms from the Bay Area, but any grocery-store whole milk ricotta will do), strain it in the fridge overnight to remove any excess whey, then blend it in the food processor with a little Parmigiano-Reggiano, nutmeg, salt, and sometimes pepper, until creamy and smooth. By straining out the excess liquid, or whey, you get a thicker, fattier ricotta, which will result in a creamier, richer filling. A quick blend in the food processor aerates the cheese and ensures a luscious texture, even after cooking.

This whipped cheese is a real workhorse in my home and restaurant kitchens. I use it for stuffed pastas like my Kale, Ricotta, and Hot Honey filling (see page 239), but I also serve it as a dip for Rice Paper Cacio e Pepe Chips (page 38) or Santorini-Style Tomato Fritters (page 40), pipe it onto roasted radicchio (see Radicchio, Whipped Ricotta, and Macadamia Nuts on page 161), or smear it under roasted squash (see Squash, Whipped Ricotta, and Spicy Pumpkin Seed Crumble Rumble on page 162). I'm partial to ricotta, but you could use this basic technique to make any whipped soft cheese.

Breaking the Rules

# WHIPPED RICOTTA

*Makes about 2 cups*

1 pound (about 1¾ cups) ricotta
½ cup freshly grated Parmigiano-Reggiano
⅛ teaspoon freshly grated nutmeg
Kosher salt
Freshly ground black pepper (optional)

**1** Place the ricotta in a fine-mesh sieve set over a large bowl (or wrap in cheesecloth and hang over a large bowl) and place in the fridge overnight. This is optional, but because less water means more fat, straining off any excess liquid will help you achieve a creamier whip.

**2** Place the strained ricotta, the Parmigiano, and nutmeg in the bowl of a food processor. Blend until very smooth and creamy, 20 to 30 seconds. Season with salt and black pepper (if using) and either use immediately or store in the fridge for up to 5 days.

VARIATIONS

## WHIPPED FETA

*MAKES ABOUT 1 CUP*

8 ounces feta cheese
½ cup whole milk yogurt
Juice of 1 medium lemon
Kosher salt and freshly ground black pepper

Place the feta, yogurt, and lemon juice in the bowl of a food processor. Blend until very smooth and creamy, 30 to 40 seconds. Season with salt and black pepper, and either use immediately or store in the fridge for up to 5 days.

## WHIPPED GOAT CHEESE

*MAKES ABOUT 1 CUP*

8 ounces goat cheese
Zest of 1 medium orange
Kosher salt and freshly ground black pepper

Place the goat cheese and orange zest in the bowl of a food processor. Blend until very smooth and creamy, 30 to 40 seconds. Season with salt and black pepper and either use immediately or store in the fridge for up to 5 days.

## CHEESY TIPS

**USE WHOLE MILK CHEESE:** This is the star of the show, so make it count and try your best to use high-quality cheese for the tastiest results. "Light" cheese won't whip as fluffy and hold up as well to being processed.

**MAKE SURE THE CHEESE IS COLD:** I recommend removing it from the refrigerator just before whipping. That way, more air will be incorporated into the cheese for fluffier results.

**EXPERIMENT WITH TOPPINGS** and add-ins based on what cheese you choose, how you plan to use it, what season it is, and what you're craving. Dried fruit, roasted vegetables like carrots or cabbage, or spices like curry or paprika would all be great.

❊ Lots of people shy away from bitter greens like radicchio, but if you know how to treat these chicories—either by balancing the bitterness with lots of acid or, counterintuitively, creating more bitterness through a hard sear, grill, or high-temp oven roast—you'll change a lot of skeptics' minds. Here, I get that high-heat char in the oven, then toss with tons of olive oil, salt, pepper, orange zest, and aged balsamic (ideally one that's old enough to vote). To balance all those bitter flavors, I serve them dolloped with creamy Whipped Ricotta (page 159) and top with buttery, rich macadamia nuts (hazelnuts would also be great).

# RADICCHIO, WHIPPED RICOTTA,
## AND MACADAMIA NUTS

Serves 4 to 6

1 large head radicchio

2 tablespoons plus 1 tablespoon extra-virgin olive oil

Kosher salt and freshly ground black pepper

1 tablespoon aged balsamic vinegar

½ small orange, zest grated

Flaky salt

½ cup Whipped Ricotta (page 159)

¼ cup toasted macadamia nuts, roughly chopped

1 Preheat the oven to 425°F and line a large sheet pan with parchment paper.

2 Remove any wilted leaves from the outside of the radicchio and cut into 8 wedges, making sure to leave the core intact. Toss in a large bowl with 2 tablespoons of the olive oil and season generously with salt and pepper. Arrange on the prepared sheet pan (set aside the mixing bowl to use later) and roast until wilted and charred, about 20 minutes, flipping halfway through. Finish under the broiler if you like a little more color.

3 Transfer the cooked radicchio back to the large bowl and toss with the remaining olive oil, balsamic vinegar, and orange zest. Season to taste with more black pepper and flaky salt.

4 Spread the whipped ricotta out in an even layer on a serving dish, arrange the radicchio on top, and garnish with chopped macadamia nuts.

## BREAK THE RULES

Instead of spreading the whipped ricotta underneath the radicchio, use a piping bag (or zip-top bag) to pipe little dollops on top of the finished dish.

�֍ This dish always reminds me of my San Francisco kitchen days. I put a version of it on the menu at Lazy Bear (where I helped run the kitchen from 2016 to 2018) one autumn day and it became a staple technique, year after year. It's a true celebration of fall and winter squashes—like red kuri, kabocha, and honeynut—and really leans into their warm, cozy flavors. At the restaurant, I salt-cured the squash the same way I do for a piece of fish or a pork chop before roasting it (see Breaking the Rules, below), which helps draw out the moisture so it crisps up beautifully, seasons the flesh, and makes the skin super tasty. If you've got a little extra time, I highly recommend this technique; if you need this on the table in 30 minutes, skip it.

# SQUASH, WHIPPED RICOTTA, AND SPICY PUMPKIN SEED CRUMBLE RUMBLE

Serves 4 to 6

## Squash
2 small red kuri or acorn or 1 medium kabocha squash
1 tablespoon extra-virgin olive oil
Kosher salt and freshly ground black pepper

## Crumble Rumble
1 tablespoon Calabrian chile paste
1 tablespoon unsalted butter
5 fresh sage leaves
1/2 tablespoon honey
1/4 cup Garlic Streusel (page 68)
2 tablespoons pumpkin seeds
Kosher salt

## To Finish
1/2 cup Whipped Ricotta (page 159)

**1** Preheat the oven to 425°F and line a large sheet pan with parchment paper.

**2** *Roast the Squash:* Cut the squash in half, remove the stem, scoop out the seeds, then cut into roughly 1½-inch wedges (leaving the skin on). Toss in a large bowl with the olive oil and season with salt and pepper to taste. Arrange on the parchment-lined baking sheet and roast until tender, 20 to 25 minutes, flipping halfway through.

**3** *Make the Crumble Rumble:* Heat the chile paste and butter in a small skillet over medium heat. When bubbling, add the sage leaves and honey and cook for 30 seconds or so, until the honey is bubbling and the sage is fragrant. Stir in the Garlic Streusel and pumpkin seeds, cook for another 30 seconds, stirring constantly, and turn off the heat. Season to taste with salt and set aside.

**4** Spread the whipped ricotta out in an even layer on a serving dish, arrange the squash pieces on top, and garnish with the spicy pumpkin seed Crumble Rumble.

## BREAK THE RULES

If you have an extra hour, give your squash a quick cure or dry brine: Toss the cut squash pieces in a large bowl with 2 teaspoons kosher salt and 1 teaspoon white sugar. Arrange on a wire rack set over a sheet pan and leave to drip and drain at room temperature for 1 hour. Pat to dry very well with paper towels or a clean dish towel and follow the recipe as written (just don't season with salt when you toss with the olive oil).

✿ Shishitos are kind of like the Russian roulette of peppers—they say one out of every ten is spicy. So if you like to live a little dangerously, these are the peppers for you. For me, these make the perfect aperitivo/drinking snack—they're salty, charred, spicy, sweet, and just really refreshing and delicious. I love pairing these blistered peppers with Dashi Mayo (page 43), which has a salty, umami backbone that perfectly complements their natural heat and brightness. But you could also dip them in any of the Fancy Mayos on page 43 or plain old Kewpie and be a very happy snacker.

# Blistered
# SHISHITOS
## AND DASHI MAYO

### Serves 4 to 6

3/4 pound shishito peppers

Neutral oil

Kosher salt

Extra-virgin olive oil

1 small lemon, zest grated

Flaky salt

1/2 cup Dashi Mayo (page 43) or mayonnaise (preferably Kewpie), for dipping

**1** Set a large, dry skillet (it should be able to hold all the peppers in an even layer) over high heat. When the pan is scorching hot, add the peppers and cook, dry and undisturbed, for 1 to 2 minutes, until just starting to squeak and very lightly blister in places. Toss and cook for another 1 to 2 minutes. (Be ready to move quickly after this next step . . .)

**2** Add a splash of neutral oil and, pulling the handle of the pan back and forth vigorously, immediately start tossing the peppers. Continue cooking, adding kosher salt and tossing frequently (either shaking the pan by the handle or tossing with a wooden spoon) to keep the peppers moving, until softened and very charred and blistered in spots, 1 to 2 minutes.

**3** Immediately transfer to a large mixing bowl and toss with a splash of olive oil, lemon zest, and flaky salt to taste. Serve hot with Dashi Mayo for dipping.

## BREAK THE RULES

Add some extra texture with the Seedy, Tingly, or Extra Crunchy Garlic Streusel from the Crumble Rumbles on page 68.

✿ This makes a nice starchy little side dish for everyone to munch and nom on—I mean, you can't go wrong with french fries and ranch. I love the sweeter, slightly less starchy sweet potatoes here, but good old russets would also work well. This is one of those filling dishes that could be served on the side, but my wife and I have eaten this for dinner on its own many times. And a little-known tidbit: Celery seed is that quintessential "ranch" flavor that we all gravitate toward and is often missing from homemade ranch.

# SWEET POTATO WEDGES

## AND LEMONY RANCH

*Serves 4 to 6*

### Potatoes

2 pounds sweet or russet potatoes (skin on), scrubbed and cut into 3/4-inch wedges (think steak fries)

2 tablespoons extra-virgin olive oil

1 tablespoon finely chopped fresh rosemary

1 tablespoon finely chopped fresh thyme

1 medium garlic clove, minced

Kosher salt and freshly ground black pepper

### Ranch

1/4 cup mayonnaise (preferably Kewpie)

1/4 cup sour cream

1 teaspoon grated lemon zest (optional)

2 tablespoons fresh lemon juice

1 medium garlic clove, minced or grated

1/2 teaspoon granulated onion

1/2 teaspoon dried dill

1/2 teaspoon dried parsley

1/2 teaspoon ground celery seed

Kosher salt and freshly ground black pepper

**1** Preheat the oven to 425°F and line a large sheet pan with parchment paper.

**2** *Roast the Potatoes:* In a large bowl, toss together the potato wedges, olive oil, rosemary, thyme, and garlic and season generously with salt and pepper. Transfer to the prepared sheet pan and roast until golden brown and tender, about 20 minutes, flipping halfway through.

**3** *Make the Ranch:* In a medium bowl, whisk together the mayonnaise and sour cream until smooth. Stir in the lemon zest (if using), lemon juice, garlic, onion powder, dill, parsley, and celery seed. Whisk to combine everything and season to taste with salt and pepper.

**4** Serve the hot potato wedges with cool ranch dressing for dipping.

## BREAK THE RULES

Toss the potato wedges with 3 tablespoons Herby Garlicky Paste (page 273) and swap in fresh or bottled yuzu juice for the lemon juice in the ranch dressing.

❄ If you know me, you know how I feel about corn. Spoiler alert: It's my favorite vegetable. I think this might be the dish that made me fall in love with it in the first place. The simple technique of blending up raw corn, then cooking it as you would a dried ground corn polenta—simmering it gently to let the natural starches in the fresh kernels activate and thicken the mixture—showcases the vegetable's beauty and creates the sweetest, creamiest polenta imaginable. Plus, it only takes about 15 minutes altogether, versus sweating over the stove for hours when making dried polenta.

Serve this alongside Pork Chops with Mustard Berry Jus (page 144) or Weeknight Short Ribs (page 134), or just eat the whole bowl with a spoon, or straw. If you're using out-of-season corn, you should add a pinch of sugar to help bring out its natural sweetness.

# Fresh Corn
# POLENTA
## WITH BUTTER
## AND CHIVES

Serves 4 to 6

5 large cobs corn, husks removed

Salt and freshly ground black pepper

2 tablespoons unsalted butter

2 tablespoons Black Garlic Butter (page 141), at room temperature (optional)

¼ cup finely chopped fresh chives

**1** Set an ear of corn down flat on a cutting board and use a sharp knife to carefully slice off one side cheek of the kernels. Transfer the cut kernels to a bowl and turn the cob so that the flat side is now on the cutting board. Continue slicing and turning until all four sides have been cut, then continue with the remaining ears of corn.

**2** Transfer the kernels to a powerful blender and blend until mostly smooth but not pureed (you still want a little texture), about 30 seconds.

**3** Pour the blended kernels into a medium sauté pan or Dutch oven and cook, stirring constantly with a spatula, until the mixture has thickened and you start to see the bottom of the pot when you drag the spatula through it, 5 to 7 minutes.

**4** Season to taste with salt and pepper and stir in the unsalted butter. Transfer to a serving dish, spoon over the Black Garlic Butter (if using), garnish with chives, and serve immediately.

## BREAK THE RULES

Save your tender inner corn husks and silks to make corn powder: Arrange the husks and silks in an even layer on 2 sheet pans. Top each sheet pan with a metal cooling rack to keep the husks in place and cook in a 225°F oven until dried out and golden brown, about 2 hours. Cool, then blend in a powerful blender until pulverized. You can now add this corn powder to pasta dough or salad dressings, or dust on top of chicken, fish, or veggies. Store in an airtight container with a silica desiccant packet to prevent clumping.

�֎ This is one of those crowd-pleasing comfort-food appetizers that's great to have in your back pocket (and not only for a group . . . I've made this for myself when I needed a cheesy hug). Like any tomato dish, this is most delicious when made with ripe, late-summer tomatoes, but because they get sautéed and then roasted, the tomato flavor and natural sweetness will be coaxed out of even the saddest, out-of-season grocery store ones. Feel free to play around with the amount of Calabrian chile paste—if I know my friends like heat, I'll add more to make it extra "alla diavola," or devilishly spicy.

# BAKED BURRATA
## alla Diavola

### Serves 2 to 4

- 1 medium baguette, thinly sliced
- 3 tablespoons extra-virgin olive oil
- 1 garlic clove, thinly sliced
- 1 small spring onion or 2 scallions, thinly sliced
- 1 pound cherry tomatoes, cut in half
- 1 teaspoon Calabrian chile paste, or more to taste
- 1 teaspoon dried oregano
- 6 sprigs fresh basil, leaves torn or roughly chopped
- Kosher salt and freshly ground black pepper
- 1 (8-ounce) ball burrata

**1** Preheat the oven to 425°F and arrange the baguette slices on a sheet pan.

**2** Heat the oil in a medium sauté pan over medium heat. Add the garlic and spring onion and cook, stirring often, until just golden, about 1 minute. Stir in the tomatoes and cook, stirring often and using a wooden spoon or potato masher to crush them, until soft, about 5 minutes. Add the chile paste, oregano, and half of the basil leaves. Stir to combine and season to taste with salt and pepper.

**3** Transfer to a medium oven-safe baking dish and place the burrata in the center. Bake for 8 to 10 minutes, or until the burrata is gooey and the tomatoes are bubbling. Add the baguette slices to the oven for the last 3 to 5 minutes of cooking, just to lightly toast.

**4** Garnish the tomatoes and cheese with the remaining basil and serve with sliced baguette for dipping.

**LEFTOVERS?** Toss any leftovers with pasta or dilute with chicken stock and blend into a cheesy roasted vegetable soup.

�֎ Ever wondered how to make any vegetable taste even more like itself? Cook it in its own juices! This method lends itself especially well to asparagus and is by far my favorite way to cook it. I picked up this technique while cooking in San Francisco. We had access to some of the best asparagus in the country, grown in the Sacramento Delta. Once you try this, it's hard to eat asparagus any other way. For best results you need to peel off the outer layer of skin to expose the porous, sponge-like interior of each piece of asparagus, so look for bunches with nice, thick spears. (Save those thin pencil stalks for the grill.)

# Asparagus
# COOKED IN ITS OWN JUICES

### Serves 4 to 6

1 large bunch asparagus

2 tablespoons extra-virgin olive oil

Kosher salt

**1** Hold one asparagus spear in your hands and bend it until it snaps naturally—one inch down from this point toward the root is now your guide. Arrange the spears on a cutting board with their tips in line and cut at the guide point of that first piece. Reserve the woody stems.

**2** Use a small sharp knife or peeler to peel the skin from each spear, starting about 1 inch down from where the tip ends, making sure not to press too hard so you only remove the tough outer layer.

**3** If you have a juicer, juice the stems. If not, put the stems in a powerful blender with 3 tablespoons of water. Blend on high until smooth, 1 to 2 minutes. Pour into a fine-mesh strainer set over a bowl, but don't press or scrape too much—you just want the juice, not the pureed asparagus.

**4** Heat the olive oil in a large skillet or sauté pan with a lid. When the oil is hot, add the asparagus and season generously with salt while tossing the pan. Quickly pour in the asparagus juice, cover the pan, and reduce the heat to maintain a gentle simmer. Cook until tender, 2 to 4 minutes depending on how big your spears are. Use tongs to transfer the asparagus to a platter, spoon over a little bit of the cooking liquid, and serve immediately.

**PRO TIP** The best way to store asparagus is standing upright in a jar with a little bit of water in the fridge. And please remove those grocery store rubber bands—they squeeze and hurt the vegetable!

✻ You may have noticed a trend in this chapter: cooking a vegetable until it develops caramelization (either by grilling, roasting, or sautéing), serving it with something creamy (burrata or some sort of whipped cheese are usually my go-tos), and then adding a little texture, whether that be with a nut, a seed, or any sort of Crumble Rumble (page 68). Here, broccolini is cooked slowly on the grill until tender and beautifully charred, then served over Whipped Ricotta (page 159) and garnished with seeded Crumble Rumble (page 68)—it's everything your heart and palate desires.

## Grilled BROCCOLINI, Stracciatella, AND SEEDED CRUMBLE RUMBLE

*Serves 4 to 6*

### Broccolini

1 large or 2 small bunches broccolini (about 3/4 pound)

2 tablespoons plus 1 tablespoon extra-virgin olive oil

1/2 medium lemon, zest grated and juiced

1 teaspoon granulated garlic

Kosher salt and freshly ground black pepper

Flaky salt

### Crumble Rumble

1/4 cup Garlic Streusel (page 68)

1 tablespoon toasted sesame seeds

1 teaspoon flax seeds

1 teaspoon hemp seeds

1 teaspoon poppy seeds

### To Finish

1 (4-ounce) ball burrata

Extra virgin olive oil

**1** Heat an outdoor grill or grill pan to medium heat.

**2** *Cook the Broccolini:* In a large bowl, toss the broccolini with 2 tablespoons of the olive oil, the lemon juice, and the granulated garlic. Season with salt and pepper to taste. Arrange the broccolini on the grill or grill pan in an even layer (set aside the mixing bowl to use later). Cook low and slow, turning every 5 minutes or so, until charred and tender, 20 to 25 minutes.

**3** *Make the Crumble Rumble:* In a small bowl, mix together the Garlic Streusel, sesame seeds, flax seeds, hemp seeds, and poppy seeds. Set aside.

**4** *Back to the Broccolini:* Transfer the cooked broccolini back to the large bowl and toss with the remaining olive oil, the lemon zest, and flaky salt.

**5** Arrange the broccolini on a serving platter, top with big dollops of burrata, drizzle with a little olive oil, and garnish with the seeded Crumble Rumble.

✿ We all know and love *elotes*, the Mexican street corn slathered with mayo and sprinkled with cotija cheese, chile, and fresh lime. This is my different, but equally delicious, Italian version. It's all about the contrast of the sweet, juicy corn, punchy pesto, and salty cheese.

# Pesto-Rubbed CORN ON THE COB

### Serves 4 to 6

6 large cobs corn with husks

½ cup Classic Pesto (page 104) or your favorite store-bought pesto

½ cup grated Pecorino Romano or crumbled cotija

**1** Preheat a grill or grill pan to medium heat.

**2** While the grill heats up, place the corn cobs in a large bowl, cover with water, and soak for 10 to 15 minutes. Drain and place on the hot grill.

**3** Cook the corn, turning every few minutes to cook evenly, until the husks are slightly charred and the kernels are just tender, 12 to 15 minutes. Remove to a large plate to cool.

**4** When cool enough to handle, shuck the cobs, brush each one with a couple tablespoons of Classic Pesto, and sprinkle with the Pecorino or cotija.

## BREAK THE RULES

Use cilantro as the main green component in your pesto (see page 102) and level up your presentation by garnishing the finished cobs with edible flowers.

Chapter Six

# DRIED PASTA IS YOUR BEST FRIEND

MOST ITALIANS WILL INSIST that, when it comes to dried pasta, each sauce should be paired with a specific shape—carbonara with bucatini or Bolognese with tagliatelle, for example. As you may have guessed from the title of this book, I'm not big on those types of prescriptive rules. I say choose whichever pasta shape inspires you (or use whatever you have in your pantry). Think of this chapter as a guidebook for making yummy sauces and use them however you'd like. If you start with a delicious sauce, made with care and good ingredients—like my creamy Corn Cacio e Pepe (page 196), classic Pasta alla Norcina (page 186), or my famous Sasto Bolo (page 178)—it's always going to be good. So go for spaghettini, fusilli, or campanelle; cook your pasta very al dente or give it a little more time. As long as you remember to save some starchy pasta cooking water to toss everything together with, you can't go wrong.

Or heck, I'm not going to call the Italian police if you skip the starchy water and serve a pile of plain noodles with big ladlefuls of sauce spooned over the top—which, by the way, is how my dad insists it should be eaten. After all my years cooking in Michelin-starred Italian restaurants, it's still the way I make it for him every time I go back home.

❊ Italian Bolognese is a rich and unctuous meat sauce originally made in Bologna, the capital of the Emilia-Romagna region. The term "Bolognese" has become synonymous with a meaty tomato sauce in much of the world, but Italians—especially ones from this region—have very strong opinions about what qualifies. A classic Bolognese typically starts with a simple soffritto of onion, carrot, and celery, then meat (usually beef or a mix of beef and pork) is added and gently simmered with milk, wine, nutmeg, and a tiny bit of tomato until thickened into an intensely flavorful ragù. My perfect version is a hybrid between a classic Bolognese and an Italian American interpretation, where tomato plays more of a starring role. Italians may tell you this isn't true Bolognese; I say it doesn't matter what you call it because it's delicious. This batch makes enough for two pounds of pasta, so I usually freeze half to have on hand for emergencies . . . you never know when you might need a warm bowl of Sasto Bolo goodness.

# SASTO BOLO

Makes about 1 quart (enough for 2 pounds of dried pasta)

3 tablespoons unsalted butter

3 tablespoons extra-virgin olive oil

½ pound ground pork

½ pound ground beef (80/20)

Kosher salt and freshly ground black pepper

1 cup Sicilian Soffritto (recipe follows)

2 tablespoons tomato paste

3 sprigs fresh thyme

½ cup dry white wine (or sub red if you prefer)

½ cup whole milk

⅛ teaspoon freshly grated nutmeg

2 cups chicken stock or water

1 medium Parmigiano-Reggiano rind (optional)

2 sprigs fresh basil

**1** Heat the butter and olive oil in a large, wide-bottomed pot or Dutch oven over medium-high heat. Add the pork and beef and cook, using a potato masher or wooden spoon to start breaking down the meat into small pieces, until no longer pink and starting to brown, 5 to 7 minutes. Season with salt and pepper.

**2** Add the soffritto and cook, stirring constantly, for 1 minute, then stir in the tomato paste and thyme sprigs. Cook, scraping the bottom to avoid burning, until the tomato mixture turns a deep brick-red color, 2 to 3 minutes. Add the wine and stir to deglaze the pan. Cook, stirring often, until the alcohol has cooked off and most of the liquid has evaporated, about 2 minutes.

**3** Add the milk and grated nutmeg and cook, stirring often, until most of the liquid has cooked off, another 2 to 3 minutes. Add the stock and Parmigiano rind (if using), lower the heat to a simmer, and cook, stirring every so often, until the sauce is thick and flavorful, at least 1 hour and up to 2.

**4** Stir in the picked basil leaves and season to taste with salt and pepper.

**BREAK THE RULES**

Grind your own pork and beef and add ¼ pound ground pancetta or other cured pork product like prosciutto or salami to the mix.

**LEFTOVERS?**

Have leftover Bolognese? Turn it into Italian shepherd's pie! Place any leftover sauce in a small baking dish and cover with mashed potatoes. Grate over some Parmigiano-Reggiano and bake in a 400°F oven until bubbling and golden brown on top, about 25 minutes.

# SICILIAN SOFFRITTO

*Makes about 2½ cups*

Italian Soffritto is a slow-cooked vegetable flavor-bomb base for soups, stews, and sauces. It is usually made with finely minced vegetables (often onion, carrot, and celery), along with garlic, fresh herbs, other vegetables, and aromatics thrown in. This is my Sicilian version, which incorporates fennel, anchovies, and colatura (see page 18) for a little extra umami flavor. You often hear about an 8-hour ragù, but because ground meat tends to get grainy if cooked for longer than 2 hours, the bulk of that cook time is used to make a really concentrated, flavorful soffritto. I cook mine for 3 to 4 hours over super low heat to make sure it doesn't catch and burn as it cooks. If you're in a rush, you can make a perfectly serviceable (if slightly less flavorful) soffritto in an hour.

1 medium fennel, diced

2 medium white onions, diced

2 celery stalks, diced

2 large carrots, peeled and diced

12 garlic cloves, peeled

½ cup plus 1½ cups extra-virgin olive oil, plus more as needed

2 tablespoons tomato paste

1 teaspoon anchovy paste

½ cup red wine

1 sprig fresh thyme

1 fresh bay leaf

1 teaspoon colatura or ½ teaspoon fish sauce

**1** Combine the fennel, onion, celery, carrot, and garlic in the bowl of a food processor. Pulse, adding some of the ½ cup of olive oil a splash at a time as needed to keep the mixture moving, and stopping to scrape down the sides several times, until a small, consistently sized paste is formed, 15 to 20 seconds. (Depending on the size of your food processor, it may be best to do this in 2 to 3 batches.)

**2** Heat what's left of the ½ cup olive oil in a large, flat-bottomed sauté pan or Dutch oven over medium heat. Add the blended vegetables and cook, stirring often, until they are tender and have released most of their liquid, about 10 minutes. Use a wooden spoon or spatula to clear a small area in the center of the pot and add the tomato paste and anchovy paste. Cook for 1 to 2 minutes, stirring everything in the pot together.

**3** Add the wine and stir to deglaze the pan. Cook, stirring often, until the alcohol has cooked off and most of the liquid has evaporated, about 5 minutes. Tie the thyme sprig and bay leaf together with twine and add to the pot.

**4** Add the remaining 1½ cups olive oil (or however much you need to just cover the vegetable mixture) and reduce the heat to medium-low. Cook, stirring often and scraping the bottom of the pot to make sure nothing is sticking or burning, for 3 to 4 hours. Add the colatura in the last 20 minutes of cooking, so the flavors have time to cook together and marry.

**5** Use immediately or cool and store in the fridge for up to 1 week or in the freezer for up to 3 months.

# COLD-WATER PASTA COOKING METHOD

I may be banned from ever entering Italy again for saying this, but I almost always use the cold-water method when cooking dried pasta (and think you should, too). It's been pounded into our heads that pasta should be cooked in big pots of "rapidly boiling water," but starting your pasta in cold water has multiple benefits: It takes less energy to heat, it takes less time since the noodles come to a boil with the water, and you end up with concentrated starchy cooking water that gives a silky, creamy finish to pasta sauces. I learned this method from the great Alton Brown, and I provide directions for this technique in all the recipes in this chapter; if the cold-water method offends you, feel free to get out that big pot of boiling water.

❊ This one has become a real Sasto tradition over the years. It's a seasonal staple that fuses modern and nostalgic—taking typical Thanksgiving flavors like turkey, sage, and white wine but presenting them in a new and interesting way. I usually serve this with sweet potato gnocchi and top with White Pepper Marshmallows (page 272; think sweet potato casserole), but this can, of course, be tossed with any type of fresh or dried pasta.

# TURKEY BOLOGNESE

### Makes about 1 quart (enough for 2 pounds of dried pasta)

1 small white onion, diced

3 small or 2 medium carrots, peeled and diced

3 medium celery ribs, diced

8 medium garlic cloves, peeled

2 tablespoons extra-virgin olive oil, plus more as needed

3 tablespoons unsalted butter

1 sprig fresh thyme, leaves removed and chopped

1 bunch fresh sage, leaves removed and thinly sliced

1 pound ground turkey (preferably dark meat)

½ pound ground pork (optional)

Kosher salt and ground white pepper

½ cup dry white wine (or sub red if you prefer)

½ cup whole milk

⅛ teaspoon freshly ground nutmeg

1½ to 2 cups chicken stock or water, plus more as needed

**1** Combine the onion, carrots, celery, and garlic in the bowl of a food processor and pulse, adding olive oil a splash at a time as needed to keep the mixture moving and stopping to scrape down the sides several times, until a small, consistently sized paste is formed, 15 to 20 seconds. (Depending on the size of your food processor, it may be best to do this in 2 to 3 batches.)

**2** Heat the butter in a large, flat-bottomed pan or Dutch oven over medium heat and cook until slightly toasted and brown. Reduce the heat to low, add the vegetables and 2 tablespoons of olive oil, and cook, stirring often and adding more oil as needed to keep things moving in the pan, until very tender and lightly brown, 30 to 40 minutes. Add the thyme and sage and cook, stirring, just until fragrant, about 1 minute. Add the ground turkey and pork (if using), increase the heat to medium-high, and cook, using a potato masher or wooden spoon to start breaking down the meat into small pieces, until no longer pink and starting to brown, 5 to 7 minutes. Season generously with salt and pepper.

**3** Add the wine and stir to deglaze the pan. Cook, stirring often, until the alcohol has cooked off and most of the liquid has evaporated, about 2 minutes.

**4** Add the milk and grated nutmeg and cook, stirring often, until most of the liquid has cooked off, another 1 to 2 minutes. Add enough chicken stock to just cover the mixture, lower the heat to a simmer, and cook, stirring every so often, for 30 to 45 minutes. Taste for seasoning, adding salt and pepper if desired.

**5** Use immediately, or cool and store in the fridge for up to 1 week or in the freezer for up to 3 months.

BREAK THE RULES

Top each serving with White Pepper Marshmallows (page 272).

✿ I ate a lot of mac n cheese as a kid and still crave it when I need a bowl of comfort. Here, I skip the roux, relying instead on the natural starches in squash to provide the creamy base for the sauce. You're essentially making a Fonduta (page 143), working in roasted squash to increase the volume and tone down the richness. I usually opt for butternut squash, but any variety—pumpkin, acorn, kabocha, honeynut—would work well. This is also a great way to use up leftover boiled, steamed, or roasted squash. But don't let your creativity end there—any starchy vegetable (potato to parsnip) can be turned into a thickener for fonduta!

# Butternut
# MAC N CHEESE

### Serves 4 to 6

1 very small or ½ small/medium butternut squash (about 1½ pounds)

1 tablespoon extra-virgin olive oil

Kosher salt and freshly ground black pepper

3 sprigs fresh sage

1 pound dried pasta (I like elbow or campanelle)

2 cups whole milk

12 tablespoons (6 ounces) unsalted butter, melted

¼ teaspoon freshly grated nutmeg, or to taste

1½ cups freshly grated sharp cheddar

¾ cup freshly grated Gruyère

1 cup finely grated Parmigiano-Reggiano

½ cup Garlic Streusel (page 68)

**1** Preheat the oven to 425°F and line a sheet pan with parchment paper.

**2** Cut the squash in half and discard the seeds. Drizzle the flesh side with the olive oil and season with salt and pepper to taste. Transfer to the prepared sheet pan, flesh side down on a bed of sage, and roast until tender when pierced with a knife, about 25 minutes.

**3** Place the pasta in a large, wide pot with a lid and cover with cold water (you want a ratio of 4:1 water to dried pasta). Season with salt, cover with the lid, and bring to a boil, stirring often to avoid sticking. When the water boils, remove the lid and cook, stirring often, until the pasta is al dente, about 4½ minutes.

**4** Meanwhile, bring the milk and butter to a simmer in a small saucepan over medium heat, then turn off the flame. Use a large spoon to scoop the flesh out of the squash and transfer to a high-powered blender. Add the milk, butter, nutmeg, and a good pinch of salt. Open the vent and cover with a clean dish towel (to allow steam to escape). Turn the machine to high and blend for 30 seconds or so, just to combine everything. Add in the cheddar, Gruyère, and Parmigiano, and blend again until the cheese is fully incorporated, about 30 seconds. Pour the sauce into a large sauté pan or Dutch oven over low heat.

**5** When the pasta is ready, use a spider or tongs to transfer it to the sauce. Toss to combine and add starchy pasta cooking water as needed to make it smooth and creamy. Season to taste with salt and pepper. Divide among serving bowls, sprinkle over the Garlic Streusel, and top with crispy sage from the roasting tray.

# BREAK THE RULES

Add a pinch (about ¹⁄₁₆ teaspoon) of xanthan gum (see page 21) to the blender. It will make the cheese sauce even silkier and more stable.

✿ This dish originates from the town of Norcia in Umbria, a region in central Italy that borders Tuscany and is famous for its hill towns, wild boar, and black truffles. Classically made with homemade Norcia-style sausage (which showcases wine and garlic rather than the typical fennel seed and chile flake) and fresh truffles, this creamy pasta is still delicious with store-bought Italian sausage. If you can track down truffle oil or paste (it's available online or at most grocery stores these days), its fragrant earthiness really plays well and elevates the dish. If not, don't sweat it; rules are meant to be broken.

# PASTA alla NORCINA

Serves 4 to 6

1 pound dried pasta (I like rigatoni or cavatappi)

1/4 cup extra-virgin olive oil

1 pound mild Italian pork sausage, casings removed

2 large shallots, minced (about 3/4 cup)

2/3 cup white wine

1 cup heavy cream

2 tablespoons unsalted butter

1 teaspoon (or more to taste) truffle paste or oil (optional)

1 cup freshly grated Parmigiano-Reggiano, plus more for serving

3/4 cup freshly grated Pecorino Romano, plus more for serving

Kosher salt and freshly ground black pepper

1 Place the pasta in a large, wide pot with a lid and cover with cold water (you want a ratio of 4:1 water to dried pasta). Season with salt, cover with the lid, and bring to a boil, stirring often to avoid sticking. When the water boils, remove the lid and cook, stirring often, until the pasta is al dente, about 4½ minutes.

2 Heat the olive oil in a large, flat-bottomed sauté pan or Dutch oven over medium-high heat. Divide the sausage into 8 even pieces, press into loose patties, and cook in the hot pan until deeply caramelized on the first side, 6 to 8 minutes. Use a wooden spoon to flip the patties, then begin breaking them into small pieces. Cook until nicely browned all over, another 2 to 3 minutes.

3 Add the shallots and cook, stirring constantly to make sure they don't burn, until fragrant and just starting to brown, 1 to 2 minutes. Add the white wine and cook, scraping the bottom of the pan to release any brown bits, until the raw alcohol has cooked off, 1 to 2 minutes. Stir in the heavy cream and cook, stirring often, until it has reduced and thickened slightly, 2 to 3 minutes. Reduce the heat to low while the pasta finishes cooking.

4 Use a spider or tongs to transfer the cooked pasta to the pan. Add the butter, truffle paste or oil (if using), Parmigiano, and Pecorino. Toss to combine and add starchy pasta cooking water as needed to make a smooth, creamy sauce. Season to taste with salt and pepper and serve immediately.

PRO TIP  Cooking the sausage in large pieces (rather than crumbling it into the pan) increases the surface area, allowing more of the meat to get deep caramelization and flavor.

**BREAK THE RULES**

Make your own sausage: Start with all your ingredients (and the bowl of your stand mixer) fridge-cold. Combine 1 pound ground pork, 3 minced garlic cloves, 2½ teaspoons kosher salt, 1¾ teaspoons freshly ground black pepper, and ½ teaspoon freshly ground nutmeg in the cold bowl of a stand mixer and mix to combine. Slowly drizzle in ¼ cup cold red wine, with the mixer running on medium speed, until the mixture is sticky and emulsified, no more than 2 minutes. Cover with plastic wrap and chill in the fridge for at least 1 hour and up to overnight (if you're short on time, you can use the sausage right away, but it will have a less developed flavor), then follow the recipe as written.

Dried Pasta Is Your Best Friend

❄ This dish feels like a perfect melding of my Italian heritage and Californian upbringing. I build flavor with a base of classic soffritto but swap out the traditional meat for a staple Californian ingredient: beets. I'm on a mission to convert all the beet skeptics out there and I think this magenta-hued pasta might be just the dish to do it. So please, grab a bunch of beets from the farmers' market (heck, even try this recipe with precooked grocery store beets!) and give beets a chance. They have a beautiful, natural, earthy flavor that not only pairs so well with the pasta, but also the tomatoes and all the other notes in the soffritto.

# BEET BOLOGNESE

### Serves 4 to 6

- 1 medium bunch red beets (about 1 pound), tops and stems reserved
- 1 cup extra-virgin olive oil, plus more as needed
- Kosher salt and freshly ground black pepper
- 1 bunch fresh rosemary
- 6 medium garlic cloves, peeled
- 1 small yellow onion, finely diced
- 2 large shallots, diced
- 1 large carrot, peeled and diced
- 1 sprig fresh thyme
- 2 tablespoons tomato paste
- 1 pound dried pasta (I like pappardelle)
- Freshly grated Parmigiano-Reggiano, for serving

**1** Preheat the oven to 350°F.

**2** Wash the beet roots and greens very well. Set the greens on a clean dish towel to dry and toss the roots on a large piece of aluminum foil with about 1 tablespoon of the olive oil. Season with salt and pepper, add 1 sprig of rosemary, and wrap up the edges to make a tight foil packet. Place on a sheet pan, transfer to the oven, and cook until the beets are easily pierced with a knife, but not mushy, about 1 hour.

**3** Combine the garlic, onion, shallots, and carrot in the bowl of a food processor. Blend, adding some of the olive oil a splash at a time as needed to keep the mixture moving, and stopping to scrape down the sides several times, until a small, consistently sized paste is formed, 15 to 20 seconds. (Depending on the size of your food processor, it may be best to do this in 2 to 3 batches.)

*RECIPE CONTINUES*

**4** Transfer the vegetable mixture to a large, flat-bottomed sauté pan or Dutch oven and add the remaining oil (or however much you need just to cover the vegetable mixture). Season with salt and pepper. Tie the thyme sprig and remaining rosemary with twine and add to the pot. Turn the heat to medium-low and cook, stirring and scraping often, for about 45 minutes, or until the vegetables are soft, translucent, and starting to brown. Add the tomato paste and continue to cook over medium-low heat, stirring often, until very dark but not burned, 30 more minutes. Remove the herb bundle.

**5** Once cooked, open the foil packet and allow the beet roots to cool on the sheet pan. Roughly chop the beet greens (optionally reserve the stems for pickling—see "Break the Rules" box below) and set aside.

**6** Place the pasta in a large, wide pot with a lid and cover with cold water (you want a ratio of 4:1 water to dried pasta). Season with salt, cover with the lid, and bring to a boil, stirring often to avoid sticking. When the water boils, remove the lid and cook, stirring often, until the pasta is al dente, about 4½ minutes.

**7** When the beets are just cool enough to handle, use a clean kitchen towel to rub off their skins and cut them into large pieces. Add the roasted beets to the food processor and pulse, adding olive oil a splash at a time as needed to keep the mixture moving and stopping to scrape down the sides a few times, until chopped into small pieces but not mushy (the texture should be similar to ground beef). Transfer to the pot with the soffritto and stir in the beet greens.

**8** Use a spider or tongs to transfer the cooked pasta to the sauce. Toss to combine and add starchy pasta cooking water as needed to make it smooth and creamy. Season to taste with more salt and pepper, top with Parmigiano, and serve immediately.

**BREAK THE RULES**

Add an extra layer of flavor to the dish with pickled beet stems (follow the Pickle Liquor recipe and technique on page 193).

# PICKLE LIQUOR

What is pickle liquor? I'm so glad you asked! It's the liquid you use to make pickles and it's one of my secret weapons for adding a bright, sweet-and-salty component to dishes. I start with my base pickle liquor ratio, then tweak it with different vinegars and spices. Depending on what I'm pickling and when I want to eat it, I'll also vary the temperature of the liquor and the pickle time. (If I want to pickle something firmer like a carrot and/or want to eat it sooner, I'll pour over the liquor while it's still warm; if I'm working with something a little more delicate, like shallots or cucumbers, and have a day or two to leave it in the fridge, I'll cool the liquor off first.) You can pickle just about anything—crunchy veg like carrots, cauliflower, turnips, or fennel, softer ones like cucumbers or beet stems, alliums like shallots, garlic, or ramps.

But the pickle party doesn't stop there. Have you ever tried pickling roasted vegetables (like mushrooms or broccoli), or even fruits like blueberries or strawberries?! Here is my base pickle liquor recipe with simple directions, plus a mini guide to quick pickling.

PRO TIP   The best part? Leftover pickle liquor that has now been infused with the flavor of your pickled vegetable can be reused for a new pickle (I usually only do this once) or used to season a vinaigrette or sauce.

# BASE PICKLE LIQUOR

*Makes about 3½ cups*

2¼ cups vinegar
1¼ cups water
¾ cup white sugar
¼ cup kosher salt
2 tablespoons spices (optional)

Combine the vinegar, water, sugar, salt, and spices (if using) in a medium saucepan over medium-high heat. Bring the mixture up to a simmer and cook, stirring constantly, until the salt and sugar have dissolved. Either use immediately or cool before using.

# A MINI GUIDE TO QUICK PICKLING

**1.** **What is the initial texture of the vegetable you want to pickle?**

HARD: A harder vegetable, like carrot or cauliflower, is going to take longer to pickle and will benefit from a hot pickle liquor. If you're in a hurry or want a softer, more consistent texture, it's helpful to blanch or steam these hard veggies before placing them in a heat-proof container (such as a glass jar or plastic container with a lid) and carefully pouring or ladling over the pickle liquor.

SOFT: A softer vegetable like a cucumber, onion, or mushroom typically responds better to a cold pickle liquor. You can cut these into any shape (or leave smaller ones whole), transfer to any container with a tight-fitting lid, and pour over the cooled pickle liquor.

**2.** **When do you want to use your pickle?**
If you want to use your pickle right away, cut your veg into smaller pieces and pour the liquor over when it's still hot. This will break down the cells of harder vegetables quickly and softer vegetables very quickly, so you can "quickle" something like chopped cauliflower in 30 minutes or sliced onions in 5 to 10 minutes. If you have a little more time, consider what texture you're looking to achieve . . .

### 3. Are you looking for all crunch or a little softness?

If you want to retain the crunchy texture of the vegetable (whether it be soft or hard), a cold, 48-to-72-hour pickle is going to be best. If you want the vegetable to break down and soften a bit (like red onions or shallots for a salad or sandwich), use a hot liquid.

### 4. How to choose a vinegar?

I generally reach for rice wine vinegar (unseasoned) but, depending on the vegetable and the final use of my pickle, I will often make some adjustments. White balsamic and rice wine vinegar make a beautiful blend for sweet vegetables like carrots or fennel. Rice and red wine vinegar together have a beautiful pink hue and natural acidity that works really well with red onions and shallots. I go for champagne vinegar (which has a less sweet, more acidic flavor than straight rice wine vinegar) when I'm looking for a sharper pickle.

### 5. What about aromatics?

There are endless combinations of pickling aromatics, so feel free to play around with whatever whole spices and fresh herbs you have in your kitchen. Here are a few of my favorite mixes:

CLASSIC DILL PICKLE: 1 teaspoon chile flakes, 1 teaspoon fennel seed, 2 teaspoons coriander seed, 2 teaspoons whole black peppercorns, and 4 crushed garlic cloves.

SPICY PICKLE: 1 tablespoon whole black peppercorns, 1 tablespoon Calabrian chile paste, and 4 crushed garlic cloves.

FUNKY PICKLE: 1 tablespoon whole black peppercorns, 2 teaspoons colatura, 1 teaspoon chile flakes, 2 teaspoons coriander seeds.

FRESH DILL PICKLE: 1 tablespoon whole black peppercorns, 4 crushed garlic cloves, ½ bunch fresh dill.

❋ Yep, corn again. My favorite vegetable is back. This time, I use it to add sweetness, creaminess, and freshness to the Roman classic Cacio e Pepe. Like all corn dishes, this is best made in the summertime with sweet, peak-season corn. If you do decide to make it in November, I'd recommend using frozen corn, which is consistently sweeter and more flavorful than off-season fresh corn.

# CORN CACIO E PEPE

*Serves 4 to 6*

### Corn Sauce

2 ears corn, shucked (about 1½ cups)

4 tablespoons unsalted butter

1 sprig fresh basil

Kosher salt and white sugar

4 ounces mascarpone

### To Finish

1 pound dried pasta (I like cavatelli or ziti)

1 tablespoon freshly ground black pepper, plus more for garnish

2 tablespoons freshly grated Parmigiano-Reggiano, plus more as needed

Freshly grated Pecorino Romano, to garnish

**1** *Make the Corn Sauce:* Set an ear of corn down flat on a cutting board and use a sharp knife to carefully slice off one side cheek of the kernels. Transfer the cut kernels to a bowl and turn the cob so that the flat side is now on the cutting board. Continue slicing and turning until all four sides have been cut, then continue with the remaining ears of corn.

**2** Melt the butter in a large skillet over medium heat. Add the corn and the whole basil sprig, and season to taste with salt and a pinch of sugar. Cook, stirring often, until the corn is just tender, about 5 minutes. (Try not to get any color on the butter or the corn; this will help preserve its fresh flavor.) Remove and discard the basil sprig and any leaves that fell off and set aside about ⅓ cup of the corn for garnish.

## BREAK THE RULES

Use the cut corn cobs to make corn stock: Use a spoon to scrape all the starch and milk from the cobs into a medium saucepan or Dutch oven. Add the cobs, cover with cold water, and bring to a simmer. Cook gently, uncovered, for 20 minutes, then turn off the heat and let steep for at least 30 minutes and up to 2 hours. Strain the stock and add a few tablespoons to the pasta in step 6. Add any leftover stock to soups, pastas, or anything that could use a little natural corn sweetness and starch.

**3** While hot, transfer the corn (minus the ⅓ cup reserved) to a high-powered blender and blend on high until smooth, 1 to 2 minutes. Add the mascarpone and continue blending until very smooth, another minute or so. Taste for seasoning and add more salt and/or sugar if desired. A slight sweetness is ideal, so you might want a little more sugar depending on the seasonality of the corn. Either strain through a fine-mesh sieve first (if you prefer a smoother sauce) or just set aside.

**4** *Cook the Pasta:* Place the pasta in a large, wide pot with a lid and cover with cold water (you want a ratio of 4:1 water to dried pasta). Season with salt, cover with the lid, and bring to a boil, stirring often to avoid sticking. When the water boils, remove the lid and cook, stirring often, until the pasta is al dente, about 4½ minutes.

**5** Just before the pasta is ready, toast the black pepper in a dry sauté pan or Dutch oven over medium-high heat until fragrant, about 30 seconds, then add a spoonful of starchy pasta cooking water to prevent it from burning.

**6** Use a spider or tongs to transfer the cooked pasta to the pan. Add the corn sauce, reserved sautéed corn, and Parmigiano. Toss to combine and add more Parmigiano and starchy water as needed to make a smooth, creamy sauce.

**7** Taste for seasoning, divide among serving plates or bowls, and top with a few cracks of freshly ground black pepper and grated Pecorino.

LEFTOVERS? Have leftover corn sauce? Make corn crepes! In a large bowl, whisk together 1½ cups corn sauce, ¼ cup rice flour, and ¼ cup all-purpose flour. Follow the directions for cooking crepes on page 264 and serve with sweet or savory fillings. Some of my favorites are bacon and eggs, spinach and melted cheese, or ground beef and diced tomatoes.

✤ Spaghetti alla Nerano is one of those dishes that really speak to the magic of Italian cooking. It sounds so simple—zucchini, pasta, garlic, olive oil, basil, and cheese—but there's a reason the small fishing village it was named after is now famous for this dish. Before I made it myself, I didn't believe the hype. But like so many seemingly simple Italian dishes, there's some mysterious alchemy at play. The different elements (the golden fry on the zucchini, the perfect amount of starchy sauce, the freshness of the basil, the salty bite from the cheese) combine to make something so much greater than the sum of its parts.

The dish is traditionally made with Provolone del Monaco, a delicious, semi-hard provolone cheese produced exclusively on the Sorrento Peninsula. If you can get it, use it, but because it is nearly impossible to find in the States, I use Pecorino Romano or any salty sheep's milk cheese in its place.

# PASTA
## alla
# NERANO

### Serves 4 to 6

1/2 cup extra-virgin olive oil

1 whole garlic clove, peeled

3 large zucchini, very thinly sliced

1 pound dried pasta (I like spaghetti or bucatini)

Kosher salt

4 tablespoons unsalted butter

3/4 cup freshly grated Pecorino Romano

1 handful fresh basil leaves

Freshly ground black pepper

**1** Heat the olive oil and garlic clove in a large skillet or sauté pan over medium-high heat and place a paper towel–lined plate or sheet pan fitted with a wire rack near the stove.

**2** When the oil is hot but not smoking (325°F—the garlic clove will start to sizzle), add a single layer of zucchini slices, making sure not to overcrowd the pan (you want the slices to fry and not steam). Cook, stirring often to make sure they're not overlapping, until lightly brown and crispy in places, 3 to 5 minutes depending how thin your zucchini slices are. Use tongs or a slotted spoon to remove to the prepared plate or wire rack and season immediately with salt. Continue shallow frying in batches until all the zucchini is cooked.

**3** Place the pasta in a large, wide pot with a lid and cover with cold water (you want a ratio of 4:1 water to dried pasta). Season with salt, cover with the lid, and bring to a boil, stirring often to avoid sticking. When the water boils, remove the lid and cook, stirring often, until the pasta is al dente, about 4½ minutes.

**4** *Back to the zucchini pan:* Lower the heat, remove and discard the garlic clove, and add the zucchini back into the pan with the infused olive oil. Quickly add a ladleful (about ⅓ cup) of starchy pasta water. Use a wooden or metal spoon to gently mash the zucchini until a loose sauce begins to form.

**5** Use a spider to remove the pasta from the boiling water and transfer to the sauce. Add the butter, Pecorino, and basil leaves. Toss to combine and add starchy pasta cooking water as needed to make a smooth, creamy sauce. Season to taste with salt and pepper and serve immediately.

❈ This is inspired by one of my favorite breakfasts: an everything bagel with cream cheese. Because I'm me, I decided to take those flavors and transform them into a pasta dish. I gotta say, I think I nailed it. The silky cauliflower puree provides the richness of the cream cheese and the spiced streusel evokes the flavor and slight crunch of the everything bagel. If you're feeling fancy, some salmon or trout roe (think lox on a bagel sandwich) takes this dish to a whole new level.

# WHIPPED
## Cauliflower
### AND
### EVERYTHING BAGEL
### CRUMBLE RUMBLE

Serves 4 to 6

### Whipped Cauliflower
2 tablespoons unsalted butter

2 tablespoons extra-virgin olive oil

1 small head cauliflower, quartered and thinly sliced

2 large garlic cloves, minced

1 medium shallot, finely chopped

1 dried bay leaf

1/2 cup heavy cream

Kosher salt and freshly ground black pepper

### Crumble Rumble
1/4 cup Garlic Streusel (page 68)

2 tablespoons everything bagel spice mix

### To Finish
1 pound dried pasta (I like penne or fusilli)

Kosher salt and freshly ground black pepper

1 small lemon, zest grated

2 tablespoons finely chopped fresh chives

**1** *Make the Whipped Cauliflower:* Heat the butter and olive oil in a large skillet or Dutch oven over medium heat. Add the cauliflower and cook, stirring often, just until it starts to soften, about 5 minutes. Stir in the garlic, shallot, and bay leaf and cook, stirring often, until the shallot has softened and is fragrant, another 3 to 4 minutes.

**2** Pour in 1/2 cup of water and cook, stirring often, until the cauliflower is tender and almost all the water has evaporated from the pan, 2 to 3 minutes. Add the heavy cream and cook, stirring often, until the flavors have melded and the cream has reduced by half, about 2 minutes. Remove and discard the bay leaf.

**3** Transfer the mixture to a powerful blender and blend until smooth and creamy, 2 to 3 minutes. Season to taste with salt and pepper. Place the cauliflower puree in a large sauté pan and warm over low heat.

**4** *Make the Crumble Rumble:* In a small bowl, mix together the Garlic Streusel and everything bagel spice mix.

**5** *To Finish:* Place the pasta in a large, wide pot with a lid and cover with cold water (you want a ratio of 4:1 water to dried pasta). Season with salt, cover with the lid, and bring to a boil, stirring often to avoid sticking. When the water boils, remove the lid and cook, stirring often, until the pasta is al dente, about 4½ minutes. Use a spider to remove the pasta from the boiling water and transfer to the cauliflower puree. Toss to combine and add starchy pasta cooking water as needed to make a smooth, creamy sauce. Season to taste with salt and pepper and finish with lemon zest.

**6** Divide the pasta among serving bowls and garnish each with a good sprinkle of Crumble Rumble and chives.

**LEFTOVERS?**

I often make a double batch of the cauliflower puree and use it as a base for just about any protein (it goes especially well with the Weeknight Short Ribs on page 134). It also makes a great stand-alone veggie side dish—just finish with a little Parmigiano-Reggiano and chopped fresh chives.

**BREAK THE RULES**

Top each serving with ½ to 1 ounce salmon or trout roe.

✿ If you like alla vodka, you'll love alla mezcal. In the classic vodka version, the ethanol in the alcohol is used as an emulsifier in the sauce but doesn't really add any flavor. Since more flavor is more better, I decided to try swapping out my favorite adult beverage, and the result was a smoky take on the Italian American classic. This creamy marinara sauce is great tossed with any dried pasta for a quick and easy weeknight dinner that will leave you thinking, "Why didn't anyone try this sooner?"

# PASTA alla MEZCAL

Serves 4 to 6

3 tablespoons extra-virgin olive oil

1 medium white onion, sliced in ½-inch rings

4 medium garlic cloves, peeled

2 tablespoons tomato paste

1 (28-ounce) can crushed tomatoes

1 teaspoon dried oregano

1 teaspoon dried thyme

1 teaspoon dried parsley

½ cup mezcal

1 cup heavy cream

Kosher salt and freshly ground black pepper

1 pound dried pasta (I like penne or spaghetti)

Freshly grated Parmigiano-Reggiano, for serving

Fresh basil leaves, to garnish (optional)

**1** Heat the olive oil in a large saucepan or Dutch oven over medium heat. Add the onion and garlic and fry, stirring occasionally, until golden brown, 5 to 8 minutes. Use a spider or slotted spoon to remove the onions and garlic to a plate and set aside.

**2** Add the tomato paste to the pan and cook, stirring constantly to ensure it doesn't burn, until fragrant, 1 to 2 minutes. Add the crushed tomatoes, oregano, thyme, and parsley and bring the sauce to a simmer. Cook, stirring occasionally, until the sauce has reduced slightly and the raw tomato flavor has cooked off, about 15 minutes.

**3** Place the pasta in a large, wide pot with a lid and cover with cold water (you want a ratio of 4:1 water to dried pasta). Season with salt, cover with the lid, and bring to a boil, stirring often to avoid sticking. When the water boils, remove the lid and cook, stirring often, until the pasta is al dente, about 4½ minutes.

**4** *Back to the sauce:* Add the mezcal to the tomato sauce and cook until the alcohol has evaporated, 2 to 3 minutes. Add the cream and cook, stirring occasionally, until the sauce has reduced slightly and smells amazing, 8 to 10 minutes. Season to taste with salt and pepper.

**5** Use a spider or tongs to transfer the cooked pasta to the pan. Toss to combine and add starchy pasta cooking water as needed to make a smooth, creamy sauce. Season to taste with salt and pepper and garnish with Parmigiano and basil (if using).

## Chapter Seven

# MADE BY HAND

*I LOVE MAKING FRESH PASTA.* So much so, I even have a prominent tattoo that reads "*fatto a mano*," which translates to "made by hand" in Italian. You've likely heard that only certain pasta fillings can go with certain pasta shapes. But where's the fun in that?? Rather than getting caught up in that "traditionalist" approach, I'm giving you my go-to pasta dough recipe, sheeting and shaping directions for three of my favorite shapes, and a whole bunch of different fillings to mix and match as you please. Think of it as a choose-your-own-adventure fresh pasta chapter; play around and have some fun.

All these stuffed pastas are designed to be enjoyed with a simple glaze of starchy pasta water and butter. If that sounds like too much work, spoon over some melted butter and call it a day. And last but not least, don't forget you can always make a batch of this dough, roll it out into sheets, and cut it into noodles to toss with your favorite sauce or filling.

✿ This is my desert island pasta dough. It's simple to make, quick to sheet, and can easily be cut and folded into any stuffed pasta shape. I call it Grano Treiso because *grano* means grain in Italian and Treiso is the commune in the Piedmont region of Italy where I first discovered this unique style of egg-yolk-rich dough and was lucky enough to learn the technique.

This dough, like all doughs, will vary slightly every time you make it. The perfectionist in you will dislike it, but the artist in you will love it. There is no "perfect" formula for pasta dough, as there are too many variables to account for: Everything from the time of day, the weather and humidity, the altitude, and the type of flour or eggs will affect the final product. An average "large" egg yolk weighs 18 grams, but every egg is slightly different, so you may need 12 yolks one day and 14 the next. Once you've made this dough a few times, you'll know what to look for and be able to adjust as needed. And trust me, with a little practice and a spray bottle of water at your side, you'll soon be able to bring together a perfect pasta dough every time.

# GRANO TREISO DOUGH

*Makes enough dough for 2 to 4 portions of any stuffed pasta shape*

12 large (218g) egg yolks
1 large (50g) whole egg
2¾ cups (325g) 00 flour
1 teaspoon (3g) kosher salt

**1** Prepare a spray bottle with water and keep it near your workstation.

**2** If using a stand mixer, add all the egg yolks and the whole egg to the bowl fitted with the dough hook and pour the flour and salt on top. Place on the stand mixer fitted with the dough hook and mix on medium-low speed. For the first 3 minutes, watch the dough slowly come together. If it still looks dry, add a spritz or two of water as needed to keep the dough moving (it will be quite stiff and your mixer might struggle just a bit). Mix until smooth and pliable, 12 to 15 minutes.

**3** If mixing by hand, mix together the flour and salt on a large, clean surface and make a well in the center. Add the egg yolks and whole egg to the well and slowly beat with a fork, gradually incorporating flour from around the edges of the well. When the dough starts to come together, switch to your hands and knead until the dough is smooth and supple, 20 to 30 minutes.

**4** Wrap the dough tightly in plastic wrap. If using that day, let it rest at room temperature for at least 1 hour and up to 3 hours. If making in advance, transfer to the fridge for up to 2 days and bring out to room temp 2 hours before using.

**PRO TIP** If your dough starts to form small black dots after a day in the fridge, that is only the oxidation from the air and the sulfur from the egg yolks. This tends to happen if the flour you used is high in sulfur content. Don't worry—this doesn't affect the taste and is safe to eat.

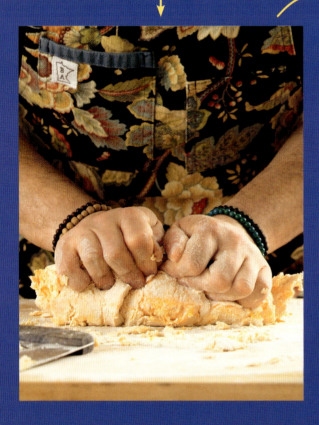

# SHEETING AND SHAPING FRESH DOUGH

## SHEETING

The exact technique for rolling out pasta will vary a bit depending on what dough you make and which machine you are using. A lot of different pasta sheeting instructions use and refer to numbers—which correspond to the notches that control the width between the rollers—as a guide, but because each machine is different, I always just tell people to start with the widest setting and work your way down. If you're using my Grano Treiso Dough (page 206), which is heavy with egg yolks, you can stop when you see your hand through the dough and be confident it will stay about that thickness when it cooks. If you're using a dough with lots of whole eggs, it will puff and soufflé slightly as it cooks, so you may want to roll it out a little more. As a rule of thumb, I tend to go to the second or third thinnest setting, depending on my filling and the shape I am making. For most home pasta machines, you will likely have to cut the dough into 2 (or even 4) pieces—you want to make sure that it comfortably fits between the rollers without pressing and forcing the dough out the sides. Like everything, rolling out pasta takes practice and patience and will change a little each time you do it, but here's a basic guide:

# A BASIC GUIDE TO SHEETING

1 Set up your pasta rolling machine, keep some 00 flour nearby, and start with a batch of room-temperature dough. The pasta sheeter can only do so much with its small plastic gears—if your dough is too cold, stiff, or thick, it will tear and rip as you try to roll it through the machine.

2 Divide the dough into 2 equal pieces. Wrap one in plastic wrap or place in a gallon-size zip-top bag, and set aside. Use a rolling pin to roll the first piece into a rectangle, about 8 inches (or about double the width of your machine) wide and 12 inches long. (Keep in mind the pasta sheeter will exaggerate whatever shape you start with. A clean, even rectangle will be exaggerated into a large, clean, neat rectangle; a funky crater shape will . . . well, you get the idea.) Roll until the dough is as thin as the widest setting of the machine, using your hands to adjust and pull the edges as you work, to ensure the rectangle is even.

3 Lightly dust your dough with flour and cut it in half vertically (think hot dog). Place half the dough in the zip-top bag to stay fresh while you roll out the other half.

4 Set the machine to the widest setting and pass the pasta dough through once. If the dough doesn't move through with ease, pass it through again.

5 Turn the knob to the second thickest setting and pass the dough through, catching it as it comes out the bottom. Continue adjusting the setting, one level at a time, passing through the dough until it moves through the machine without any resistance and dusting lightly with flour as needed to make sure it doesn't stick.

6 About halfway down your settings, as your dough sheet gets long and harder to manage, liberally dust it with flour and divide in half (think hamburger). Fold one half into quarters and place into the zip-top bag, while you focus on the remaining quarter sheet of dough.

7 Continue rolling the quarter sheet until you can see your hand through the dough. Now you're ready to shape.

8 Once you've cut and shaped everything from the first quarter of dough, you can go back to the quarter that was partially rolled thin. Repeat step 7 for that quarter sheet, then return to step 4 to roll out the remaining half of the dough.

PRO TIP  When sheeting, focus on the hand that is holding the dough as it goes into the machine. As the machine pulls the dough in, it's your hand's job to actively guide the dough and pull back gently as needed, creating tension, keeping it straight, and stopping it from bunching up, rippling, or getting caught in the sides. The hand catching the dough coming out of the machine is less important in the guiding process and can be used secondarily.

# MY THOUGHTS ON SHEETING AND LAMINATING

Some chefs and pastaio will tell you to laminate and trifold your dough, rerolling it throughout the sheeting process. I am not a proponent of this method for a few reasons:

**1** You are pushing all the air that you've worked into the dough out, essentially pressing the life out of your precious dough baby.

**2** Lamination will cover up and make *pasta ruvida* or "textured pasta" impossible. The slight drying and leathering (looking like a crocodile skin) is a sign of a seasoned pasta technician. This texture allows the sauce and condiment to stick to the cooked pasta shapes.

**3** It takes more time. If you already spent the time creating a smooth, round, even dough ball before resting, and the time shaping the dough into a rectangle with your pin before sheeting, then you shouldn't need to spend additional time laminating to make a nice, even rectangle.

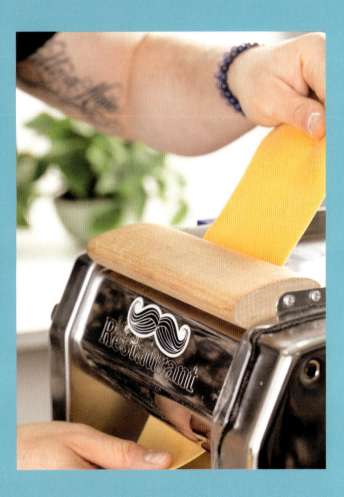

# SHAPING

When it comes to shaping, many pasta recipes will give you specific measurements and guidelines to follow. I decided to keep things loose—after all, this book is about breaking the rules (and life is too short to be measuring squares of pasta with a ruler). For all these shapes, you can make them as big or as small as you like and keep things simple with straight edges or add a little flair with a fluted pasta cutter. I will say that it is usually easier to start with larger squares when filling pasta and work your way smaller. And start with shorter sheets of dough, as you work your way up to longer portions in one go.

Once shaped, the parcels can either be cooked immediately or transferred to a parchment-lined and semolina-dusted baking sheet in a single layer, loosely covered with a dry kitchen towel, and stored in the fridge for up to 2 days.

PRO TIP  My favorite way to store fresh, uncooked pasta is in a clean cardboard pizza box. It stacks in the fridge and the cardboard whisks away excess moisture, prevents sticking, and protects the pasta from the cold blowing air of the fridge.

# TRIANGOLI OR MEZZALUNA

## SHAPING METHOD

1 Use a knife, pizza cutter, pasta cutter, or ring mold to cut the sheeted pasta into even circles or squares (they can be any size). Pipe some filling into the center (the larger your piece of dough, the more filling you can stuff inside), leaving a generous border on all sides. Use a spray bottle to spritz the air above the pasta sheets, allowing the water to gently and evenly fall and spread across the dough.

2 Fold the dough over in half, making a triangle or semicircle. Seal the dough as close as possible to the filling (you don't want any air gaps) and use your fingers to firmly press the folded-over edges to the original thinness of the sheeted dough. (If you skip this step, the edges of your filled pasta will be chewy.)

# TORTELLINI OR TORTELLONI

## SHAPING METHOD

1 Use a knife, pizza cutter, or pasta cutter to cut the sheeted pasta into even squares (they can be any size, but tortelloni will be larger than tortellini). Pipe some filling into the center, leaving a generous border on all sides. Use a spray bottle to spritz the air above the pasta sheets, allowing the water to gently and evenly fall and spread across the dough.

2 Fold the dough over in half, making a triangle or semicircle. Seal the dough as close as possible to the filling (you don't want any air gaps) and use your fingers to firmly press the folded-over edges to the original thinness of the sheeted dough. (If you skip this step, the edges of your filled pasta will be chewy.)

3 Pick up a parcel and, while gently holding one end of the triangle in each hand, press your thumb into the stuffed center of the pasta, creating some space between the filled center and the ends (it should look almost like an open fortune cookie).

4 Depending how big your tortellini or tortelloni are, place one, two, or three of your fingers from your opposite hand in the opening and loop the triangle ends around them to touch. Squeeze and press the ends to seal.

# 1

MAKE A TRIANGOLI OR MEZZALUNA.

# NOW YOU CAN EITHER MAKE:

TORTELLINI (OR TORTELLONI)          **OR**          CAPPELLETTI

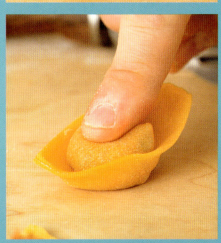

# CAPPELLETTI

## SHAPING METHOD

**1** Use a knife, pizza cutter, pasta cutter, or ring mold to cut the sheeted pasta into even circles or squares. Pipe some filling into the center, leaving a generous border on all sides. Use a spray bottle to spritz the air above the pasta sheets, allowing the water to gently and evenly fall and spread across the dough.

**2** Fold the dough over in half, making a rectangle or semicircle. Seal the dough as close as possible to the filling (you don't want any air gaps) and use your fingers to press the folded-over edges to the original thinness of the sheeted dough. (If you skip this step, the edges of your filled pasta will be chewy.)

**3** Stand the pasta parcel up flat on the work surface, with the stuffed bottom end closest to you and the folded top end facing away. Use your thumb or index finger to press into the filling, so the two bottom edges can meet. Squeeze and press the two pointed ends together, slightly overlapping and bringing the inner portion together, and pinch firmly to seal. You can then either leave as is or press down on the filling to make a dimple.

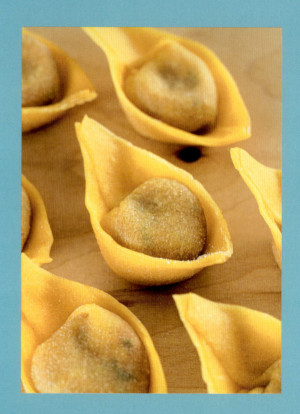

Spicy Pork with Pistachio Crumble Rumble, PAGE 238

# AGNOLOTTI

## SHAPING METHOD

**1** Use a knife, pizza cutter, or pasta cutter to cut the sheeted pasta into very long, narrow rectangles. Pipe one long line of filling down the center of the pasta, leaving a generous border on the top and bottom. Use a spray bottle to spritz the air above the pasta sheets, allowing the water to gently and evenly fall and spread across the dough. Fold the dough up and over in half, covering the line of filling.

**2** Using the back of your thumbs, run them along the length of the dough, lightly pressing the dough together as close as possible to the filling (you don't want any air gaps).

**3** With the stuffed bottom end closest to you and the folded top end facing away, use your thumb and index fingers to pinch the filled part of the dough into little individual parcels, making sure the dough is sealed between each one. Press firmly to ensure the pinched spots are the original thinness of the sheeted dough. (If you skip this step, the edges of your filled pasta will be chewy.) Use a knife, pizza cutter, or fluted pasta cutter to trim the top edge of the dough, then cut them into individual agnolotti.

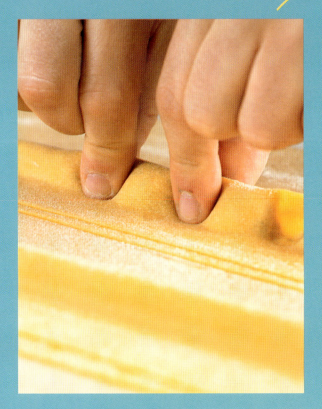

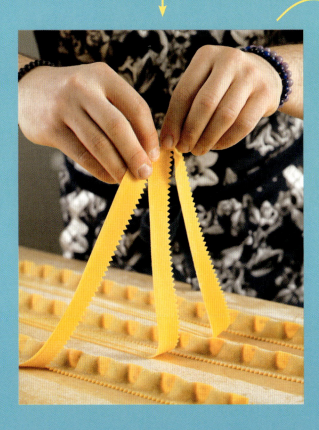

# THE FILLINGS

Braised Pork and Roasted Pepper, PAGE 226

Sweet Potato Maple Miso, PAGE 235

Spicy Pork with Pistachio Crumble Rumble, PAGE 238

Chicken Parm,
PAGE 232

Kale,
Ricotta, and
Hot Honey,
PAGE 239

FILLING NO. 1

✽ This is a great filling for anyone new to pasta making or looking to practice new shapes. Not only is it delicious, cheap, and easy to make, but its starchy potato base gives it a nice, sturdy texture so there's no risk of it squishing out the sides when you're shaping your pasta!

# BROWN BUTTER AND POTATO

Serves 4

*Filling*

4 large Yukon Gold potatoes (about 1 pound)

8 tablespoons (4 ounces) unsalted butter

1 cup freshly grated Parmigiano-Reggiano

Kosher salt and freshly ground black pepper

*To Shape and Finish*

Grano Treiso Dough (page 206)

Kosher salt

3 tablespoons unsalted butter

Freshly grated Parmigiano-Reggiano, to garnish

1 Preheat the oven to 375°F.

2 *Make the Filling:* When the oven is hot, poke a few holes in the potatoes with a knife or skewer and place directly on the oven rack. Cook until easily pierced with a cake tester or knife, about 1 hour.

3 Put the butter in a large saucepan and cook over medium heat, stirring often, to melt. When the butter has melted and begins to bubble and sizzle a bit, continue to cook, whisking constantly, until the milk solids turn golden brown and it smells nutty, 5 to 8 minutes. Immediately remove the pan from the heat and let the butter cool, scraping the bottom of the pot to release any of the toasted milk solids.

4 When the potatoes are still very hot but just cool enough to handle (latex gloves are helpful here!), use your fingers and/or a paring knife to peel off the skins. Use a food mill or potato ricer to rice the potatoes into a large bowl. Whisk in the melted but slightly cooled browned butter, and allow the mixture to cool to the touch. Stir in the Parmigiano and add salt and pepper to taste. Transfer the mixture to piping bags and chill in the fridge for at least 20 minutes and up to 2 days. (If you chill the filling completely, be sure to bring it out of the fridge an hour before using so it's easier to pipe and work with.)

**BREAK THE RULES**

Use leftover filling in place of the boiled potatoes in the Fried Potato, Cheese, and Sausage Pie (page 88). Just add a little flour to thicken the mixture so it doesn't leak out the sides of the little bread pockets.

**5** *Shape and Finish the Pasta:*
When ready to cook your pasta, bring a large pot of water to a boil. Follow the directions for sheeting and shaping (I like triangoli or cappelletti) on pages 210–21.

**6** When the pasta is ready and the water is boiling, salt your water to taste like a well-seasoned soup. Add the triangoli (or whatever shape you chose) to the pot and cook until they float to the surface, 4 to 5 minutes.

**7** Set a large sauté pan or skillet over low heat. Use a large slotted spoon or spider to transfer the pasta to the warm pan along with about ¼ cup of the starchy water.

**8** Add the butter, increase the heat, and bring the mixture up to a simmer. Cook, swirling the pan to keep everything moving while you reduce the pasta water to make a smooth glaze, 1 to 2 minutes.

**9** Divide among plates or bowls and garnish with extra grated Parmigiano.

**PRO TIP** Save your potato skins! They add great flavor to chicken or veggie stocks or can be tossed with extra-virgin olive oil, salt, and pepper and baked at 425°F for 20 minutes for a pre-dinner aperitivo.

 FILLING NO. 2

❦ *Agnolotti del plin*, which translates to "pasta with a pinch," is probably my favorite type of pasta to eat and make. In the classic Piedmontese version, the little stuffed morsels are filled with a mixture of slow-cooked meats—typically braised pork, beef, chicken, and sometimes rabbit—then glazed in the pan with some of the braising liquid, a little butter, and finished with grated Parmigiano-Reggiano. My version utilizes pork shoulder because it's delicious, affordable, and easy to find, but you could turn any tender, slow-cooked meat into a great filling. Bonus points if you save some extra braising liquid and use that in your pasta sauce glaze.

# BRAISED PORK AND ROASTED PEPPER

Serves 4

### The Filling

1½ to 2 pounds bone-in pork shoulder

Kosher salt and freshly ground black pepper

2 tablespoons extra-virgin olive oil

4 medium shallots, thinly sliced

12 whole medium garlic cloves, peeled

1 medium carrot, peeled and sliced into rounds

1 medium fennel bulb, thinly sliced

1 (16-ounce) jar roasted red peppers, drained and roughly chopped

1 medium escarole or ½ medium green cabbage, roughly chopped

1 cup dry white wine

2 cups chicken or vegetable broth

2 sprigs fresh thyme

1 dried bay leaf

1 cup freshly grated Pecorino Romano

⅛ teaspoon freshly grated nutmeg

### To Shape and Finish

Grano Treiso Dough (page 206)

Kosher salt

4 tablespoons unsalted butter

Freshly grated Pecorino Romano, to garnish

**1** Preheat the oven to 325°F.

**2** *Make the Filling:* Remove the pork from the fridge, pat it dry with paper towels, and season generously with salt and pepper on all sides. Let it sit at room temperature for 30 to 45 minutes (if you're short on time, you can skip this step). In a large, oven-safe pot or Dutch oven, heat the olive oil over medium-high heat. Once hot, add the pork shoulder and sear, turning with tongs, until nicely browned on all sides, 4 to 5 minutes per side. Remove to a large plate and set aside.

**3** In the same pot, add the shallots and garlic and cook, stirring, until fragrant, 1 to 2 minutes. Add the carrots and fennel and cook, stirring, until they start to soften and brown, about 8 minutes. Add the chopped peppers and escarole, give everything a stir, cover the pot, and let the greens steam and wilt for 2 to 3 minutes.

*RECIPE CONTINUES*

**4** Pour in the white wine and scrape up any browned bits from the bottom of the pot with a wooden spoon. Simmer for 2 to 3 minutes, until slightly reduced. Return the pork to the pot, add the broth, thyme, and bay leaf, and bring the liquid up to a simmer. Cover with a tight-fitting lid and cook in the oven for 2½ to 3 hours, or until the meat is fork-tender and falling off the bone. Discard the bone, thyme sprigs, and bay leaf and pour the mixture into a large baking dish to cool. Cover and transfer to the fridge to chill for at least 4 hours or overnight.

**5** Once chilled, remove the pork to a plate and strain the liquid into a large bowl, reserving all the braising vegetables. Either reduce the braising liquid in a saucepan (see Break the Rules, below) or cover and save to use for soup, blanching veggies, cooking rice, or braising more meat.

**6** Combine the pork and vegetables in the bowl of a food processor and pulse until uniform and broken down but not smooth (you want it to be pipeable but still have some texture), about 10 quick pulses. Stir in the Pecorino and nutmeg and season to taste with salt and pepper. Transfer to piping bags.

**7** *Shape and Finish the Pasta:* Bring a large pot of water to a boil for the pasta. Follow the directions for sheeting and shaping (I like agnolotti) on pages 210–21.

**8** When the pasta is ready and the water is boiling, salt your water to taste like a well-seasoned soup. Add the agnolotti (or whatever shape you chose) to the pot and cook until they float to the surface, 4 to 5 minutes. Set a large sauté pan or skillet over low heat. Use a large slotted spoon or spider to transfer the pasta to the warm pan along with about ¼ cup of the starchy water. Add the butter, increase the heat, and bring the mixture up to a simmer. Cook, swirling the pan to keep everything moving while you reduce the pasta water to make a smooth glaze, 1 to 2 minutes.

**9** Divide among plates or bowls and garnish with extra grated Pecorino.

**PRO TIP** Always chill your braised proteins submerged in the braising liquid. Because all the pores of the protein are wide open, it will suck up additional moisture. If it cools out of the liquid, you risk leaving your meat dry and sad.

**BREAK THE RULES**

Reduce the braising liquid by half and use some of it to glaze the cooked agnolotti along with the butter and pasta water in step 8.

Drizzle the finished pasta with parsley oil (see Green Herb Oils on page 230).

# GREEN HERB OILS

Green Herb Oil is a super easy way to make everyone think you're a professional chef. A little drizzle lends a fine dining look and feel to any dish, and only requires a powerful blender, fresh herbs, and a neutral oil to make. Use any herbs you like—I make chive oil to drizzle over Fresh Corn Polenta with Butter and Chives (page 167), fennel frond oil to garnish Summer Melon Gazpacho (page 63), and mint oil to spoon over Strawberry Cobbler (page 266)—but basil, parsley, tarragon, cilantro, chervil, rosemary, or a mix of any would be great, too.

Most herb oil recipes start by blanching the herbs in water, but I've never understood that step. By blanching the greens, you're infusing the water with their flavor, then leaving all that flavor behind when you drain them. Instead, I wash and dry my herbs very well and blend with neutral oil (grapeseed is my preferred choice, but you could use sunflower, canola, avocado, or any neutral oil) until smooth, heat the mixture in a saucepan to about 175°F (which is when the chlorophyll in the herbs gets activated, giving you that beautiful green color), then cool, chill, and strain before using. The longer you let the cooled oil mixture infuse before straining, the stronger the final flavor will be!

# GREEN HERB OIL

*Makes about 1 cup*

2 cups fresh herb leaves (such as parsley, cilantro, chives, or basil), packed
1 cup neutral oil
Kosher salt

1  Fill a large bowl with some ice and a little bit of water and set it near the stove.

2  Combine the herbs, oil, and a good pinch of salt in a powerful blender and blend until smooth, about 2 minutes.

3  Transfer to a saucepan and cook over medium heat, stirring often, until the oil turns a bright green color and reaches 175°F on a food thermometer, 2 to 3 minutes. Carefully pour the hot oil into a medium bowl and set it over the prepared ice bath. Once cold, cover and transfer to the fridge to chill and infuse overnight. The next day, strain the mixture through a very fine strainer or coffee filter.

4  Use the oil immediately or store it in a jar in the fridge for up to 1 week or in the freezer for up to 3 months.

PRO TIP  Add a few drops of liquid chlorophyll for a longer lasting, more vibrant green color. Just be sure to find a brand that is not flavored.

❦ This is one of my signature dishes and will always have a special place in my heart. The first time I made it was for an Italian friend who was in town visiting from New York. I wanted to make them something special, and because I knew they were a fan of chicken parm, I decided to turn that nostalgic dish into an elevated stuffed pasta. As soon as I tasted it, I knew I was onto something. All these little parcels need is a simple glaze of olive oil and water to evoke the flavors of the iconic dish. But if you want the full experience, "break the rules" with a creamy Fonduta (page 143) base, sweet and acidic Tomato Raisins (page 276), and crunchy Garlic Streusel (page 68) on top.

# CHICKEN PARM

Serves 4

## Filling

2 boneless skinless chicken thighs (about ½ pound)

Kosher salt and freshly ground black pepper

2 tablespoons extra-virgin olive oil, plus more as needed

¼ small yellow onion, minced

2 large garlic cloves, minced

6 tablespoons tomato paste

2 sprigs fresh basil

½ cup pre-shredded mozzarella

¾ cup freshly grated Parmigiano-Reggiano

## To Shape and Finish

Grano Treiso Dough (page 206)

Kosher salt

3 tablespoons extra-virgin olive oil

Small fresh basil leaves, to garnish (optional)

**1** *Make the Filling:* Heat a medium skillet or Dutch oven over medium-high heat and season the chicken thighs with salt and pepper. Add the 2 tablespoons of olive oil to the pan and cook the chicken, searing on one side until starting to brown, 4 minutes. Flip the chicken and sear for another 2 minutes on the second side (the chicken should be browned and only about 90 percent cooked through). Remove to a plate to cool.

**2** Add the onion and garlic to the pan (add a little more olive oil if the pan is looking dry) and cook, stirring often, until translucent and starting to brown, 5 to 7 minutes. Stir in the tomato paste and cook, stirring often, until the paste has turned a deep red color, 12 to 15 minutes. Right before removing from the heat, stir in the leaves from the basil sprigs. Transfer to a bowl to cool.

**3** Chop or tear the cooled chicken into large pieces. Transfer to a food processor and pulse about 10 times for a couple of seconds each time, stopping and scraping down the sides of the bowl as needed, until the chicken is broken down but not a paste. Add the cooled

*RECIPE CONTINUES*

tomato paste mixture, mozzarella, and Parmigiano and season with a little more salt and pepper. Pulse two more times, until just combined. Transfer to a piping bag.

**4** *Shape and Finish the Pasta:*
Bring a large pot of water to a boil for the pasta. Follow the directions for sheeting and shaping (I like tortelloni or agnolotti) on pages 210–21.

**5** When the pasta is ready and the water is boiling, salt your water to taste like a well-seasoned soup. Add the tortelloni (or whatever shape you chose) to the pot and cook until they float to the surface, 4 to 5 minutes. Set a large sauté pan or skillet over low heat. Use a large slotted spoon or spider to transfer the pasta to the warm pan along with about ¼ cup of the starchy water. Add the olive oil, increase the heat, and bring the mixture up to a simmer. Cook, swirling the pan to keep everything moving while you reduce the pasta water to make a smooth glaze, 1 to 2 minutes.

**6** Divide among plates or bowls, garnish with basil leaves (if using), and serve immediately.

**PRO TIP** If you have a grinder, grind the chicken with the tomato mixture on a 3/16 die instead of using the food processor and whip the filling together with the cheese using the paddle of the stand mixer.

**BREAK THE RULES**

To serve this dish the way we did at the restaurant or one of my pop-ups, spoon the cooked tortelloni onto a bed of Fonduta (page 143) and garnish with Garlic Streusel (page 68) and Tomato Raisins (page 276).

❁ I wouldn't necessarily call this a classic flavor combination, but it's certainly been in my arsenal for years. It's very reminiscent of the brown butter/butternut squash combo that becomes ubiquitous each fall, but I think the addition of sweet maple syrup and salty miso makes this a much more interesting interpretation. By long roasting the sweet potatoes, you're able to convert their natural sugars into caramel and you get a really deep, rich flavor. However, if you're short on time and need a little "quick & dirty," I have successfully made this with a bag of frozen, par-cooked sweet potato cubes in a pinch. Just roast them in a hot oven for 10 to 15 minutes to cook off any excess moisture.

## Sweet Potato MAPLE MISO

### Serves 4

### Filling

4 medium sweet potatoes (about 2 pounds)

16 tablespoons (8 ounces) unsalted butter

1 sprig fresh rosemary

¾ cup ricotta

¼ cup grated Parmigiano-Reggiano, plus more for garnish

2 tablespoons panko breadcrumbs

2 tablespoons white miso

1 tablespoon maple syrup

Kosher salt and freshly ground black pepper

### To Shape and Finish

Grano Treiso Dough (page 206)

Kosher salt

3 tablespoons unsalted butter

Freshly grated Parmigiano-Reggiano, to garnish

**1** Preheat the oven to 375°F and line a sheet pan with parchment paper.

**2** *Make the Filling:* Rinse and scrub the potatoes, poke a few holes in the skin with a knife or skewer, and arrange on the prepared sheet pan. Cook until easily pierced with a cake tester or knife, about 1 hour.

**3** Meanwhile, place the butter and rosemary sprig in a small saucepan and cook over medium heat, stirring often, to melt. When the butter has melted and begins to bubble and sizzle a bit, continue to cook, whisking constantly, until the milk solids turn golden brown and it smells nutty, 5 to 8 minutes. Immediately remove the pan from the heat. Let the butter cool, scraping the bottom of the pot to release any of the toasted milk solids, and discard the rosemary.

RECIPE CONTINUES

**4** When the potatoes are still very hot but just cool enough to handle (latex gloves are helpful here!), use your fingers and/or a paring knife to peel off the skins. Place the peeled potatoes in a strainer or colander to drain off any excess moisture as they cool. Once cooled to room temperature, transfer the potatoes to a food processor and blend until smooth, about 1 minute. Add the cooled brown butter, ricotta, Parmigiano, panko, miso, and maple syrup and blend again to combine. When the mixture is smooth, season to taste with salt and pepper and transfer to a piping bag.

**5** *Shape and Finish the Pasta:* Bring a large pot of water to a boil for the pasta. Follow the directions for sheeting and shaping (I like cappelletti or triangoli) on pages 210–21.

**6** When the pasta is ready and the water is boiling, salt your water to taste like a well-seasoned soup. Add the cappelletti (or whatever shape you chose) to the pot and cook until they float to the surface, 4 to 5 minutes. Set a large sauté pan or skillet over low heat. Use a large slotted spoon or spider to transfer the pasta to the warm pan along with about ¼ cup of the starchy water. Add the butter, increase the heat, and bring the mixture up to a simmer. Cook, swirling the pan to keep everything moving while you reduce the pasta water to make a smooth glaze, 1 to 2 minutes.

**7** Divide among plates or bowls and garnish with extra grated Parmigiano.

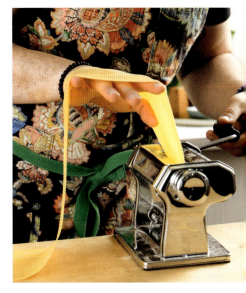

**LEFTOVERS?** Use any leftover filling to make the Sweet Potato Pie on page 259.

❁ Some of the best stuffed pasta in Italy can be found in Bologna and Modena, where they're famous for their tortellini. This is my riff on their classic filling, which is made with a mixture of mortadella, prosciutto, and ground pork. To keep it simple, I use only ground pork, and incorporate the pistachios that you would normally find inside the mortadella into the Crumble Rumble garnish. Given the relatively short ingredients list, this pasta packs a big punch, thanks to the chile crisp I fold into the filling (my friend Stephanie Izard makes the best one, This Little Goat Chile Crunch). Though certainly not traditional, it works really well here, adding heat and some umami backbone. If some of your guests don't like spice, drizzle it over individual portions instead of mixing it into the filling.

# SPICY PORK

## WITH PISTACHIO CRUMBLE RUMBLE

### Serves 4

## BREAK THE RULES

Replace half of the pork with ½ pound chopped and blended mortadella and replace 1 tablespoon of the unsalted butter with unsweetened pistachio butter in step 5 for an even richer and creamier dish.

### Filling

1 pound ground pork

1 cup freshly grated Parmigiano-Reggiano

3 tablespoons of your favorite store-bought chile crunch

Kosher salt and freshly ground black pepper

### Crumble Rumble

¼ cup Garlic Streusel (page 68)

1 teaspoon chile flakes, finely chopped or ground in a mortar and pestle

2 tablespoons crushed or roughly chopped shelled pistachios

### To Shape and Finish

Grano Treiso Dough (page 206)

Kosher salt

3 tablespoons unsalted butter

2 tablespoons finely chopped fresh chives

**1** Bring a small saucepan of water to a boil.

**2** *Make the Filling:* In a large bowl, mix together the pork, Parmigiano, and chile crunch, and season to taste with salt and pepper. Make a small meatball, add to the saucepan of boiling water, and poach until cooked through, 1 to 2 minutes. Taste the meatball and add more salt and pepper to the filling if desired, then transfer to a piping bag.

**3** *Make the Crumble Rumble:* In a small bowl, mix together the Garlic Streusel, chile flakes, and pistachios.

**4** *Shape and Finish the Pasta:* Bring a large pot of water to a boil for the pasta. Follow the directions for sheeting and shaping (I like tortelloni or tortellini) on pages 210–21.

**5** When the pasta is ready and the water is boiling, salt your water to taste like a well-seasoned soup. Add the tortelloni (or whatever shape you chose) to the pot and cook until they float to the surface, 4 to 5 minutes. Set a large sauté pan or skillet over low heat. Use a large slotted spoon or spider to transfer the pasta to the warm pan along with about ¼ cup of the starchy water. Add the butter, increase the heat, and bring the mixture up to a simmer. Cook, swirling the pan to keep everything moving while you reduce the pasta water to make a smooth glaze, 1 to 2 minutes.

**6** Divide the pasta among serving bowls and garnish each with a good sprinkle of Crumble Rumble and chives.

There is something wonderfully nostalgic about a spinach and ricotta filling. It always makes me think of the cheese ravioli my mom would make (or usually buy frozen) and serve with her famous red sauce. My version, which blends my basic Whipped Ricotta (page 159) and blanched kale, is a slightly more Californian interpretation of the Italian American classic. I pipe mine into triangoli (I think the ratio of pasta to filling works much better) and drizzle with a little hot honey; the perfect mix of old-school and modern.

# KALE, RICOTTA, AND HOT HONEY

Serves 4

## Filling
Kosher salt

1 medium bunch dino kale, ribs removed

1 cup Whipped Ricotta (page 159)

Freshly ground black pepper

## To Shape and Finish
Grano Treiso Dough (page 206)

Kosher salt

3 tablespoons unsalted butter

4 tablespoons Hot Honey (recipe follows), to garnish

**1** Prepare a large bowl of ice water and bring a large pot of salted water to a boil.

**2** *Make the Filling:* Add the kale leaves to the pot and blanch for 1 minute, just until tender. Remove to the ice bath to cool, then drain and wring dry on a clean dish towel.

**3** Transfer the kale to a food processor and blend until broken down and chopped but not pureed, about 30 seconds. Add the Whipped Ricotta and pulse a few times just to combine. Season to taste with salt and pepper and transfer to piping bags.

**4** *Shape and Finish the Pasta:* When ready to cook, bring a large pot of water to a boil for the pasta. Follow the directions for sheeting and shaping (I like triangoli or cappelletti) on pages 210–21.

**5** When the pasta is ready and the water is boiling, salt your water to taste like a well-seasoned soup. Add the cappelletti (or whatever shape you chose) to the pot and cook until they float to the surface, 4 to 5 minutes. Set a large sauté pan or skillet over low heat. Use a large slotted spoon or spider to transfer the pasta to the warm pan along with about ¼ cup of the starchy water. Add the butter, increase the heat, and bring the mixture up to a simmer. Cook, swirling the pan to keep everything moving while you reduce the pasta water to make a smooth glaze, 1 to 2 minutes.

**6** Divide among plates or bowls and drizzle over the hot honey.

## BREAK THE RULES
Finish with some pickled beet stems or other pickled vegetables (see Pickle Liquor on page 193).

# HOT HONEY

*Makes ½ cup*

Hot honey is one of those condiments that sounds intimidating but couldn't be simpler to make. All you need is 3 ingredients and a saucepan. Drizzle this over pastas, pizzas, eggs, vegetables, sandwiches, or anything that could use a little spicy sweetness.

½ cup honey
1 teaspoon Calabrian chile paste
Kosher salt

Combine the honey, chile paste, and salt in a small saucepan over medium heat. When some of the water has evaporated, the honey is beginning to caramelize and the mixture is bubbling, turn off the heat and set aside to cool slightly. Season to taste with salt and either use immediately or store in a jar in the fridge for up to 2 weeks.

✿ Potato gnocchi is notoriously one of the simplest, yet hardest pastas to make. Any chef will tell you that the best potato gnocchi is made by eye and by feel, not by following a recipe. That's because each potato has a different weight, water content, and starch content, and will therefore need a different amount of flour to bind it. But don't be intimidated! Making perfect potato gnocchi may take years of practice (I'm still honing my technique), but anyone can make good potato gnocchi; just keep these tips in mind:

1. Never make gnocchi with cold cooked potatoes. Once they cool down, the starches will set, and you'll be left with a gummy end product. If you need to keep the potatoes warm, hold them in a 250°F oven until you're ready to process and use them.

2. Think of the eggs in this recipe as a set of training wheels. They say the best potato gnocchi is made with no eggs and as little flour as possible. If you want to work your way up to that, great. While you're learning, the eggs will keep things from falling apart and on track.

3. I prefer a mix of Yukon Gold and russet potatoes for their respective flavor and starch and water content. If you're only going to use one, I would go with russets because they have that nice balance of starch, sugar, water, and flavor.

# POTATO GNOCCHI

Serves 4 to 6

4 medium or 2 large russet potatoes (about 2 pounds)

4 large Yukon Gold potatoes (about 1 pound)

Kosher salt

2 large eggs

2 to 3 cups 00 flour, plus extra for dusting

**1** Preheat the oven to 375°F.

**2** Rinse and scrub the potatoes and poke a few holes in the skin with a knife, fork, or skewer. Place on a sheet pan and toss generously with salt. Transfer to the oven and cook until easily pierced with a cake tester or knife, 1 to 1½ hours.

**3** When the potatoes are still very hot but just cool enough to handle (latex gloves are helpful here!), use your fingers and/or a paring knife to peel off the skins. Use a food mill or potato ricer to rice the potatoes onto a clean work surface. (If you don't have either of these tools, a potato masher will also work in a pinch.)

**4** Use a bench scraper to cut the potatoes, moving them around to help cool them down. When the potatoes are still warm but cool enough to comfortably touch with bare hands, season them generously with salt to taste, then mix in the eggs, using the bench scraper to mix everything together evenly.

**5** Begin dusting on the flour, ½ cup at a time, using the bench scraper to cut/chop in the flour and handling and kneading the dough as little as possible. Continue mixing, pressing together, and adding flour until the dough holds together, is less tacky, and becomes smooth, 2 to 3 minutes.

**6** Bring a large pot of water to a boil.

**7** Break the dough into 4 equal pieces and dust the work surface with flour as needed. Spread your fingers wide and roll each piece of dough into a log, roughly 24x1-inch (we all know the length doesn't matter, it's the width that counts,

so just make sure it's consistent), working from the center of the dough out to the ends. Cut the logs into 1-inch pieces, or gnocchi.

8 When the gnocchi are ready and the water is boiling, salt your water to taste like a well-seasoned soup. Add the gnocchi, being careful not to overcrowd the pot, and cook, stirring as needed to make sure none of them are sticking, until they float to the top, 2 to 3 minutes.

**PRO TIP** You can use rice flour instead of 00 flour to make these gluten free! Also, once blanched, the gnocchi can be tossed with oil, and cooled/frozen on a tray before putting in freezer bags to have microwave- and sauce-ready gnocchi ready anytime.

## BREAK THE RULES

For extra credit, use your thumb to roll the uncooked dumplings along the tines of a dinner fork or gnocchi board to make ridges; they look cool and will help whatever sauce you toss them with cling better.

❁ Although not all Italians agree with me, I firmly believe that gnocchi are pasta, too. I like to think of them as their own branch on the pasta tree—you have flour and water doughs, egg doughs, and dumplings (which includes gnocchi, strozzapreti, and canederli). I believe this ricotta gnocchi is the simplest, most forgiving of all the pasta doughs, so it's a great one to start with. Because you're not developing any gluten, it can be brought together very quickly and doesn't need to rest. And, since the main ingredient is creamy ricotta, you're pretty much guaranteed pillowy, tender dumplings every time. I love these simply tossed in a little brown butter and sage or Classic Pesto (page 104), but you could also sauté up some seasonal vegetables in butter—wild mushrooms in the fall or corn and tomatoes in summertime would be lovely—then toss with the gnocchi for something extra special.

# RICOTTA GNOCCHI

Serves 4

2 cups ricotta cheese (ideally hung overnight in cheesecloth to remove any excess moisture)

1/4 cup freshly grated Parmigiano-Reggiano

1 large egg

1 tablespoon unsalted butter, melted

Kosher salt

1 cup 00 or all-purpose flour, plus more for dusting

**1** In a large bowl, combine the strained ricotta, Parmigiano, egg, and butter, and season with salt. Add the flour, ½ cup at a time, and mix until combined, being careful not to overmix the dough—it should be sticky on the inside, but dry to the touch and not sticking to your hands or the bowl.

**2** Transfer to a clean work surface dusted with flour and sprinkle the surface of the dough with more flour to prevent it from sticking when rolling. Divide the dough into 4 equal pieces. Spread your fingers wide and roll each piece of dough into a thin log, roughly 18x¾ inches, working from the center of the dough out to the ends and adding more flour as needed to keep it from sticking to the work surface. Cut the logs into ½-inch pieces, or gnocchetti.

**3** Bring a large pot of salted water to a boil. Add the gnocchetti, being careful not to overcrowd the pot, and cook until they float to the top, 2 to 3 minutes.

**PRO TIP** Because ricotta is a natural product, the water (or whey) content will vary, and so the amount of flour used in the recipe will change every time you make it.

## Chapter Eight

# SWEET TREATS

Matcha
Tea-ramisu,
PAGE 260

*THERE'S ALWAYS ROOM FOR DESSERT.* My mom famously said that desserts fill your heart and not your stomach and, as someone with a big sweet tooth, I couldn't agree more. This chapter is full of the desserts I want to eat—pretty sweet, a little bit salty, with wonderful texture all the way through. Some are pure nostalgia (my Absolute Best Rainbow Sprinkle Cookies, page 248, taste like childhood encapsulated), while others, like my Matcha Tea-ramisu (page 260), play with somewhat more sophisticated, unexpected flavors. All of them are sure to impress your friends and keep everyone coming back for seconds (and probably thirds).

✿ I think everyone can agree—there is something magical and nostalgic about rainbow sprinkles. Just saying the words and picturing the brightly colored treats brings a smile to my face. Trust me when I say I have tasted and tested countless sugar cookie recipes, and this recipe combines all my favorite qualities: chewy, crispy around the edges, and slightly underdone in the center. The basic grocery store sprinkles work great here, but feel free to play around, incorporating a blend of your favorite sprinkles for a variety of textures and to make them your own.

# Absolute Best
# RAINBOW SPRINKLE COOKIES

### Makes 12 cookies

- 8 tablespoons (4 ounces) unsalted butter, softened
- 3/4 cup (150g) white sugar
- 1½ cups (180g) all-purpose flour
- 2 teaspoons (6g) cornstarch
- 3/4 teaspoon (5g) baking soda
- Pinch kosher salt
- 1 large egg, at room temperature (see Pro Tip on page 251)
- 1 teaspoon vanilla extract
- ½ teaspoon almond extract
- 1 cup rainbow sprinkles

**1** Using a mixer fitted with the paddle attachment, cream together the butter and sugar on medium speed, stopping to scrape down the bottom and sides of the bowl every few minutes, until light and fluffy, about 8 minutes. (Don't cheat here; the biggest mistake I see when making cookies is under-creaming.)

**2** Meanwhile, sift the flour, cornstarch, baking soda, and salt into a medium bowl.

**3** Add the egg, vanilla extract, and almond extract to the butter and sugar and mix for a minute or so, just to combine. With the mixer running on low, add the dry ingredients and mix just to combine, 5 to 10 seconds, being careful not to overmix. Stir in the rainbow sprinkles.

**4** Use an ice cream scoop or large spoon to shape the cookie dough into 12 equal balls. Cover and transfer to the fridge to chill for at least 2 hours.

**5** Preheat the oven to 350°F, place oven racks in the upper and lower thirds of the oven, and line 2 sheet pans with parchment paper.

**6** Transfer the cookies to the prepared sheet pans and bake for 9 to 11 minutes, switching positions in the oven and rotating front to back halfway through. The cookies will have no color and appear underbaked but will continue to cook as they cool.

**7** As soon as the cookies have set up enough to move (2 to 3 minutes), use a spatula to carefully transfer them to a wire cooling rack. Let rest for at least 10 minutes before eating.

**8** These will keep in an airtight container at room temperature for 4 to 5 days.

**PRO TIP** The cornstarch in the recipe helps absorb excess moisture to keep the baked cookies soft and also inhibits gluten development while mixing.

## BREAK THE RULES

My friend Christina Tosi of Milk Bar fame taught me this secret: If you want that nostalgic "cake batter" flavor from childhood, add ½ teaspoon clear imitation vanilla extract along with the other extracts. If you can't find imitation vanilla extract at your local grocery store, you can easily buy it online.

�֎ After extensive research and development—picking and choosing my favorite techniques from all the chocolate chip cookies I've tasted over the years—I finally arrived at this, the perfect chocolate chip cookie. There are a few things that make this recipe special. First up, the ice cube in the brown butter: Brown butter imparts a deep, nutty flavor, which we want. But in order to brown the milk solids, you first need to evaporate off the water in the butter (which means you're losing a lot of moisture, which we don't want). The ice cube essentially rehydrates that butter, so you get the toasty flavor without losing any moisture. Next, the mix of white and brown sugars: I use white sugar for its dissolvability (it whips up beautifully with the egg yolks) and brown sugar for its moisture, molasses flavor, and crunchy, granulated texture. For the "chip" element, I use a mix of milk and dark chocolate and always rough chop it by hand rather than using chips or morsels. And finally, as with all my cookies, I prefer to bake these slightly under and let them carry over and finish "cooking" as they cool, much as you would with a prime cut of steak. If you leave them on the hot baking sheet to cool, they'll overbake and get too crispy.

# Brown Butter
# CHOCOLATE CHIP COOKIES

### Makes 18 cookies

16 tablespoons (8 ounces) unsalted butter, cut into tablespoons

1 standard ice cube (about 2 tablespoons)

2⅓ cups (280g) all-purpose flour

¾ teaspoon (5g) baking soda

2 teaspoons (6g) kosher salt

⅔ cup (140g) white sugar

2 large eggs, at room temperature (see Pro Tip)

2 teaspoons vanilla extract

½ cup plus 2 tablespoons (140g) lightly packed light brown sugar

8 ounces (225g) milk and/or semisweet chocolate, roughly chopped with a knife into ¼- to ½-inch chunks

Flaky salt, to garnish

**1** Place the butter in a small saucepan and cook over medium heat, stirring often, to melt. When the butter has melted and begins to bubble and sizzle a bit, continue to cook, whisking constantly, until the milk solids turn a deep, golden brown and it smells nutty, 5 to 8 minutes. Transfer to a small metal bowl, making sure to get any brown bits stuck to the bottom of the pan. Let the butter cool for 2 or 3 minutes, then add the ice cube. Stir and let sit for a few minutes, then transfer to the fridge to cool, stirring every so often, for about 20 minutes (you want it to be soft and pliable, not firm and hard, so it can be easily added into the cookie dough).

**2** Sift the flour, baking soda, and salt into a medium bowl.

**3** Using a mixer fitted with the whisk attachment, whisk together the sugar, eggs, and vanilla on medium-high speed until the mixture has thickened slightly and is a pale yellow color, 5 to 7 minutes. Switch to the paddle attachment and add the cooled, softened, brown butter and brown sugar. Mix for 15 to 30 seconds, just to combine. Add the dry ingredients and mix, starting on low and increasing the speed to medium, just to combine, about 15 seconds. Use a spatula to scrape down the sides and bottom of the bowl to make sure everything is incorporated and stir in the chopped chocolate.

**4** Line a sheet pan with parchment paper. Use an ice cream scoop or large spoon to scoop the dough into 18 equal (or roughly equal) scoops. Cover with plastic wrap and transfer to the fridge for 30 minutes to firm up. Remove from the fridge and use your hands to roll the dough into round balls. Cover again and transfer to the fridge to chill for at least 2 hours (and preferably overnight).

**5** Preheat the oven to 350°F, place 3 racks in the oven, and line 3 sheet pans with parchment paper. Transfer the cookies to the prepared sheet pans (these spread a lot, so make sure they're at least 1 inch apart) and bake, switching positions in the oven and rotating front to back halfway through, until very lightly golden, 12 to 14 minutes.

**6** Remove the baking sheets from the oven and top each cookie with a hefty sprinkle of flaky salt. As soon as the cookies have set up enough to move (about 1 minute), use a spatula to carefully transfer them to a wire cooling rack. Let rest for at least 10 minutes before eating.

**7** These will keep in an airtight container at room temperature for 4 to 5 days.

**PRO TIP** Fill a glass with hot tap water and put your egg in it while you gather the rest of your ingredients. It will be room temperature and ready to bake within a few minutes!

Almond Flour and Egg White Thumbprints, PAGE 254

Brown Butter
Chocolate
Chip Cookies,
PAGE 250

Absolute
Best Rainbow
Sprinkle
Cookies,
PAGE 248

❀ If you've ever been to one of my dinners, you've gotten one of these in a little brown package with a mustache stamp. I first developed this recipe to use up all the egg whites I had accumulated in my fridge from making so much pasta dough. They were such a hit, I started making them for all my events and they became a signature sweet bite. These little thumbprints may seem intimidating, but they're actually pretty forgiving. As long as you don't overbake them, they have a beautiful, slightly crunchy, slightly chewy texture that I absolutely love.

# ALMOND FLOUR AND EGG WHITE THUMB-PRINTS

*Makes 24 cookies*

4 large (120g) egg whites
¼ teaspoon almond extract
2 teaspoons kosher salt
2 tablespoons (50g) honey
4 cups (400g) almond flour
1 cup (200g) plus ¼ cup (50g) white sugar
1 medium orange, zest grated
½ cup crushed sliced almonds

**1** Preheat the oven to 325°F and line 2 sheet pans with parchment paper.

**2** Combine the egg whites, almond extract, and salt in the bowl of a stand mixer fitted with the whisk attachment. Whisk on medium speed until the mixture holds soft peaks, 2 to 3 minutes.

**3** Bring the honey to a boil in a small saucepan over medium heat. Turn the stand mixer up to high speed and slowly stream in the hot honey. Whisk on high until the mixture is very stiff, light, and fluffy and has cooled to room temperature, 3 to 4 minutes.

**4** In a medium bowl, whisk together the almond flour, the cup of sugar, and the orange zest. Switch to the paddle attachment and add the flour mixture in 2 batches, mixing after each addition. Mix on medium speed until just combined, scraping down the sides of the bowl as needed.

**5** In a shallow bowl, mix together the remaining ¼ cup of sugar and the crushed sliced almonds. Using a 1-ounce cookie dough scoop or a spoon, scoop level balls (about 2 tablespoons) of dough into the sugar and crushed almond mixture. Roll around, making sure the nuts and sugar stick to the dough as evenly as possible and pressing to adhere. Use your hands to roll each one into an even ball and arrange on the prepared baking sheets.

**6** Use your thumb to press into the center of each cookie, making a little indentation. Transfer to the oven and bake until the cookies are just starting to brown around the edges but are still soft and chewy, 10 to 14 minutes. As soon as the cookies have set up enough to move (about 1 minute), use a spatula to carefully transfer them to a wire cooling rack and cool completely before eating.

**7** These will keep in an airtight container at room temperature for 6 to 7 days.

## BREAK THE RULES

I always add 1 teaspoon of orange blossom water and 1 teaspoon of rose water along with the almond extract to make the cookies extra special.

✻ When it comes to dessert pizzas (or folded-up pizzas, aka calzones), I think a lot of people lean toward a chocolate or chocolate hazelnut pie, but this pistachio calzone is my go-to. It's like a little hot pocket with a creamy, nutty, and oh so tasty filling. If you're a fan of Nutella, give this pistachio version a try—it just might convert you.

# Pistachio CALZONES

### Serves 4

1 ball "Quick and Dirty" Pizza Dough (page 108) or 1 store-bought ball pizza dough, at room temperature

All-purpose flour, for dusting

White rice flour, for dusting

1 large egg, at room temperature

1 tablespoon whole milk

6 tablespoons pistachio butter

1 tablespoon cocoa powder

1 tablespoon powdered sugar

Flaky salt

1/4 cup toasted shelled pistachios, finely chopped

**1** If using refrigerated pizza dough or store-bought, place the dough on a work surface dusted with a little all-purpose and white rice flour, cover with a large, inverted bowl or clean dish towel, and leave near a warm spot on the counter for at least 1 hour to rest and rise. If using freshly made and proofed pizza dough, place on a work surface dusted with a little flour and proceed to step 2.

**2** Preheat the oven to 425°F and place a sheet pan inside.

**3** Divide the dough ball into 2 equal pieces. Use a rolling pin to roll each piece into a 10-inch circle, making them as even as possible.

**4** Whisk together the egg and milk in a small bowl. Fill the center of each calzone with 3 tablespoons of the pistachio butter and brush the edges with egg wash. Fold the dough over in half, making a semicircle, then use your fingers or a fork to crimp the edges, sealing the pistachio butter inside.

**5** Carefully remove the baking sheet from the oven and line with parchment paper. Transfer the calzones to the baking sheet and brush all over with the egg wash. Bake until golden brown, 15 to 18 minutes. Let rest for 2 to 3 minutes, then dust each one with cocoa powder and powdered sugar. Sprinkle over a little flaky salt and garnish with pistachios.

❋ People are always asking me what to do with leftover Whipped Ricotta (page 159) from making filled pastas, so I came up with this recipe. The great thing about ricotta pie is how easy and versatile it is. This sweet version, based on a classic Italian ricotta pie, is flavored with sugar, vanilla, lemon, and cinnamon, but you could also make it super savory with lots of cracked black pepper and Parmigiano-Reggiano and/or Pecorino Romano cheese.

# Baked RICOTTA PIE

Serves 10 to 12

1 (9-inch) frozen pie shell

1 cup (250g) Whipped Ricotta (page 159) or whole milk ricotta

1/2 cup (100g) white sugar

2 large eggs

1 teaspoon vanilla extract

1 large or 2 small lemons, zest grated

1 large pinch ground cinnamon

Fresh berries, to garnish

**1** Preheat the oven to 350°F.

**2** Remove the frozen pie shell from the freezer and let sit at room temperature for 5 minutes. Prick the bottom of the dough with a fork, line with a piece of parchment paper, and fill with dried beans or baking pie weights. Bake until very lightly brown, 10 to 15 minutes.

**3** Meanwhile, whisk together the ricotta, sugar, eggs, vanilla, lemon zest, and cinnamon. Carefully pour the filling into the par-baked shell. Bake until the filling is just starting to brown around the edges but still jiggles slightly when you give it a shake, 30 to 32 minutes.

**4** Let cool to room temperature and serve with fresh berries.

## BREAK THE RULES

Upgrade your dessert with homemade Basic Pie Dough (page 275). Roll out the dough, place it in a 9-inch pie plate (trimming the edges as needed), then follow the recipe as written.

Add a brûléed topping: Once the pie has cooled slightly, sprinkle over 1/4 cup of white sugar and cook with a blowtorch until caramelized and bubbling. If you don't have a blowtorch, heat up a large metal spoon over your stove burner (make sure to use a towel or oven mitt, as the entire spoon will get very hot). Once scorching, press the back of the hot spoon onto the sprinkling of sugar and watch it caramelize. Repeat as needed.

❋ I often end up with some leftover filling when I make Sweet Potato Maple Miso pasta (page 235), so I came up with this recipe as a way to repurpose it. Much like the Baked Ricotta Pie on page 256, I sweeten the filling (here I use maple syrup and light brown sugar to lean into those cozy fall flavors), add some eggs to help it set, and bake off in a pie shell. It tastes like an upgraded pumpkin pie and would make a great addition to any Thanksgiving dessert spread!

1 (9-inch) frozen pie shell

1½ cups (300g) Sweet Potato Maple Miso filling (page 235)

3 tablespoons (50g) maple syrup

¼ cup (50g) light brown sugar

2 large eggs

# SWEET POTATO PIE

Serves 10 to 12

**1** Preheat the oven to 350°F.

**2** Remove the frozen pie shell from the freezer and let sit at room temperature for 5 minutes. Prick the bottom of the dough with a fork, line with a piece of parchment paper, and fill with dried beans or baking pie weights. Bake until very lightly brown, 10 to 15 minutes.

**3** Meanwhile, whisk together the sweet potato filling, maple syrup, light brown sugar, and eggs. Carefully pour the filling into the par-baked shell. Bake until the filling has just set but still jiggles slightly when you give it a shake, 35 to 38 minutes.

**4** Let cool to room temperature before serving.

## BREAK THE RULES

Top the finished pie with Praline Paste (page 274).

We all know tiramisu, or "pick me up," the classic Italian dessert made with cocoa, coffee, eggs, and ladyfingers. But have you heard of "tea" ramisu? I developed this recipe while living in California, where you'll find matcha—the grassy, slightly bitter Japanese green tea—at just about any coffee shop. It works great as a stand-in for both the espresso and cocoa powder, creating a fun and truly unique reinterpretation of the original.

# Matcha TEA-RAMISU

### Serves 10 to 12

### Soaking Syrup

1 cup hot water

2 tablespoons matcha green tea powder

½ cup white sugar

¼ cup freshly brewed espresso

### Matcha Mascarpone Filling

4 large eggs, separated

¼ cup lightly packed light brown sugar

1 teaspoon vanilla extract

8 ounces mascarpone, softened

2 tablespoons matcha green tea powder

¼ cup powdered sugar

### Assembly

1 (7-ounce) package ladyfinger cookies

Cocoa powder, to garnish

Matcha green tea powder, to garnish

**1** *Make the Soaking Syrup:* In a medium shallow bowl (large enough to hold the ladyfingers), whisk together the hot water and matcha until smooth. Add the granulated sugar and espresso and whisk to dissolve the sugar. Set aside to cool.

**2** *Make the Filling:* In a large mixing bowl, whisk together the egg yolks and brown sugar until pale and creamy, about 5 minutes. Stir in the vanilla extract. Add the softened mascarpone and matcha and beat until smooth.

**3** In a separate large mixing bowl, use a clean whisk to beat the egg whites and powdered sugar until stiff peaks form, about 5 minutes. Gently fold into the mascarpone mixture, being careful not to deflate the egg whites too much.

**4** *To Assemble:* Have an 8-inch square baking dish ready. Working one at a time, quickly dip half of the ladyfinger cookies into the soaking syrup, flipping to coat each side (don't leave them to soak for too long or they'll start to get soggy), then arrange them in an even layer in the bottom of the baking dish. Spread over half of the filling, smooth it out with a spatula, and add a dusting of cocoa powder. Repeat with the remaining ladyfingers and filling. Dust the final top layer of filling with matcha powder.

**5** Cover the dish with plastic wrap and refrigerate for at least 4 hours and preferably overnight, to allow the flavors to meld and the tiramisu to set. Serve chilled.

## BREAK THE RULES

Add ½ cup Amaro Montenegro to the soaking liquid and add a garnish of shaved white chocolate to the finished dish.

**PRO TIP** To make this dairy free, sub whipped coconut cream for the mascarpone.

✿ Panettone—a buttery, sweet cake originally from Milan—is an Italian essential around the holidays. I buy one every year from my friend Roy, the best panettone baker in the world, and turn any leftovers into my Italian version of French toast the morning after Christmas. What makes my take on this popular brunch dish Italian is, obviously, the panettone, but also the garnishes. Instead of using maple syrup, which can be cloyingly sweet, I finish mine with strawberries and aged balsamic vinegar. It's the most custardy, fluffiest "Italian" toast you can imagine. If it's an option, spring for a slightly more expensive panettone. A cheaper, commercially made version will certainly work here, but a true panettone requires time (when done properly they can take up to 3 to 4 days to make), skill, and quality ingredients, and you can really taste the difference.

# Panettone "ITALIAN TOAST" WITH STRAWBERRIES AND BALSAMIC

Serves 4 to 6

- 1 pint fresh strawberries, hulled and quartered
- 1 tablespoon plus 3 tablespoons white sugar
- 4 large eggs
- Pinch kosher salt
- Pinch ground cinnamon
- Pinch freshly grated nutmeg
- ¼ teaspoon vanilla extract
- 1½ cups whole milk
- 4 tablespoons strawberry milk powder, such as Nesquik (optional)
- 4 tablespoons unsalted butter
- ½ panettone, cut into 1-inch wedges
- 3 tablespoons aged balsamic vinegar

**1** Preheat the oven to 200°F.

**2** In a medium bowl, stir together the strawberries and 1 tablespoon of sugar. Mix well and set aside to macerate.

**3** In a large, shallow dish or bowl, whisk together the eggs, remaining 3 tablespoons of sugar, salt, cinnamon, nutmeg, and vanilla extract until smooth. Whisk in the milk and strawberry milk powder (if using).

**4** Heat 1 tablespoon of the butter in a large, cast-iron or nonstick skillet over medium heat. Briefly dip a slice of panettone into the custard mixture, letting it soak for about 5 seconds per side. Transfer to the pan and cook, flipping halfway through, until both sides are golden brown, about 2 minutes per side. Place on a sheet pan and store in the oven to keep warm.

**5** Continue dipping and frying, putting as many pieces as will comfortably fit into the pan, adding more butter as needed, and transferring cooked pieces to the baking sheet in the oven, until all the panettone is cooked.

**6** Transfer the "toast" to plates or a serving platter, top with strawberries and their juices, and drizzle over the balsamic vinegar.

## BREAK THE RULES

For a slightly more complex flavor, top with Burnt Strawberries (page 278) instead of, or in addition to, the macerated strawberries.

My mom cooked everything well, but she might be most famous for these crepes. She'd make them every weekend for my brothers, me, and any friends who'd slept over. I can still see her standing in our kitchen, pouring batter and swirling, trying to keep up with a house full of hungry boys—she couldn't make them fast enough! I'd wait by her side, grab a hot crepe just as it slid from the pan, then immediately sprinkle it with granulated sugar, roll it up like a taquito, and devour it. It's still my favorite way to eat them.

I personally like a crepe that is almost totally blond (no dark brown bubbles, color, or caramelization), which I now know is very hard to do, and not at all the way you'll find them in France. But my loving mom always indulged me. That said, if you like yours speckled, go for it. Prefer powdered sugar and lemon, jam or jelly, fresh fruit, Nutella or pistachio butter, or even ham and cheese? Be my guest. Just be sure to eat them straight from the pan and always think of Mom.

# MOM'S CREPES

### Makes 9 (8-inch) crepes

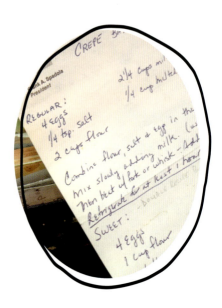

4 large eggs, at room temperature (see Pro Tip on page 251)

1 cup (227g) whole milk, at room temperature (or microwaved on high for about 45 seconds)

2 tablespoons unsalted butter, melted and slightly cooled

1 cup (120g) all-purpose flour

2 tablespoons white sugar, plus extra to serve

Pinch kosher salt

Nonstick cooking spray, for the pan

1 Preheat the oven to 200°F.

2 If using a blender, add the eggs and blend until smooth, 5 to 10 seconds. Add the milk, melted butter, ¼ cup of water, the flour, sugar, and salt and blend again until smooth, 20 to 30 seconds. If making by hand, add the eggs to a large mixing bowl and beat with a whisk until smooth. Add the milk, melted butter, ¼ cup of water, the flour, sugar, and salt and whisk until smooth.

3 Cover and rest at room temperature for 30 minutes to allow the flour to rest and hydrate. Give the batter another quick whisk or blend just before cooking.

4 Heat a 10-inch nonstick pan (don't stress over a special "crepe pan"—any nonstick pan will do) over medium heat and coat lightly in nonstick spray. When the pan is warm, add about ¼ cup of the batter (I like using a ladle; my mom had one specifically sized for her crepe pan) and immediately pick up the pan by the handle and swirl (it's all in the wrist!), allowing the batter to spread out to the edges of the pan. Let the crepe cook until just set (the top will turn more yellow and you'll start to see tiny bubbles), about 1 minute. Use a rubber spatula to carefully flip and cook for another 30 seconds.

5 Sprinkle with sugar and eat right away, while warm, or transfer to a plate, cover with a clean dish towel, and store in the warm oven while you cook the remaining crepes. Serve warm with sugar for sprinkling.

I've always loved strawberry cobbler—that combination of sweet, warm strawberries, golden cake-y topping, and a scoop of cold vanilla cream is hard to beat. My one criticism is that they can sometimes be a *little* too sweet. In this version, I add a layer of bitterness by first broiling half of the strawberries until bubbling and black on top. The slightly burnt flavor helps temper the sweetness of the strawberries and adds really nice complexity to the dish. This recipe calls for strawberries, but rules are meant to be broken, so use your favorite fruit of the season (or dare I say, even something frozen?).

# Strawberry COBBLER

### Serves 10 to 12

- 2 quarts (about 2 pounds) fresh strawberries, hulled and halved, with larger ones quartered
- 2 tablespoons (25g) plus 1/4 cup (50g) plus 3/4 cup (150g) white sugar
- 1 medium lemon, zest grated and juiced
- 8 tablespoons (4 ounces) unsalted butter, cut into tablespoons
- 1 cup (120g) all-purpose flour
- 1½ teaspoons baking powder
- ½ teaspoon kosher salt
- ¼ teaspoon baking soda
- 1 cup (227g) whole buttermilk
- 1 teaspoon vanilla extract

1 Turn the oven to broil and place a rack in the upper third of the oven.

2 Toss half of the strawberries with the 2 tablespoons sugar (or more or less, depending on how sweet your strawberries are) and transfer to a 9x13-inch baking dish. Place under the broiler and cook, without turning or moving, until very blackened and burned on the exterior, 10 to 15 minutes, depending how powerful your broiler is.

3 Meanwhile, combine the remaining strawberries, lemon zest and juice, and the ¼ cup of sugar in a large mixing bowl and stir gently. Let the mixture sit and macerate, stirring occasionally, until very juicy, about 15 minutes.

4 Remove the broiled strawberries from the oven and turn the temperature down to 350°F. Immediately add the butter to the baking dish, letting the heat from the strawberries melt it. Stir in the macerated strawberries and mix to combine.

5 In a large bowl, whisk together the remaining ¾ cup of sugar, flour, baking powder, salt, and baking soda. Stir in the buttermilk and vanilla and whisk until smooth. Pour the batter evenly over the top of the strawberries and transfer to the oven. Bake until the batter is puffed and slightly golden in the center and dark golden brown around the edges, 40 to 45 minutes. Remove from the oven and cool on a wire rack for at least 15 minutes.

## BREAK THE RULES

Serve with strawberry and rose whipped cream: Place 1 cup heavy whipping cream, ½ cup lightly crushed freeze-dried strawberries, 2 tablespoons white sugar, 1 tablespoon dried rose petals, ¼ teaspoon rose water, and a pinch of kosher salt in the bowl of a stand mixer fitted with the whisk attachment. Beat, starting on low and increasing the speed to high as it thickens, until the cream holds soft peaks, 2 to 3 minutes.

Drizzle with mint oil (see Green Herb Oils on page 230) just before serving.

I came up with this creamy banana ice cream while looking for dairy-free desserts that satisfy that sugary craving, while also feeling "healthy." I find some banana ice cream recipes to be a little one-note, but this one is special—the oats and tahini add roundness and texture, the honey and dates bring a little extra sweetness, and the cinnamon and walnuts give it a slight banana bread vibe. I always keep some bananas in a zip-top bag in my freezer so I can quickly blend up this last-minute dessert, especially when vegan or gluten-free friends come over!

# Banana "ICE CREAM"

## WITH CINNAMON, WALNUTS, AND DATES

### Serves 6

5 large bananas, broken into 2-inch pieces and frozen overnight (or at least a few hours)

¼ cup rolled oats

¼ cup honey

1 tablespoon tahini

1 teaspoon vanilla extract

1 teaspoon ground cinnamon

½ teaspoon kosher salt

Oat milk, as needed

¼ cup crushed walnuts, to garnish

¼ cup medjool dates, sliced into rings, to garnish

**1** Combine the frozen banana pieces, oats, honey, tahini, vanilla, cinnamon, and salt in a high-powered blender or food processor. Process on high speed, using a tamper to press the mixture into the blades or pausing to scrape down the sides of the food processor and adding a splash or two of oat milk as needed to get the mixture moving, until the "ice cream" is smooth and creamy, 1 to 2 minutes.

**2** Spoon into serving bowls and garnish with crushed walnuts and sliced dates.

**PRO TIP** Don't prematurely add the oat milk or you'll end up with a banana milkshake and not ice cream.

Chapter Nine

# ESSENTIAL BASIC
## RECIPES

Tomato
Raisins,
PAGE 276

THESE ARE MY "break the rules" basics—recipes that I lean on time and again to add a little extra flavor, texture, oomph, or pizzazz to my dishes. Most can be made in advance and stored in the cupboard, fridge, or freezer. Make them when you have a little extra time, so you can be like me and elevate just about any dish with minimal effort.

✿ I'm always looking for new and fun ways to use the leftover egg whites from all the Grano Treiso Dough (page 206) I make. You can only eat so many omelets. These white pepper marshmallows are essentially a stable and versatile Swiss meringue. The recipe only requires a few easy steps; it can be adjusted to make sweet or savory, and flavored with any extracts, juices, vinegars, or colors you like. Make it savory or sweet, torched, baked, or dehydrated.

# White Pepper MARSH- MALLOWS

Makes about 60 (1-inch) marshmallows

2 large egg whites

½ cup plus 1 tablespoon white sugar

¼ teaspoon cream of tartar (optional)

Juice of ½ medium lemon

Kosher salt and ground white pepper

**1** Combine the egg whites, sugar, and cream of tartar (if using) in the bowl of your stand mixer. Fill a medium pot with 1 inch of water (choose one that will hold the bowl comfortably without letting the bottom touch the water) and set over medium heat. When the water is simmering, set the mixing bowl on top and reduce the heat as needed to maintain a gentle simmer. Cook, stirring constantly with a spatula, until the egg whites reach 175°F on a food thermometer, 4 to 5 minutes.

**2** Immediately transfer to a stand mixer fitted with the whisk attachment and stir in the lemon juice. Whisk on high speed until the mixture has cooled completely and holds stiff peaks, 6 to 8 minutes. Season to taste with salt and pepper and transfer to a piping bag. Congratulations, you just made a Swiss meringue!

**3** *To toast:* Pipe little marshmallow kisses onto any dish (I especially love them on the Turkey Bolognese on page 182) and either toast with a blowtorch or quickly broil until they look like little roasted marshmallows. If you don't have a blowtorch, heat up a large metal spoon over your stove burner (make sure to use a towel or oven mitt, as the entire spoon will get very hot). Once scorching, press the back of the hot spoon onto the meringue and watch it toast. Repeat as needed.

**4** *To dehydrate:* Pipe, spread, or scoop the meringues onto a parchment-lined baking sheet and cook in a 200°F oven for 2 to 4 hours, or until crispy and dehydrated. Use them to garnish pasta, salads, or vegetables, or just eat them as a snack.

**5** Store uncooked meringue in the fridge for up to 3 days and dehydrated meringues in an airtight container at room temperature for 1 to 2 days.

This is my go-to marinade and condiment. I use it as a base recipe but end up using whatever I have in my fridge. Scallion bottoms? Half an onion? Or the butt end of a shallot?—toss it in. Cilantro stems? Wilted parsley? Leftover jalapeño quarter? Yep, that works, too. You can cook it, use it as a marinade, toss pasta with it, or spread it on a sandwich. I'll even keep some frozen in vacuum-sealed bags or ice cube trays to have on hand at all times, whenever I want a marinade or to season roasted or grilled vegetables.

# Herby Garlicky Paste

Makes about 1 1/3 cups

- 1 cup extra-virgin olive oil
- 1/2 cup whole garlic cloves, peeled
- 4 sprigs fresh thyme, picked
- 2 sprigs fresh rosemary, picked
- 1 teaspoon black peppercorns

Combine the olive oil, garlic, thyme and rosemary leaves, and peppercorns in a blender or food processor. Blend until smooth, about 30 seconds. Use immediately, or transfer to an airtight container and store in the fridge for up to 1 week (or in the freezer for up to 3 months).

✾ What is not to love about caramelized sugar and toasted nuts? We all know and love peanut butter; praline is its sweet cousin. This technique (making a caramel, mixing in nuts to make a brittle, then blending into a paste) can be applied to any nut or seed, and the consistency can be adjusted with water or oil to make it thicker or thinner. Sandwich this sweet, nutty paste between two cookies, use it as a filling for cakes or donuts, or just eat it by the spoonful.

# PRALINE PASTE

*Makes about 1 cup*

**Nonstick cooking spray**

**5 tablespoons plus 2 teaspoons (70g) white sugar**

**3 tablespoons (60g) light corn syrup**

**1 scant cup (120g) toasted blanched hazelnuts**

**1/4 teaspoon kosher salt**

**1/4 teaspoon baking soda**

1 Lightly grease a rimmed sheet pan (9x13-inch is ideal, but 13x18-inch will also work) with cooking spray and set aside.

2 In a 2-quart stainless-steel saucepan or saucier, combine 3 tablespoons of water with the sugar, corn syrup, hazelnuts, and salt. Cook over medium heat, stirring frequently with a heat-resistant spatula to ensure that the sugar dissolves but doesn't scorch, until the mixture darkens to a tawny brown and registers 320°F on a food thermometer, about 10 minutes.

3 Remove from the heat, then immediately stir in the baking soda, folding with the heat-resistant spatula until the candy is evenly foamy. Pour onto the prepared baking sheet and let cool to room temperature, about 30 minutes.

4 Once cool, break the praline into pieces and transfer to the bowl of a food processor. Pulse several times to pulverize, then let the food processor run continuously, stopping to scrape down the sides of the bowl as needed, until the praline transforms into a thick, peanut butter–like paste, 5 to 7 minutes. If you want a spreadable praline, add a little water, 1 tablespoon at a time, until you reach your desired consistency. Transfer the paste to a small bowl and either use immediately or cover and store at room temperature for up to 2 weeks.

**PRO TIP** Look for blanched hazelnuts (which have been quickly blanched to remove their skins) in the baking or nuts section at your grocery store. If you can only find skin-on hazelnuts, warm them in a 350°F oven for about 5 minutes, then use a dish towel to rub off their skins.

✿ Yes, frozen pie dough is just a click away, but making your own is surprisingly easy, and the difference is tenfold. Unlike some other pie doughs, this recipe has you manipulate the ingredients as little as possible (simply pressing each piece of butter between your fingers once), which results in the flakiest, most buttery, tender crust imaginable. I keep pre-portioned pie dough rounds in my freezer, so I always have one ready to defrost and roll, whether it be for Baked Ricotta Pie (page 256) or a rustic galette made with Burnt Strawberries (page 278).

3/4 cup plus 1 tablespoon (113g) all-purpose flour, plus more for dusting

1½ teaspoons (6g) white sugar

½ teaspoon (2g) kosher salt

1 stick (4 ounces) cold unsalted butter, cut into ½-inch cubes

¼ cup (58g) cold water

# Basic PIE DOUGH

*Makes 1 (9-inch) pie shell*

**1** In a medium bowl, whisk together the flour, sugar, and salt. Toss in the cubed butter and use your fingertips to smash each cube flat. Stir in the water and use your hands to knead the dough, mixing until it comes together in a shaggy ball (be careful not to over-knead or heat up and melt the butter with your hands).

**2** Transfer to a clean work surface dusted with flour. Use your hands to mix and press the dough together until smooth, 1 to 2 minutes. Wrap in plastic wrap and chill in the refrigerator for 20 to 30 minutes until firm.

**3** Dust a clean work surface with flour and roll the dough into a 12-inch circle. Transfer to a 9-inch pie plate. Lightly press the dough into the bottom edges of the plate with your thumbs. Use scissors or a sharp knife to trim off any excess dough, leaving a 1-inch overhang. Fold the overhang up over the edge of the dough and crimp the top with your fingers or a fork. Wrap in plastic wrap and refrigerate for at least 2 hours and up to overnight before baking.

**PRO TIP** Make a double batch! Extra dough can be wrapped and frozen to use for anything from potpie to Pop-Tarts to a rustic galette.

✿ Making Tomato Raisins is one of those high-end restaurant techniques that everyone can do at home. A commercial dehydrator is perfect for these, but if you're not a fruit leather or jerky connoisseur and don't have a dehydrator, your home oven on low works just as well. The low-temp bake draws out the moisture in the tomatoes, which concentrates and intensifies their flavor, creating nature's little sweet-and-sour candy. These are great on a sandwich, in a salad, tossed into pasta, or spooned over Fancy Toast (page 114) and scrambled eggs.

# TOMATO RAISINS

*Serves 4 to 6*

2 bunches on-the-vine or 1 basket cherry tomatoes

1 tablespoon extra-virgin olive oil

1 teaspoon kosher salt

**1** Preheat the oven to 200°F (with the convection fan on, if possible) and line a sheet pan with parchment paper.

**2** In a large bowl, gently toss the tomatoes with the olive oil and salt. Transfer to the prepared sheet pan and spread out evenly.

**3** Cook, stirring and rotating the baking sheet as needed for even cooking, until the tomatoes are wrinkled and partially dried, 2 to 3 hours depending on your oven. Use immediately or store in an airtight container in the fridge for up to 3 days.

✿ This is another staple I always keep in the fridge door and in the freezer. You don't always want the spice and pungency of raw garlic in a recipe, especially since it blooms over time. Enter garlic confit. This umami-rich, sweet-and-savory version of garlic is the answer to your prayers. Much like swapping brown butter for regular butter, try using garlic confit in any recipe that calls for raw garlic to give it a slightly rounder, more complex flavor.

# GARLIC CONFIT

*Makes about 25 cloves*

**2 large heads garlic, cloves separated and peeled**

**Extra-virgin olive oil**

*1* Place the garlic cloves in a small saucepan. Add enough oil to cover them and turn the heat to medium. Bring the oil to a simmer, then reduce slightly to maintain a very gentle simmer (you want the garlic to soften and only barely start to turn golden). Cook, adjusting the heat as needed to maintain a gentle simmer, until the garlic is very tender, 25 to 30 minutes.

*2* Use immediately or cool and store in an airtight container in the fridge for up to 2 weeks.

❀ It may sound counterintuitive to intentionally burn something, but we do it in the restaurant all the time, charring onions for stock or burning beets for puree. Strawberries are naturally sweet, so when you hard-roast one side (caramelizing the natural sugars), you simultaneously concentrate all that strawberry goodness and balance it with a natural bitterness from the char. I use them to garnish Panettone "Italian Toast" with Strawberries and Balsamic (page 263), as a base for my Strawberry Cobbler (page 266), or serve them on a cheese plate or Fancy Toast (page 114).

# BURNT STRAW-BERRIES

*Makes about 2 cups*

1 quart (about 1 pound) fresh strawberries, hulled and halved, with larger ones quartered

2 tablespoons white sugar

1 Turn the oven to broil and place a rack in the upper third of the oven.

2 In a large bowl, toss the strawberries with sugar and transfer to a rimmed sheet pan or 9x13-inch baking dish. Place under the broiler and cook, without turning or moving, until very blackened and burned on the exterior, 10 to 15 minutes (depending how powerful your broiler is). Keep an eye on them. Depending on how much moisture is in your strawberries, they might bubble up. If they do, put another pan underneath to catch any drippings—cleaning up a sugar burn from the bottom of your oven is no fun!

3 Remove from the oven and stir with a wooden spoon or heat-proof spatula to combine with all the juices, mashing the now cooked strawberries slightly.

4 Use immediately or cool and store in an airtight container in the fridge for up to 5 days.

# ACKNOWLEDGMENTS

Sitting here and writing a page of people to acknowledge, for a book that has always been a dream of mine, is a very surreal feeling. I'm overcome with emotions when I think about who to thank, who to acknowledge, and, ultimately, who helped make this dream a reality. As someone who never went to culinary school but always felt a passion for hospitality and feeding others, publishing a cookbook is a dream come true.

First and foremost, I want to thank you, the reader. I wouldn't be fortunate enough to do what I do every day if it wasn't for people out there like you: the supporters, the fans, the followers, and the culinary curious. From the bottom of my heart, thank you.

Second, I have to acknowledge Sean, my best friend and Tantos cofounder. I'm not sure if this book would ever have come to be if it wasn't for his continued pressure, pestering, nagging, and, most of all, support and belief in me. I had always thought that I needed a restaurant, a brick-and-mortar, in order to publish a cookbook. I couldn't have been more wrong. Sean pushed me to start the proposal process, helped me find a literary agent, and sparked the journey toward writing this book.

Speaking of literary agents, a huge thank-you to Nicole for guiding me through this entire process and forcing me to work harder for her support and attention. After taking multiple calls with lots of agents, all eager to represent me and assist in writing a book, none of them felt like the right fit. Nicole, on the other hand, did *not* think I was ready to write a book. She told me I needed more time to work on my proposal, my vision, and my ideas. It was that motivation and push to be better that I needed. I knew she was the one to help me see this through. After all, it was Nicole who helped find this book a home at Simon Element and got it into the helping hands of Justin and Gina, who believed in it from the beginning.

Which leads me to the next instrumental person on this adventure, my coauthor, Thea. As a cookbook collector, it's easy to take for granted the amount of writing, organization, formatting, and editing that goes into actually writing a cookbook. None

of this would have been possible without her. Thea transformed countless voice memos, scribbled recipe notes, and kitchen journals into what you see before you.

A good cookbook is filled with great recipes; a great cookbook is filled with great recipes and beautiful photos. None of this would have been possible without Huge, his assistants Jack and Eric, and everyone else on the photo shoot team. The most daunting and intimidating part of the process was deciding on the vibe, the color palette, the props, and the styling of the book. Janelle somehow managed to distill everything I was thinking and feeling about each recipe into a perfect place setting and design. I learned something new every day about food styling, organization, and preparation from Mollie. And Joon was our secret culinary weapon, keeping us clean and soigné. Joon, who has been with me since he started as a cook seven years ago, deserves an extra-special thanks. He not only helped me grow as a mentor and a chef but also flew across the country to be my sous chef for the shoot.

And last but certainly not least are my two biggest cheerleaders and taste-testers, Tito and Kait. They have been my rocks, kept me sane, talked me off the edge, and done so much more to help bring this book to life.

# INDEX

## 00 flour
about, 17
Grano Treiso Dough, 206–9
Potato Gnocchi, 242–43
"Quick and Dirty" Pizza Dough,
108–9
Ricotta Gnocchi, 244–45

## A
acorn squash, in Squash, Whipped
Ricotta, and Spicy Pumpkin Seed
Crumble Rumble, 162
aged balsamic vinegar, 18
Agnolotti, 220–21
aioli, 42
All the Peppercorns Sauce, Ribeye,
Crispy Fingerlings, and, 137–39
Almond Flour and Egg White
Thumbprints, 254
almonds
Almond Flour and Egg White
Thumbprints, 254
Kale Salad with Blueberry and
Lemon Dressing, 83
Summer Melon Gazpacho, 63
anchovies
Good Bread, Good Butter, Good
Anchovies, 115
Mozzarella en Carrozza, 50
anchovy paste
about, 20
Crunchy Caesar and Garlic Streusel,
79
Rosemary Chicken Thighs,
Raspberry Bomba, and Anchovy
Grilled Romaine, 146–48
Sicilian Soffritto, 180
apriums, in Grilled Apriums, Vinegary
Simple Syrup, Burrata, and Brown
Butter Crumble Rumble, 66
Aquerello carnaroli rice, 18
artichoke hearts/paste, in Roasted
Snap Peas and Artichoke Yogurt,
76
Asparagus Cooked in Its Own Juices,
171
avocado, in Green Goddess Mayo, 43

## B
bacon, in Pistachio Butter & Bacon,
118
baguette, in Baked Burrata alla Diavola,
168
Baird, Carrie, 114
Baked Burrata alla Diavola, 168
Baked Clams and Rice "Casino," 127–28
Baked Ricotta Pie, 256
balsamic vinegars, 18

bananas, in Banana "Ice Cream" with
Cinnamon, Walnuts, and Dates,
268
Base Pickle Liquor, 193
Basic Pie Dough, 275
basil, fresh
Baked Burrata alla Diavola, 168
Charred Zucchini Dip, Basil, and
Cherry Tomatoes, 62
Chicken Parm, 232–34
Classic Pesto, 104
Corn Cacio e Pepe, 196
Green Herb Oil, 231
Grilled Apriums, Vinegary Simple
Syrup, Burrata, and Brown Butter
Crumble Rumble, 66
Mom's Red Sauce, 54
Pasta alla Nerano, 199
Pasta all Mezcal, 203
Santorini-Style Tomato Fritters,
40–41
Sasto Bolo, 178
Summer Melon Gazpacho, 63
Tomato Paste & 'Nduja, 118
BBQ Shrimp, Calabrian Chile Paste,
Orange, and Fresh Herbs, 80
beef. See also ground beef
Grilled Short Rib Lettuce Wraps, 72
Ribeye, Crispy Fingerlings, and All
the Peppercorns Sauce, 137–39
Weeknight Short Ribs, 134–36
Beet Bolognese, 188–91
beets, in Beet Bolognese, 188–91
berries
Baked Ricotta Pie, 256
Blueberries & Caramelized Onions,
119
Burnt Strawberries, 278
Kale Salad with Blueberry and
Lemon Dressing, 83
Panettone "Italian Roast" with
Strawberries and Balsamic, 263
Pork Chops with Mustard Berry Jus,
144–45
Rosemary and Blackberry Focaccia
with Whipped Mortadella,
91–92
Rosemary Chicken Thighs,
Raspberry Bomba, and Anchovy
Grilled Romaine, 146–48
Strawberry Cobbler, 266–67
black garlic
about, 20
black Caesar dressing, 79
Black Garlic Butter, 141
Black Garlic Mayo, 43
Black Garlic Butter
Black Garlic Butter Branzino, 140
Fresh Corn Polenta with Butter and
Chives, 167

for Garlic Knots, 112
recipe, 141
Black Garlic Mayo
Black Garlic Egg Salad, 114
recipe, 43
Blistered Shishitos and Dashi Mayo, 163
Bloomsdale, in Black Garlic Butter
Branzino, 140
blueberries
Blueberries & Caramelized Onions,
119
Kale Salad with Blueberry and
Lemon Dressing, 83
Bolognese
Beet Bolognese, 188–91
Sasto Bolo, 178
Turkey Bolognese, 182
bourbon, in Pork Chops with Mustard
Berry Jus, 144–45
Braised Pork and Roasted Pepper
pasta, 226–29
bread(s). See also "Quick and Dirty"
Pizza Dough; sourdough bread
Baked Burrata alla Diavola, 168
BBQ Shrimp, Calabrian Chile Paste,
Orange, and Fresh Herbs with, 80
day old, in Summer Melon
Gazpacho, 63
Fancy Toasts, 114–15
Fried Potato, Cheese, and Sausage
Pie, 88–90
Mini Salami Meatballs with Whipped
Ricotta and Pesto, 149–51
Mozzarella en Carrozza, 50
Pesto Pinwheel Pull-Apart bread
and Fonduta, 98–101
Rosemary and Blackberry Focaccia
with Whipped Mortadella,
91–92
Sesame Semolina Flatbread, 106
Staff-Favorite Cornbread, 107
breadcrumbs. See also panko
breadcrumbs
Baked Clams and Rice "Casino,"
127–28
Fried Castelvetrano Olives, 39
Mozzarella en Carrozza, 50
bread flour, 17
Pesto Pinwheel Pull-Apart Bread,
98–101
"Quick and Dirty" Pizza Dough,
108–9
Rosemary and Blackberry Focaccia,
91–92
Sesame Semolina Flatbread, 106
broccolini, in Grilled Broccolini,
Stracciatella, and Seeded
Crumble Rumble, 173
Brown, Alton, 181
Brown Butter and Potato pasta, 224–25

281

Brown Butter Chocolate Chip Cookies, 250–51
Burnt Strawberries, 278
burrata
    Baked Burrata alla Diavola, 168
    Grilled Apriums, Vinegary Simple Syrup, Burrata, and Brown Butter Crumble Rumble, 66
    Grilled Broccolini, Stracciatella, and Seeded Crumble Rumble, 173
butternut squash, in Butternut Mac n Cheese, 185

## C

Caesar dressing, 79
Calabrian chile paste
    about, 17
    Baked Burrata alla Diavola, 168
    BBQ Shrimp, Calabrian Chile Paste, Orange, and Fresh Herbs, 80
    Carrots with Spicy Yogurt and Carrot Top Pesto, 154
    Crunchy Caesar and Garlic Streusel, 79
    Grilled Short Rib Lettuce Wraps, 72
    Honey Butter Fried Chicken, 48–49
    Hot Honey, 239
    Lamb Chops with Agrodolce Glaze, Walnuts, and Feta, 122
    Mom's Meatballs, 130–31
    Rosemary Chicken Thighs, Raspberry Bomba, and Anchovy Grilled Romaine, 146–48
    Spicy Lemon Mayo, 43
    Spicy Pickle, 195
    Squash, Whipped Ricotta, and Spicy Pumpkin Seed Crumble Rumble, 162
cantaloupe, in Summer Melon Gazpacho, 63
Cappelletti pasta, 218
Caramelized Onions, Blueberries and, 119
Carnaroli rice
    about, 18
    Baked Clams and Rice "Casino," 127–28
    Risotto, 125–26
carrot(s)
    Beet Bolognese, 188–91
    Braised Pork and Roasted Pepper pasta, 226–29
    Carrots with Spicy Yogurt and Carrot Top Pesto, 154
    Grilled Short Rib Lettuce Wraps, 72
    pickling, 194
    Sicilian Soffritto, 180
    Turkey Bolognese, 182–83
    Weeknight Short Ribs, 134–36
Castelvetrano Olives, Fried, 39

cauliflower
    pickling, 194
    Whipped Cauliflower and Everything Bagel Crumble Rumble, 200–201
celery
    Black Garlic Egg Salad, 114
    Pepperoncini Tuna Salad, 119
    Sicilian Soffritto, 180
    Turkey Bolognese, 182–83
    Weeknight Short Ribs, 134–36
Charred Zucchini Dip, Basil, and Cherry Tomatoes, 62
cheese. See also feta cheese; mozzarella cheese; Parmigiano-Reggiano cheese; Pecorino Romano cheese; ricotta
    Butternut Mac n Cheese, 185
    Fried Potato, Cheese, and Sausage Pie, 88–90
    grated, 23
    in pesto, 103
    types of, 23
    Whipped Goat Cheese, 159
cherry tomatoes
    Baked Burrata alla Diavola, 168
    Charred Zucchini Dip, Basil, and Cherry Tomatoes, 62
    Tomato Paste & 'Nduja, 118
    Tomato Raisins, 276
chicken
    Chicken Parm, 232–34
    Honey Butter Fried Chicken, 48–49
    Lemon Pepper Chicken Wings, 46–47
    Rosemary Chicken Thighs, Raspberry Bomba, and Anchovy Grilled Romaine, 146–48
Chicken Parm, 232–34
chile crunch, in Spicy Pork with Pistachio Crumble Rumble, 238
Chipotle Mayo, 43
chives
    Fresh Corn Polenta with Butter and Chives, 167
    Fried Halibut and Savory Zabaglione, 32–34
    Fried Maitake Mushrooms with Onion Dip, 45
    Green Herb Oil, 231
    Honey Butter Fried Chicken, 48–49
    Marinated Tomato "Amatriciana," 75
    Ribeye, Crispy Fingerlings, and All the Peppercorns Sauce, 137–39
    Spicy Pork with Pistachio Crumble Rumble, 238
    Whipped Cauliflower and Everything Bagel Crumble Rumble, 200–201

chocolate, in Brown Butter Chocolate Chip Cookies, 250–51
Churros and Fonduta, 57–58
cilantro
    Chipotle Mayo, 43
    Green Herb Oil, 231
    Grilled Short Rib Lettuce Wraps, 72
    Summer Melon Gazpacho, 63
clams, in Baked Clams and Rice "Casino," 127–28
Classic Dill Pickle, 195
Classic Pesto
    Carrots with Spicy Yogurt and Carrot Top Pesto, 154
    Green Eggs & Ham, 115
    Mini Salami Meatballs with Whipped Ricotta and Pesto, 149–51
    Pesto Pinwheel Pull-Apart bread and Fonduta, 98–101
    Pesto-Rubbed Corn on the Cob, 174
    recipe, 104
cocoa powder, in Pistachio Calzones, 255
cognac, in Ribeye, Crispy Fingerlings, and All the Peppercorns Sauce, 137–39
colatura
    about, 18
    Funky Pickle, 195
    Grilled Short Rib Lettuce Wraps, 72
    Sicilian Soffritto, 180
    Spicy Salty Mayo, 43
cold proofing dough, 109
cookies
    Brown Butter Chocolate Chip Cookies, 250–51
    Rainbow Sprinkle Cookies, 248–49
Cornbread, Staff Favorite, 107
Corn Cacio e Pepe, 196–97
corn cobs
    corn stock, 196
    Fresh Corn Polenta with Butter and Chives, 167
corn crepes, 197
cornmeal, in Staff-Favorite Cornbread, 107
Corn on the Cob, Pesto-Rubbed, 174
corn powder, 167
corn stock, 196
crème fraîche
    Fried Maitake Mushrooms with Onion Dip, 45
    Ribeye, Crispy Fingerlings, and All the Peppercorns Sauce, 137–39
    Staff-Favorite Cornbread, 107
Crepes, 264
Crispy Churros and Fonduta, 57–58
Crumble Rumble
    adding to Grilled Short Rib Lettuce Wraps, 72

Grilled Apriums, Vinegary Simple Syrup, Burrata, and Brown Butter Crumble Rumble, 66
Grilled Broccolini, Stracciatella, and Seeded Crumble Rumble, 173
recipe, 68
Spicy Pork with Pistachio Crumble Rumble, 238
Squash, Whipped Ricotta, and Spicy Pumpkin Seed Crumble Rumble, 162
variations, 68
Whipped Cauliflower and Everything Bagel Crumble Rumble, 200–201
Crunchy Caesar and Garlic Streusel, 79
cucumber(s)
Cucumber and Plum Salad with Pistachio and Wasabi, 71
Grilled Short Rib Lettuce Wraps, 72
Pepperoncini Tuna Salad, 119
pickling, 194
Summer Melon Gazpacho, 63
Cucumber and Plum Salad with Pistachio and Wasabi, 71
cutting board, 28

**D**

Dashi Mayo
Blistered Shishitos and Dashi Mayo, 163
recipe, 43
digital food scale, 26
digital food thermometer, 26
dill, fresh
BBQ Shrimp, Calabrian Chile Paste, Orange, and Fresh Herbs, 80
Endive Salad with Roasted Red Pepper Italian Vinaigrette, Horseradish, and Hazelnuts, 84
Fresh Dill Pickle, 195
Garlic Knots, 112
Green Goddess Mayo, 43
Marinated Tomato "Amatriciana," 75
Santorini-Style Tomato Fritters, 40–41
dough scrapers, 28
dressings
Blueberry and Lemon Dressing, 83
Caesar, 79
Endive Salad, 84
Grilled Romaine and Anchovy, 146
leftover, 79
Ranch, 164
Roasted Red Pepper Italian Vinaigrette, 84
dried plum powder, 71
dry brine
for halibut, 34
for pork chops, 145

for squash, 162
duck fat, in Carrots with Spicy Yogurt and Carrot Top Pesto, 154

**E**

egg(s)
Baked Ricotta Pie, 256
Black Garlic Egg Salad, 114
Brown Butter Chocolate Chip Cookies, 250–51
Crispy Churros and Fonduta, 57–58
Fancy Mayo, 43
Fried Castelvetrano Olives, 39
Green Eggs & Ham, 115
Matcha Tea-Ramisu, 260
Mom's Crepes, 264
Mom's Meatballs, 130–31
Mozzarella en Carrozza, 50
Panettone "Italian Roast" with Strawberries and Balsamic, 263
Pepperoni Stromboli, 113
Pesto Pinwheel Pull-Apart bread and Fonduta, 98–101
Pistachio Calzones, 255
Potato Gnocchi, 242–43
Rainbow Sprinkle Cookies, 248–49
Ricotta Gnocchi, 244–45
Egg Salad, Black Garlic, 114
egg whites
Almond Flour and Egg White Thumbprints, 254
White Pepper Marshmallows, 272
egg yolks
Fried Halibut and Savory Zabaglione, 32–34
Grano Treiso Dough, 206–9
Pesto Pinwheel Pull-Apart Bread and Fonduta, 98–101
endives, in Endive Salad with Roasted Red Pepper Italian Vinaigrette, Horseradish, and Hazelnuts, 84
espresso, in Matcha Tea-Ramisu, 260
everything bagel spice mix, in Whipped Cauliflower and Everything Bagel Crumble Rumble, 200–201

**F**

Fancy Mayo
about, 42
Pepperoncini Tuna Salad, 119
recipe, 43
variations, 43
Fancy Toasts, 114–19
fennel bulb
Braised Pork and Roasted Pepper pasta, 226–29
Sicilian Soffritto, 180
fennel pollen
about, 20

adding to Fried Ceci Beans, 35
Fried Halibut and Savory Zabaglione, 32–34
feta cheese
Kale Salad with Blueberry and Lemon Dressing, 83
Lamb Chops with Agrodolce Glaze, Walnuts, and Feta, 122
Whipped Feta, 159
finocchiona, in Mini Salami Meatballs with Whipped Ricotta and Pesto, 149–51
fish and seafood
Baked Clams and Rice "Casino," 127–28
BBQ Shrimp, Calabrian Chile Paste, Orange, and Fresh Herbs, 80
Black Garlic Butter Branzino, 140
Fried Halibut and Savory Zabaglione, 32–34
Pepperoncini Tuna Salad, 119
flaky salt, 21
flax seeds, in Grilled Broccolini, Stracciatella, and Seeded Crumble Rumble, 173
flours, types of, 17
Focaccia, Rosemary and Blackberry, 91–92
Fonduta
about, 142
adding to Chicken Parm, 234
adding to Ribeye, Crispy Fingerlings, and All the Peppercorns Sauce, 139
Crispy Churros and Fonduta, 57–58
Fonduta & Herb Oil, 115
Pesto Pinwheel Pull-Apart bread and Fonduta, 98–101
recipe, 143
food mill, 28
food scale, 25
food thermometer, 25
Fresh Corn Polenta with Butter and Chives, 167
Fresh Dill Pickle, 195
fresh mozzarella, in Mozzarella en Carrozza, 50
Fried Castelvetrano Olives, *36*, 39
Fried Ceci Beans, 35, *36*
Fried Halibut and Savory Zabaglione, 32–34
Fried Maitake Mushrooms with Onion Dip, *36*, 45
Fried Potato, Cheese, and Sausage Pie, 88–90
Funky Pickle, 195

**G**

garbanzo beans, in Fried Ceci Beans, 35

Garlic Confit
  adding to Black Garlic Butter, 141
  black Caesar dressing, 79
  Charred Zucchini Dip, Basil, and
    Cherry Tomatoes, 62
  Fonduta, 143
  Garlic Streusel, 68
  Pepperoni Mayo, 43
  recipe, 277
  Spicy Lemon Mayo, 43
Garlic Knots, 112
Garlic Streusel
  adding to Blistered Shishitos and
    Dashi Mayo, 163
  adding to Chicken Parm, 234
  adding to Grilled Short Rib Lettuce
    Wraps, 72
  Butternut Mac n Cheese, 185
  Crunchy Caesar and Garlic Streusel,
    79
  Grilled Apriums, Vinegary Simple
    Syrup, Burrata, and Brown Butter
    Crumble Rumble, 66
  Grilled Broccolini, Stracciatella,
    and Seeded Crumble Rumble,
    173
  recipe, 68
  Spicy Pork with Pistachio Crumble
    Rumble, 238
  Squash, Whipped Ricotta, and
    Spicy Pumpkin Seed Crumble
    Rumble, 162
  variations, 68
  Whipped Cauliflower and
    Everything Bagel Crumble
    Rumble, 200–201
Gazpacho, Summer Melon, 63
ginger, fresh
  Grilled Short Rib Lettuce Wraps,
    72
  Lamb Chops with Agrodolce Glaze,
    Walnuts, and Feta, 122
gnocchi
  Potato Gnocchi, 242–43
  Ricotta Gnocchi, 244–45
Goat Cheese, Whipped, 159
Good Bread, Good Butter, Good
  Anchovies, 115
Grano Treiso Dough
  Braised Pork and Roasted Pepper
    pasta, 226–29
  Brown Butter and Potato pasta,
    224–25
  Chicken Parm, 232–34
  Kale, Ricotta, and Hot Honey, 239
  recipe, 206–9
  Spicy Pork with Pistachio Crumble
    Rumble, 238
  Sweet Potato Maple Miso, 235–37

Greek yogurt
  Carrots with Spicy Yogurt and
    Carrot Top Pesto, 154
  Roasted Snap Peas and Artichoke
    Yogurt, 76
Green Eggs & Ham, 115
Green Goddess Mayo, 43
Green Herb Oil, 230–31
Grilled Apriums, Vinegary Simple
  Syrup, Burrata, and Brown Butter
  Crumble Rumble, 66
Grilled Broccolini, Stracciatella, and
  Seeded Crumble Rumble,
  173
Grilled Short Rib Lettuce Wraps, 72
ground beef
  Mom's Meatballs, 130–31
  Sasto Bolo, 178
ground pork
  homemade pork sausage, 187
  Mini Salami Meatballs with Whipped
    Ricotta and Pesto, 149–51
  Mom's Meatballs, 130–31
  Sasto Bolo, 178
  Spicy Pork with Pistachio Crumble
    Rumble, 238
ground turkey, in Turkey Bolognese,
  182–83
Gruyère cheese, in Butternut Mac n
  Cheese, 185
guanciale, in Marinated Tomato
  "Amatriciana," 75

**H**
halibut, in Fried Halibut and Savory
  Zabaglione, 32–34
hazelnuts
  Endive Salad with Roasted Red
    Pepper Italian Vinaigrette,
    Horseradish, and Hazelnuts, 84
  Praline Paste, 274
heavy cream
  Fonduta, 143
  Pasta alla Mezcal, 203
  Pasta alla Norcina, 186–87
  strawberry and rose whipped
    cream, 267
  Whipped Cauliflower and
    Everything Bagel Crumble
    Rumble, 200–201
  Whipped Mortadella, 97
hemp seeds, Grilled Broccolini,
  Stracciatella, and Seeded
  Crumble Rumble, 173
Herby Garlicky Paste
  adding to Ribeye, Crispy
    Fingerlings, and All the
    Peppercorns Sauce, 139
  adding to Roasted Snap Peas and
    Artichoke Yogurt, 76

  adding to Sweet Potato Wedges
    and Lemony Ranch, 164
  recipe, 273
honey
  Almond Flour and Egg White
    Thumbprints, 254
  Banana "Ice Cream" with Cinnamon,
    Walnuts, and Dates, 268
  Carrots with Spicy Yogurt and
    Carrot Top Pesto, 154
  Charred Zucchini Dip, Basil, and
    Cherry Tomatoes, 62
  Cucumber and Plum Salad, 71
  Honey Butter Fried Chicken, 48–49
  Kale Salad with Blueberry and
    Lemon Dressing, 83
  Lamb Chops with Agrodolce Glaze,
    Walnuts, and Feta, 122
  Pork Chops with Mustard Berry Jus,
    144
  Sesame Semolina Flatbreads, 106
  Squash, Whipped Ricotta, and
    Spicy Pumpkin Seed Crumble
    Rumble, 162
horseradish, in Endive Salad with
    Roasted Red Pepper Italian
    Vinaigrette, Horseradish, and
    Hazelnuts, 84
Hot Honey
  Kale, Ricotta, and Hot Honey, 239
  recipe, 240

**K**
kabocha squash, in Squash, Whipped
    Ricotta, and Spicy Pumpkin Seed
    Crumble Rumble, 162
kale
  Kale, Ricotta, and Hot Honey, 239
  Kale Salad with Blueberry and
    Lemon Dressing, 83
  Weeknight Short Ribs, 134–36
KitchenAid mixer, 26
kitchen tools, 25–28
kosher salt, 21

**L**
ladyfinger cookies, in Matcha Tea-
    Ramisu, 260
Lamb Chops with Agrodolce Glaze,
    Walnuts, and Feta, 122
leftovers, 15
  Baked Burrata, 168
  Bolognese, 178
  Brown Butter and Potato filling, 224
  Caesar dressing, 79
  cauliflower puree, 201
  churro dough, 58
  corn sauce, 197
  fried onions and garlic, 54
  Mini Salami Meatballs, 151

risotto, 126
short ribs, 136
simple syrup, 67
Sweet Potato Maple Miso filling, 237
lemongrass, in Grilled Short Rib Lettuce
    Wraps, 72
lemon/lemon zest
    Baked Ricotta Pie, 256
    Black Garlic Butter, 141
    Blistered Shishitos and Dashi Mayo,
        163
    Charred Zucchini Dip, Basil, and
        Cherry Tomatoes, 62
    Classic Pesto, 104
    Crunchy Caesar and Garlic Streusel,
        79
    Fancy Mayo, 43
    Fried Maitake Mushrooms with
        Onion Dip, 45
    Good Bread, Good Butter, Good
        Anchovies, 115
    Grilled Broccolini, Stracciatella, and
        Seeded Crumble Rumble, 173
    Kale Salad with Blueberry and
        Lemon Dressing, 83
    Marinated Tomato "Amatriciana," 75
    Pork Chops with Mustard Berry Jus,
        144
    Roasted Snap Peas and Artichoke
        Yogurt, 76
    Rosemary Chicken Thighs,
        Raspberry Bomba, and Anchovy
        Grilled Romaine, 146–48
    Strawberry Cobbler, 266–67
    Sweet Potato Wedges and Lemony
        Ranch, 164
    Whipped Cauliflower and
        Everything Bagel Crumble
        Rumble, 200–201
    Whipped Feta, 159
    White Pepper Marshmallows, 272
Lemon Pepper Chicken Wings,
    46–47
lettuce(s)
    Crunchy Caesar and Garlic Streusel,
        79
    Grilled Short Rib Lettuce Wraps, 72
    Rosemary Chicken Thighs,
        Raspberry Bomba, and Anchovy
        Grilled Romaine, 146–48
lime juice/zest
    Black Garlic Mayo, 43
    Dashi Mayo, 43
    Fried Ceci Beans, 35
    Spicy Salty Mayo, 43

M

Madeira, in Ribeye, Crispy Fingerlings,
    and All the Peppercorns Sauce,
    137–39

Maple Miso Sweet Potato filling
    recipe, 235–37
    Sweet Potato Pie, 259
Marcato Atlas 150 pasta rolling
    machine, 26
Marinated Tomato "Amatriciana," 75
Marshmallows, White Pepper, 272
mascarpone
    Corn Cacio e Pepe, 196–97
    Matcha Tea-Ramisu, 260
matcha green tea powder, in Matcha
    Tea-Ramisu, 260
mattarello (rolling pin), 26
mayonnaise. See Fancy Mayo
meatballs
    Mini Salami Meatballs with Whipped
        Ricotta and Pesto, 149–51
    Mom's Meatballs, 130–31
medjool dates, in Banana "Ice Cream"
    with Cinnamon, Walnuts, and
    Dates, 268
melon, in Summer Melon Gazpacho, 63
mezcal, in Pasta alla Mezcal, 203
Mezzaluna pasta, 215–16
Mini Salami Meatballs with Whipped
    Ricotta and Pesto, 149–51
mint, fresh
    Grilled Apriums, Vinegary Simple
        Syrup, Burrata, and Brown Butter
        Crumble Rumble, 66
    Grilled Short Rib Lettuce Wraps, 72
    Santorini-Style Tomato Fritters,
        40–41
    Summer Melon Gazpacho, 63
mint oil, 230, 267
miso paste
    Black Garlic Butter, 141
    Lamb Chops with Agrodolce Glaze,
        Walnuts, and Feta, 122
    Sweet Potato Maple Miso filling,
        235–37
Mom's Crepes, 264
Mom's Meatballs, 130–31
Mom's Red Sauce
    about, 52–53
    Mozzarella en Carrozza, 50
    Pepperoni Stromboli, 113
    recipe, 54
mortadella
    Mini Salami Meatballs with Whipped
        Ricotta and Pesto, 151
    Spicy Pork with Pistachio Crumble
        Rumble, 238
    Whipped Mortadella, 97
mozzarella cheese
    Chicken Parm, 232–34
    Mozzarella en Carrozza, 50
    Pepperoni Stromboli, 113
Mozzarella en Carrozza, 50

mushrooms
    Fried Maitake Mushrooms with
        Onion Dip, 45
    pickling, 194
    Weeknight Short Ribs, 134–36
Mustard Berry Jus, Pork Chops with,
    144–45

N

'nduja
    adding to Baked Clams and Rice
        "Casino," 128
    Tomato Paste & 'Nduja, 118
nonstick cooking spray, 21
nuts. See also almonds; hazelnuts;
        pistachios; walnuts
    adding to Garlic Streusel, 68
    Classic Pesto, 104
    in pesto, 102
    Radicchio, Whipped Ricotta, and
        Macadamia Nuts, 161

O

oils, 20
Olives, Fried Castelvetrano, 39
orange/orange zest
    Almond Flour and Egg White
        Thumbprints, 254
    BBQ Shrimp, Calabrian Chile Paste,
        Orange, and Fresh Herbs, 80
    Radicchio, Whipped Ricotta, and
        Macadamia Nuts, 161
    Whipped Goat Cheese, 159

P

pancetta
    adding to Sasto Bolo, 178
    Marinated Tomato "Amatriciana,"
        75
panettone, in Panettone "Italian Roast"
    with Strawberries and Balsamic,
    263
panko breadcrumbs
    Fried Castelvetrano Olives, 39
    Garlic Streusel, 68
    Mom's Meatballs, 130–31
    Sweet Potato Maple Miso, 235–37
pantry items, 17–23
"Parmesan" cheese, 23
Parmigiano-Reggiano cheese, 23
    Baked Clams and Rice "Casino,"
        127–28
    Beet Bolognese, 188–91
    Brown Butter and Potato pasta,
        224–25
    Butternut Mac n Cheese, 185
    Carrots with Spicy Yogurt and
        Carrot Top Pesto, 159
    Chicken Parm, 232–34
    Classic Pesto, 104
    Corn Cacio e Pepe, 196–97

Parmigiano-Reggiano cheese (*cont.*)
    Crunchy Caesar and Garlic Streusel, 79
    Fonduta, 143
    Mini Salami Meatballs with Whipped Ricotta and Pesto, 149–51
    Mom's Meatballs, 130–31
    Pasta alla Mezcal, 203
    Pasta alla Norcina, 186–87
    Rice Paper Cacio e Pepe Chips, 38
    Ricotta Gnocchi, 244–45
    Risotto, 125–26
    Sasto Bolo, 178
    Spicy Pork with Pistachio Crumble Rumble, 238
    Sweet Potato Maple Miso, 235–37
parsley, fresh
    Baked Clams and Rice "Casino," 127–28
    BBQ Shrimp, Calabrian Chile Paste, Orange, and Fresh Herbs, 80
    Fried Halibut and Savory Zabaglione, 32–34
    Fried Potato, Cheese, and Sausage Pie, 88–90
    Garlic Knots, 112
    Green Goddess Mayo, 43
    Green Herb Oil, 231
    Marinated Tomato "Amatriciana," 75
    Mini Salami Meatballs with Whipped Ricotta and Pesto, 149–51
    Mom's Meatballs, 130–31
    Pork Chops with Mustard Berry Jus, 144–45
    Ribeye, Crispy Fingerlings, and All the Peppercorns Sauce, 137–39
    Santorini-Style Tomato Fritters, 40–41
Pasta alla Mezcal, 203
Pasta alla Nerano, 199
Pasta alla Norcina, 186–87
pasta dough, fresh fillings for. *See* stuffed pasta
    Grano Treiso Dough, 206–9
    laminating, 213
    shaping, 214–20
    sheeting, 210–13
    storing, 214
pasta, dried, 21
    Beet Bolognese, 188–91
    Butternut Mac n Cheese, 185
    cold-water cooking method, 181
    Corn Cacio e Pepe, 196–97
    Pasta alla Mezcal, 203
    Pasta alla Nerano, 199
    Pasta alla Norcina, 186–87
    shapes of, 177

Whipped Cauliflower and Everything Bagel Crumble Rumble, 200–201
pasta rolling machine, 26, 210, 212
pasta shapes, 177
peas
    in Mini Salami Meatballs with Whipped Ricotta and Pesto, 151
    Risotto variation, 126
Pecorino Romano cheese, 23
    Braised Pork and Roasted Pepper pasta, 226–29
    Corn Cacio e Pepe, 196–97
    Endive Salad with Roasted Red Pepper Italian Vinaigrette, Horseradish, and Hazelnuts, 84
    Fonduta, 143
    Garlic Knots, 112
    Marinated Tomato "Amatriciana," 75
    Mini Salami Meatballs with Whipped Ricotta and Pesto, 149–51
    Mom's Meatballs, 130–31
    Pasta alla Nerano, 199
    Pasta alla Norcina, 186–87
    Rice Paper Cacio e Pepe Chips, 38
pepperoncini, in Pepperoncini Tuna Salad, 119
pepperoni
    Pepperoni Mayo, 43
    Pepperoni Stromboli, 113
pesto, elements of, 102–3. *See also* Classic Pesto
Pesto Pinwheel Pull-Apart bread and Fonduta, 98–101
Pesto-Rubbed Corn on the Cob, 174
pickle liquor, 192–93
pickling, guide to quick, 194–95
Pie Dough, 275
pies
    Baked Ricotta Pie, 256
    Fried Potato, Cheese, and Sausage Pie, 88–90
    Sweet Potato Pie, 259
pine nuts, in Classic Pesto, 104
pistachio butter
    about, 21
    Cucumber and Plum Salad with Pistachio and Wasabi, 71
    Pistachio Butter & Bacon, 118
    Pistachio Calzones, 255
    for Spicy Pork with Pistachio Crumble Rumble, 238
Pistachio Butter & Bacon, 118
Pistachio Calzones, 255
pistachios
    adding to Garlic Streusel, 68
    Cucumber and Plum Salad with Pistachio and Wasabi, 71
    Pistachio Calzones, 255

Spicy Pork with Pistachio Crumble Rumble, 238
pizza dough. *See* "Quick and Dirty" Pizza Dough
pizza/pasta cutters, 26
plums, in Cucumber and Plum Salad with Pistachio and Wasabi, 71
poppy seeds, in Grilled Broccolini, Stracciatella, and Seeded Crumble Rumble, 173
pork. *See also* ground pork
    Braised Pork and Roasted Pepper pasta, 226–29
    Pork Chops with Mustard Berry Jus, 144–45
pork sausage, in Pasta alla Norcina, 186–87
potatoes
    Brown Butter and Potato pasta, 224–25
    Fried Potato, Cheese, and Sausage Pie, 88–90
    Potato Gnocchi, 242–43
    Ribeye, Crispy Fingerlings, and All the Peppercorns Sauce, 137–39
    Sweet Potato Wedges and Lemony Ranch, 164
Potato Gnocchi, 242–43
Praline Paste, 274
preserved lemon, in Spicy Lemon Mayo, 43
pro tips, 15
    on adding baking soda to potato water, 139
    on adding salt for yeasted dough, 92
    adding vodka to fry batters, 34
    on bringing your eggs to room temperature, 251
    on churro dough, 58
    on cooking bacon, 118
    cooking eggs, 115
    on cooking sausage, 186
    on double fry method, 49
    on electric pressure cooker for short ribs, 136
    on gluten free gnocchi, 243
    on Grano Treiso dough, 206
    on grinding chicken, 234
    on liquid chlorophyll, 231
    on Mom's Red Sauce, 54
    on oil temperature for fried foods, 47
    on pie dough, 275
    on potato skins, 225
    on prepared flour for pizza dough, 109
    on ricotta gnocchi, 244
    on risotto, 126

on sheeting, 212

on storing asparagus, 171

on storing fresh, uncooked pasta, 214

on tangzhong, 101

provolone cheese, in Fried Potato, Cheese, and Sausage Pie, 88–90

pumpkin seeds, in Squash, Whipped Ricotta, and Spicy Pumpkin Seed Crumble Rumble, 162

**Q**

"Quick and Dirty" Pizza Dough

cold proofing, 109

Garlic Knots, 112

Pepperoni Stromboli, 113

Pistachio Calzones, 255

recipe, 108–9

**R**

Radicchio, Whipped Ricotta, and Macadamia Nuts, 161

radishes, in Grilled Short Rib Lettuce Wraps, 72

Rainbow Sprinkle Cookies, 248–49

Ranch, Sweet Potato Wedges and, 164

raspberries, in Rosemary Chicken Thighs, Raspberry Bomba, and Anchovy Grilled Romaine, 146–48

red kuri squash, in Squash, Whipped Ricotta, and Spicy Pumpkin Seed Crumble Rumble, 162

red wine

homemade pork sausage, 187

Sicilian Soffritto, 180

Weeknight Short Ribs, 134–36

Ribeye, Crispy Fingerlings, and All the Peppercorns Sauce, 137–39

rice flour

corn crepes, 197

Garlic Knots, 112

for Potato Gnocchi, 243

Rice Paper Cacio e Pepe Chips, 37, 38

rice paper wrappers, in Rice Paper Cacio e Pepe Chips, 38

ricer, 28

ricotta. See also Whipped Ricotta

Baked Ricotta Pie, 256

Mom's Meatballs, 130–31

Ricotta Gnocchi, 244–45

Sweet Potato Maple Miso filling, 235–37

Risotto

recipe, 125–26

variations, 126

Roasted Garlic Mayo, 43

roasted red peppers

Braised Pork and Roasted Pepper pasta, 226–29

Endive Salad with Roasted Red Pepper Italian Vinaigrette, Horseradish, and Hazelnuts, 84

Roasted Snap Peas and Artichoke Yogurt, 76

Robbins, Missy, 156

rolled oats, in Banana "Ice Cream" with Cinnamon, Walnuts, and Dates, 268

rolling pin, 26

Rosemary and Blackberry Focaccia with Whipped Mortadella, 91–92

Rosemary Chicken Thighs, Raspberry Bomba, and Anchovy Grilled Romaine, 146–48

rosemary, fresh

Beet Bolognese, 188–91

Fried Potato, Cheese, and Sausage Pie, 88–90

Grilled Short Rib Lettuce Wraps, 72

Herby Garlicky Paste, 273

Ribeye, Crispy Fingerlings, and All the Peppercorns Sauce, 137–39

Rosemary and Blackberry Focaccia with Whipped Mortadella, 91–92

Rosemary Chicken Thighs, Raspberry Bomba, and Anchovy Grilled Romaine, 146–48

Staff Favorite Cornbread, 107–8

Sweet Potato Maple Miso filling, 235–37

Sweet Potato Wedges and Lemony Ranch, 164

Weeknight Short Ribs, 134–36

rye flour, adding to churro batter, 58

**S**

saffron

Risotto variation, 126

Saffron Mayo, 43

sage, fresh

Butternut Mac n Cheese, 185

Squash, Whipped Ricotta, and Spicy Pumpkin Seed Crumble Rumble, 162

Turkey Bolognese, 182–83

Weeknight Short Ribs, 134–36

salads

Crunchy Caesar and Garlic Streusel, 79

Cucumber and Plum Salad with Pistachio and Wasabi, 71

Endive Salad with Roasted Red Pepper Italian Vinaigrette, Horseradish, and Hazelnuts, 84

Kale Salad with Blueberry and Lemon Dressing, 83

salami

Green Eggs & Ham, 115

Mini Salami Meatballs with Whipped Ricotta and Pesto, 149–51

salt, 21

salt cure, for halibut, 34

San Marzano tomatoes, 18, 20

Santorini-Style Tomato Fritters, 37, 40–41

Sasto Bolo, 178

sausage

Fried Potato, Cheese, and Sausage Pie, 88–90

making your own, 187

Pasta alla Norcina, 186–87

scallions

Baked Burrata alla Diavola, 168

Fried Maitake Mushrooms with Onion Dip, 45

Grilled Short Rib Lettuce Wraps, 72

Honey Butter Fried Chicken, 48–49

Santorini-Style Tomato Fritters, 40–41

seeds. See also sesame seeds

Crumble Rumble, 68

Grilled Broccolini, Stracciatella, and Seeded Crumble Rumble, 173

in pesto, 102

Squash, Whipped Ricotta, and Spicy Pumpkin Seed Crumble Rumble, 162

sesame seeds

adding to Garlic Streusel, 68

Grilled Broccolini, Stracciatella, and Seeded Crumble Rumble, 173

Pepperoni Stromboli, 113

Sesame Semolina Flatbread, 106

Sesame Semolina Flatbread, 106

sheet pans, 25

shio koji, 145

shiro dashi, 20

shishito peppers, in Blistered Shishitos and Dashi Mayo, 163

shower caps, resting and proofing yeasted dough with, 28

shrimp, in BBQ Shrimp, Calabrian Chile Paste, Orange, and Fresh Herbs, 80

Sicilian oregano, 17

Sicilian Soffritto

adding to Weeknight Short Ribs, 136

recipe, 180

Sasto Bolo, 178

Simple Syrup

Grilled Apriums, Vinegary Simple Syrup, Burrata, and Brown Butter Crumble Rumble, 66

leftover, 67

snap peas, in Roasted Snap Peas and Artichoke Yogurt, 76

sourdough bread
  Black Garlic Egg Salad, 114
  Blueberries & Caramelized Onions, 119
  Fonduta & Herb Oil, 115
  Good Bread, Good Butter, Good Anchovies, 115
  Green Eggs & Ham, 115
  Pepperoncini Tuna Salad, 119
  Pistachio Butter & Bacon, 118
  Tomato Paste & 'Nduja, 118
Spicy Lemon Mayo
  recipe, 43
  Santorini-Style Tomato Fritters, 40–41
Spicy Pickle, 195
Spicy Pork with Pistachio Crumble Rumble, 238
Spicy Salty Mayo, 43
spider strainer, 25
spinach, in Black Garlic Butter Branzino, 140
spray water bottle, 26
Squash, Whipped Ricotta, and Spicy Pumpkin Seed Crumble Rumble, 162
squid ink, adding to Weeknight Short Ribs, 136
Staff-Favorite Cornbread, 107
strawberries
  Burnt Strawberries, 278
  Panettone "Italian Roast" with Strawberries and Balsamic, 263
  Strawberry Cobbler, 266–67
Strawberry Cobbler, 266–67
stuffed pasta
  Braised Pork and Roasted Pepper, 226–29
  Brown Butter and Potato, 224–25
  Chicken Parm, 232–34
  Kale, Ricotta, and Hot Honey, 239
  Spicy Pork with Pistachio Crumble Rumble, 238
  Sweet Potato Maple Miso, 235–37
Summer Melon Gazpacho, 63
sweet potatoes
  Sweet Potato Maple Miso, 235–37
  Sweet Potato Pie, 259
  Sweet Potato Wedges and Lemony Ranch, 164

**T**
tangzhong, for Pesto Pinwheel Pull-Apart bread and Fonduta, 98–101
thyme, fresh
  Beet Bolognese, 188–91
  Braised Pork and Roasted Pepper pasta, 226–29
  Carrots with Spicy Yogurt and Carrot Top Pesto, 154

Charred Zucchini Dip, Basil, and Cherry Tomatoes, 62
Herby Garlicky Paste, 273
Pork Chops with Mustard Berry Jus, 144–45
Ribeye, Crispy Fingerlings, and All the Peppercorns Sauce, 137–39
Sasto Bolo, 178
Sicilian Soffritto, 180
Sweet Potato Wedges and Lemony Ranch, 164
Turkey Bolognese, 182–83
Weeknight Short Ribs, 134–36
tomatoes, canned, 18, 20
  Mom's Red Sauce, 54
  Pasta alla Mezcal, 203
tomatoes, fresh. See also cherry tomatoes
  Marinated Tomato "Amatriciana," 75
  Santorini-Style Tomato Fritters, 40–41
  Summer Melon Gazpacho, 63
tomato paste, 18
  Baked Clams and Rice "Casino," 127–28
  Beet Bolognese, 188–91
  Chicken Parm, 232–34
  Mom's Meatballs, 130–31
  Pasta alla Mezcal, 203
  Pepperoni Mayo, 43
  Sasto Bolo, 178
  Sicilian Soffritto, 180
  Tomato Paste & 'Nduja, 118
  Weeknight Short Ribs, 134–36
Tomato Raisins, 276
  adding to Chicken Parm, 234
tomato sauce, in Fried Potato, Cheese, and Sausage Pie, 88–90
tongs, 25
Tortellini pasta, 215
Tortelloni pasta, 215
Triangoli pasta, 215–16
tuna, in Pepperoncini Tuna Salad, 119
Turkey Bolognese, 182–83

**U**
umami flavor, in pesto, 104

**V**
vodka
  Fried Halibut and Savory Zabaglione, 32–34
  Fried Maitake Mushrooms with Onion Dip, 45

**W**
walnuts
  Banana "Ice Cream" with Cinnamon, Walnuts, and Dates, 268
  Lamb Chops with Agrodolce Glaze, Walnuts, and Feta, 122

wasabi paste/peas, in Cucumber and Plum Salad with Pistachio and Wasabi, 71
Weeknight Short Ribs, 134–36
Whipped Cauliflower and Everything Bagel Crumble Rumble, 200–201
Whipped Feta, 159
Whipped Goat Cheese, 159
Whipped Mortadella
  recipe, 97
  Rosemary and Blackberry Focaccia with Whipped Mortadella, 91–92
Whipped Ricotta, 156–57
  Baked Ricotta Pie, 256
  Kale, Ricotta, and Hot Honey, 239
  Mini Salami Meatballs with Whipped Ricotta and Pesto, 149–51
  Radicchio, Whipped Ricotta, and Macadamia Nuts, 161
  recipe, 159
  Squash, Whipped Ricotta, and Spicy Pumpkin Seed Crumble Rumble, 162
White Pepper Marshmallows, 272
white wine
  Braised Pork and Roasted Pepper pasta, 226–29
  Pasta alla Norcina, 186–87
  Risotto, 125–26
  Sasto Bolo, 178
  Turkey Bolognese, 182–83
wine. See red wine; white wine
wire cooling racks, 26
wooden cutting board, 28

**X**
xanthan gum, 21
  adding to Butternut Mac n Cheese, 185
  adding to Charred Zucchini Dip, 62
  Fonduta, 142, 143

**Y**
yogurt, in Whipped Feta, 159. See also Greek yogurt
Yondu, 145
yuzu juice/yuzu marmalade
  about, 20
  for Lemon Pepper Chicken Wings, 47

**Z**
zucchini
  Charred Zucchini Dip, Basil, and Cherry Tomatoes, 62
  Pasta alla Nerano, 199